ECOTHERAPY

ECOTHERAPY

THEORY, RESEARCH AND PRACTICE

EDITED BY MARTIN JORDAN
AND JOE HINDS

First published 2016 by
PALGRAVE

Palgrave in the UK is an imprint of Macmillan Publishers Limited,
registered in England, company number 785998, of 4 Crinan Street,
London, N1 9XW.

Palgrave Macmillan in the US is a division of St Martin's Press LLC,
175 Fifth Avenue, New York, NY 10010.

Palgrave is a global imprint of the above companies and is represented
throughout the world.

Palgrave® and Macmillan® are registered trademarks in the United States,
the United Kingdom, Europe and other countries.

ISBN 978-1-137-48687-5   ISBN 978-1-137-48688-2 (eBook)
DOI 10.1007/978-1-137-48688-2

This book is printed on paper suitable for recycling and made from fully
managed and sustained forest sources. Logging, pulping and manufacturing
processes are expected to conform to the environmental regulations of the
country of origin.

A catalogue record for this book is available from the British Library.

A catalog record for this book is available from the Library of Congress.

Joe Hinds
To Nina, Erin and Freya – creatures of the outdoors

Martin Jordan
To Cara, Mary and Gemma, for all the happy times spent in nature,
and to all the participants in my ecotherapy workshops,
who have taught me so much

CONTENTS

LIST OF FIGURES AND TABLES

Figures

Tables

THE CONTRIBUTORS

Martin Jordan, PhD, is a HCPC-registered counselling psychologist, UKCP-registered psychotherapist and counsellor. For the past seven years, he has been taking his therapeutic work outdoors into natural spaces. He trains and works with a range of mental health professionals who wish to explore the healing potential of nature in their therapeutic practice. Dr. Jordan's research and practice interests in this area culminated in the publication of *Nature and Therapy: Understanding Counselling and Psychotherapy in Outdoor Spaces* in 2014 with Routledge, the first book of its kind to explore the theory and practice of outdoor counselling and psychotherapy. For training and courses in ecotherapy, see www.ecotherapy.co.uk.

Joe Hinds (DPhil) is a senior lecturer in psychology at Canterbury Christ Church University in the United Kingdom, an integrative psychotherapist with a core existential humanistic training and a member of the BACP and UPCA. He combines research and teaching in environmental psychology, counselling and psychological well-being with maintaining a small therapeutic practice in East Sussex. He has published a number of papers on his interests, including those relating to horticulture, wilderness, nature connection and identity. He has a passion for the outdoors and spends time in nature as a therapist, and for relaxation and inspiration as often as he can. JoeHCP@Yahoo.co.uk

Thomas Doherty is a licensed psychologist, fellow of the American Psychological Association (APA) and past president of *The Society for Environmental, Population and Conservation Psychology*. Thomas was the founding editor of the journal *Ecopsychology* and also founded and directs the Ecopsychology Certificate Program at Lewis and Clark Graduate School. He has published research on the psychological impacts of global climate change and was a member of the APA Climate Change Task Force. Thomas provides psychotherapy and consultation about environmental aspects of mental health and well-being through his practice, Sustainable Self. He lives with his family in Portland, Oregon. thomas@selfsustain.com

Caroline Brazier is a psychotherapist with over 20 years of experience. She is course leader of the Tariki Psychotherapy Training Programme in Other-centred Approach and the Ten Directions training in ecotherapy and is engaged in offering both attendance-based and online training (http://www.buddhistpsychology. info). Caroline is author of six books on Buddhism and psychotherapy, including *Buddhist Psychology* (2003, Constable Robinson), *Acorns Among the Grass* (2011, Earth Books) and *Other-Centred Therapy* (2009, O-Books), as well as many articles, chapters and papers on the subject. Email: courses@tarikitrust.org

Linda Buzzell has been a psychotherapist for 40 years, and since 2000 she has specialized in ecopsychology and ecotherapy. She is co-editor (with Craig Chalquist) of *Ecotherapy: Healing with Nature in Mind* (2009) and is on the editorial board of *Ecopsychology*, a peer-reviewed journal in the field. She is adjunct faculty at Pacifica Graduate Institute in Santa Barbara, California, teaching ecopsychology and ecotherapy. In 2002, she founded the online organization The International Association for Ecotherapy and edits its journal *Ecotherapy News*. Linda and her husband have created a backyard food forest around their home that serves as her ecotherapy office. www.ecotherapyheals.com

Deborah Kelly is a UKCP-registered psychotherapist, having trained as an integrative arts psychotherapist (MA) at the Institute for Arts in Therapy and Education, where she now works as a tutor and course leader. She has a private practice in East Sussex, working with couples, individuals and groups. With a background in nursing and shiatsu, she has run groups and workshops with a variety of foci, including palliative care, bereavement, suicide, women's groups, Five Elements and the Wheel of the Year. She is particularly interested in working with nature and imagination, which is a focus of her doctoral research. deborah@ wildmercury.co.uk

Eva Sahlin received her PhD in environmental psychology at the Swedish University of Agricultural Sciences in Alnarp, Sweden. Her research has focused on the effects of nature-based therapy for rehabilitation and prevention of stress-related disorders. She has recently been affiliated to the Institute of Stress Medicine in Gothenburg to continue her research work. Eva.Sahlin@slu.se

Anna María Pálsdóttir has a PhD in landscape planning and environmental psychology and is a lecturer at the Swedish University of Agricultural Science at Alnarp. Her interests have centred on the use of gardens for rehabilitation for individuals with stress-related mental disorders. In addition, her research has focused on the design of outdoor environments for health promotion for a number of different service user groups, as well as developing more general nature-based interventions. She has applied the results of her research to a number of real-world situations, including contributing towards guidelines for quality assurance of nature-based interventions. http://www.slu.se/ and anna.maria .palsdottir@slu.se

Matthew Adams lectures in psychology at the University of Brighton, with a particular focus on ecopsychology, critical, social and cultural psychology. His predominant research focus is the human-to-non-human–nature relationship, leaning towards interdisciplinary understandings of how humans respond to ongoing ecological crisis. He has published numerous articles and book chapters on these subjects in the last few years. He is presently writing a book for Palgrave Macmillan entitled *Sustainability, Ecological Crisis and the Psychosocial Subject.* Matthew.Adams@brighton.ac.uk

Patricia Hasbach, PhD, is a private practitioner/owner of Northwest Ecotherapy in Eugene, Oregon; a faculty member in the Graduate School of Education and Counseling at Lewis and Clark College; and a consultant and trainer on various topics related to the human–nature relationship. Her work has appeared in numerous journals and popular magazines, and she is the co-author of two books published by MIT Press: *Ecopsychology: Science, Totems, and the Technological Species* (2012) and *The Rediscover of the Wild* (2013). Her recent research, which involves measuring the impact of nature imagery on inmates in solitary confinement, was named as one of the '25 Best Inventions in 2014' by *Time* Magazine. www.northwestecotherapy.com

Hayley Marshall MSc (TA Psych) CTA PTSTA is a UKCP-registered psychotherapist and supervisor based in Buxton and South Manchester. She has 20 years' clinical experience as a psychotherapist and supervisor, and is a TA trainer at the South Manchester Centre for Psychotherapy. She also has eight years' experience as an outdoor psychotherapist, supervisor and trainer, working both in her home landscape of the Peak District and in wilder settings as consultant psychotherapist for the Wilderness Foundation UK. She is a founder member of Counsellors and Psychotherapists Outdoors and regularly co-facilitates outdoor residential trainings for therapists with Martin Jordan. www.hayleymarshallcounselling.co.uk

Vanessa Jones has over 17 years' experience as an art psychotherapist. Recognizing the emotional and spiritual benefits of developing a deeper connection with nature, she has worked tirelessly to develop a range of nature-based outdoor therapy groups specifically for adults with serious mental health illness within mainstream NHS Services. She is a trained mindfulness instructor and currently works in London and the South East. Vanessa has published several articles within her profession and facilitates art therapy outdoors workshops for trainee art psychotherapists at the University of Hertfordshire. She has a small private practice in west Kent, England. www.vanessajones.org.uk

Brian Thompson is an occupational therapist with eight years' experience working in acute and crisis mental health services. After three years of post-graduation practice, he spent a ten-year period based at a Buddhist retreat centre, which included teaching Buddhism on retreats. Since returning to work In mental health in 2008, this experience has translated into the integration of mindfulness within many aspects of his occupational therapy practice, including mindfulness-based ecotherapy. brianfrancisthompson@gmail.com

Julie Watson is an art therapist working with adults with learning disabilities. Here, Julie writes from the perspective of a service user in crisis, which allows an insightful contribution to the understanding of theory and writing. Her experiences as a service user have also informed and supported her clinical work. watsonjulie44@gmail.com

Ronen Berger, PhD, is the founder of the Nature Therapy Center and the Nature Therapy Training Program at Tel Aviv University and is head of the Drama Therapy master's programme at the College of Arts and Social Work, Israel. He teaches nature therapy, art therapy and creative group work in Israel and around the world while researching, organizing and attending conferences and publishing on these topics. He lives on Kibbutz Snir in the north of Israel, where he tries to combine life as an academic and therapist with a close connection to nature, creativity and community. www.naturetherapy.org and ronenbw@gmail.com

Louise Ranger (MSc, BA, PgDip) is a humanistic therapist with a particular interest in animal-assisted therapy and pet bereavement. Louise is drawn to the value of working outside with a sentient being in the here and now. Her main focus of interest is related to working with clients assisted by horses, and the profound impact this can have on the individual both developmentally and systemically. Louise is trained in intergenerational mediation, human and equine shiatsu, and mindfulness practices. She uses this training to deepen her understanding of therapy from relational and body sense perspectives. walkalongside@hotmail.co.uk

ACKNOWLEDGEMENTS

The authors and publisher wish to thank Petra Thorpert and Anders Busse Nielsen for kind permission to reproduce the drawing of Alnarp Garden, Figure 8.1, page 113.

ECOTHERAPY: AN INTRODUCTION

Joe Hinds and Martin Jordan

The use of nature to affect positive change in the well-being of people has been around in many forms for many years (e.g. Metzner, 2009). An emphasis on the healing of the split between nature and human nature has long formed part of some psychological traditions (Jung, 1989; Sabini, 2008; Searles, 1960). More recently, however, there has been a growing interest in, and development of, ecopsychology as an explicit field (Roszak, Gomes and Kanner, 1995). This has largely been orientated towards the 'greening of psychology' such as developing a human identity with, and compassion for, the natural world (Roszak, 1995, p. 16), alongside the recognition that human psychological distress is bound with the ecological destruction inflicted by humankind upon the natural world.

A strongly related concept that has adopted some key features from ecopsychology is ecotherapy (Buzzell and Chalquist, 2009). Although both approaches have drawn on a number of different disciplines and perspectives in their development, particularly psychology, a central aspect to both is developing a reciprocal relationship with nature to ensure both psychological and environmental well-being. Whereas ecopsychology is about the psyche and the greening of psychology, ecotherapy focuses on the total mind–body–spirit relationship (e.g. Clinebell, 1996).

Clinebell (1996) first coined the term *ecotherapy*, positing a form of 'ecological spirituality' whereby a holistic relationship with nature encompasses both nature's ability to nurture us, through our contact with natural places and spaces, and our ability to reciprocate this healing connection through our ability to nurture nature. Recent developments, particularly in North America, tend to describe ecotherapy as 'applied' or clinical ecopsychology, just as psychotherapy can be described as applied or clinical psychology (Jordan, 2009). Ecotherapy is positioned as healing the human–nature relationship and includes a range of therapeutic and reconnective practices such as horticultural therapy, 'green' exercise, animal-assisted therapy, wilderness therapy, natural lifestyle therapy, eco-dreamwork, community ecotherapy and dealing with eco-anxiety and eco-grief with others (Buzzell and Chalquist, 2009).

Ecotherapy may be seen as an umbrella term for nature-based methods of physical and psychological healing representing a new form, or a new modality, of psychotherapy that enlarges the traditional scope of treatment to include the human–nature relationship (Chalquist, 2013; Hasbach, 2012). Traditional therapy approaches have not tended to explicitly recognize these relationships with the other-than-human world (Totton, 2011; i.e. living things such as animals) as an important part of how the client's story and healing intertwine (Hegarty, 2010).

However, amid this variety, there remains a question concerning what 'nature' is. For this collection of essays on therapeutic and psychological effects of nature, we take the position that nature is both material in its form and a historical construct. Moreover, given that we as a species are part of nature, 'mind', in the form of interiors, and 'nature', in the form of an exterior, are not so easily separated. Nature can be understood through its processes and forms as a biotic and ecological system of interaction and also as a historically contingent understanding. Furthermore, nature and people (although fully acknowledging that this is a false dichotomy) may be viewed as spiritual entities that are undeniably connected (e.g. Macy, 2009). Nature has emerged historically through its articulation in the natural sciences (Latour, 1993) and through the practices and economic developments of modernity (Bluhdorn, 2001) as well as through ancient indigenous practices, beliefs and rituals (e.g. Abrams, 1996), and therefore it is impossible to situate nature as a singular entity (Macnaghten and Urry, 1998). In these merging and emerging movements, we do not find a distinct 'mind' coming into contact with a distinct 'nature'; both are in a relational process. And undoubtedly these perceptions, and indeed changes in perceptions, of both nature and self are part of the therapeutic journey. The following collection of essays seeks to explore the relationship between humans and nature and the effect both have upon one another as an emerging and relational process.

Moreover, we are not advocating an anthropocentrism here in that nature is perceived as merely a 'resource' to be exploited for therapeutic ends. We take the position that the large majority of ecotherapy practices, including those in this book, fundamentally represent and practise a reciprocal relationship with nature, one that promotes and enhances sustainable practices (psychological and ecological). For some chapters (notably Buzzell, chapter 5), this is in the foreground, and for others it is less so; nonetheless, it is the relational and reciprocal aspect of ecotherapy that we wish to acknowledge here that is genuinely healing for both people and the planet.

Our goal in this collection is to establish a grounding of ecotherapy in a theory-based understanding in order that this multifaceted discipline might grow further. We attempt to do so by developing epistemologies of a broad ecotherapy based on sound practice and coherent research. We are particularly interested here in how ideas from contemporary psychotherapy theory and practice interweave with ideas from the emerging fields of ecopsychology and ecotherapy, for instance, how conventional ideas regarding the therapeutic frame (e.g. the therapeutic hour) are challenged and managed by the practicalities of taking people into natural environments. Overall, we are keen to present and articulate the therapeutic effects of the natural world and our relationships to it from an ecotherapy standpoint while also acknowledging that this broad approach does not constitute a panacea: undoubtedly there are situations when ecotherapy will not be appropriate.

Nevertheless, the following chapters, we feel, are a firm step towards building a robust theoretical, experiential and practice-driven understanding of ecotherapy by bringing together a diverse and international array of researchers and practitioners, and thus drawing on a broad range of philosophies and positions. We recognize, however, that among the approaches presented some material will be at odds with certain readers' ideas of what constitutes evidence; on one hand, the richness of the more personal chapters may not be perceived as being part of an empirical evidence base; on the other hand, the phenomenological nature of these accounts may be seen as central to a depth understanding. Undoubtedly, this book is an endeavour that attempts to bring together both. They of course interact and are part of the holistic process of understanding: both the positivist and inductivist positions of this growing discipline are important, and we cannot be without either. Moreover, although we recognize that the preceding chapters cover and contain aspects of one or more of the book's key areas of theory, research and practice, we have made a judgement regarding the main components or aspects of each chapter and allocated them to the most appropriate section: some chapters are stronger in one or more of these aspects than others. Again, this collection attempts to both unify the field under the umbrella term *ecotherapy* while also recognizing the idiosyncratic nature of each contribution. Therefore, as with other aspects of human inquiry, how these various chapters both converge and diverge will be interpreted differently, and our aim is not to provide prescriptive direction here about these patterns of interrelation, but to provide, as far as possible, what we feel is an informed and deliberate attempt at buttressing the practice of ecotherapy. A brief synopsis of each chapter within its given section is outlined below.

Theory

An important epistemological basis for the practice and theory of ecotherapy is ecopsychology, and Thomas Doherty's chapter 1 introduces some of the fundamental tenets to the growing practice and theoretical understanding of how and why ecotherapy works. Starting with a definition of ecotherapy as intrinsically linked to psychotherapy, he describes the fundamental ecological focus of ecotherapy at the planetary, societal, group and individual levels. Outlining some of the fundamental dichotomies in ecotherapeutic practice, his chapter gives an in-depth exploration of the history of the field, the practice and the underpinning epistemologies that inform ecotherapy, and it sets the scene for what is to follow.

In chapter 2, Caroline Brazier explores nature-based therapeutic practice from a Buddhist perspective, placing particular emphasis on the role of mindfulness in the therapeutic relationship outdoors. She discusses the therapist's own quality of mindful attention and capacity for role modelling this quality for the client. Caroline draws from her own unique model, which she calls an other-centred approach, that sees the troubled person existing in an isolated and alienated condition which is then explored through embodied awareness, addressing the conditioned mind and how this drives perceptions, thoughts and relationships. She presents a thoughtful and well-researched chapter which will be of use to those seeking to understand ecotherapy from a Buddhist perspective.

Joe Hinds describes in his chapter 3 an underpinning theoretical position which can account for the therapeutic power of human–nature connection. Drawing on the concept of eudemonia, in other words, attaining a good life and living well in accordance with one's own truth, he locates himself within humanistic and existential frameworks in order to explore how nature is central to promoting eudemonic well-being. However, within this philosophy, there is the recognition that experience of nature can promote fear, arduousness and suffering which may contribute to a more insightful shift in people's perceptions and understandings. This sense of 'terrible joy' captures something of the complexity of our relationship to nature in terms of holistic well-being and the challenges required to reconfigure world views to elicit psychological and therapeutic benefits.

In chapter 4, Martin Jordan explores ecotherapy as a psychotherapy. He critiques the current notion of what ecotherapy is, particularly within the United Kingdom, where it is seen as more of an occupational therapy than a psychotherapy. He proposes that by understanding the place and process of early developmental experience in the aetiology of distress and trauma, and drawing in particular from the work of Donald Winnicott, we are better able to understand how space is felt emotionally in therapy. Martin concludes by locating nature as a 'third space' within which psychotherapy is conducted and which can be a holding and containing space for both therapist and client alike.

Chapter 5 offers a critical exploration of the role and position of ecotherapy, with particular reference to ecopsychology. Linda Buzzell makes a distinction between Level 1 and Level 2 ecotherapies. Level 1 ecotherapies are located within traditional scientific world views of human–nature relationships, where nature is viewed as a utility to be used by humans, thereby arguably continuing the psychic, social and emotional problems which underpin our current environmental crisis. Level 2 ecotherapies, in contrast, promote a reciprocal healing relationship between humans and nature. Drawing upon the work of several writers in the field of ecopsychology and deep ecology, she presents a multilevel version of ecotherapy in the service of healing both human and planetary distress as reciprocal circles of healing.

Research

The following chapters focus on research carried out in order to understand the healing and psychological effects of contact with nature. In chapter 6, Deborah Kelly presents research which focuses on the area of palliative care and how nature can be used in working with this particular client group. Drawing upon Michael Kearney's work and the concept of Asklepian healing, the importance of symbolism and the idea that illness is a quest for healing, she articulates how nature represents a powerful space within which to explore the central issue of life and death in palliative care. Her research findings show that nature plays a central role in the healing and supportive work of palliative care and how it acts as a container for the work, in particular the rhythm of the seasons and the mirror of life and death reflected within these. Of special importance for eco-therapy practice and research is how nature can represent a sacred space through which rituals can be performed in order to make sense of life, death and illness.

Eva Sahlin presents part of her completed doctoral thesis research conducted within the nature-based rehabilitation programme in the Gothenburg Botanical Garden in Sweden. Her research is representative of the exciting and progressive work that is happening in Scandinavia, originating from the Alnarp Rehabilitation Garden research programme being conducted at the Swedish University of Agricultural Sciences near Malmo in southern Sweden. Drawing from existential ideas, she presents verbatim quotes from participants which articulate the psychological and emotional benefits of participating in a healing garden programme. One such is how nature provides helpful metaphors for people's expression of emotional conditions and promotes deeper spiritual connections which are experienced as profoundly healing. Her chapter presents clear and concise links between theory and practice, explaining how nature helps in the rehabilitation process.

Anna Maria Pálsdóttir also discusses research from Sweden's Alnarp Rehabilitation Garden project. Her focus is on how particular design aspects of the garden facilitate recovery in those experiencing mental health problems such as burnout and depression. Her chapter draws upon and further develops the significant body of research carried out in Sweden and Scandinavia into the healing effects of particular garden designs and spaces. She outlines how stages of recovery develop through a relationship to nature within the garden and describes a new and important concept of 'social quietness' which details a strong need to be alone in nature. This includes a profound non-verbal communication with nature which is not only a source of restoration but also seems to positively affect complex mental processes experienced by participants throughout the rehabilitation process.

Matt Adams and Martin Jordan discuss their research carried out with an organization called *Grow*, located in Brighton in the United Kingdom. *Grow* works with people experiencing mental distress and provides mental health support within a natural space. The project is unique in that it does not utilize horticultural therapy, but provides a safe, supportive group space in nature to aid recovery. The eight-week programme is evaluated in order to understand participants' experience of *Grow*. Although nature is articulated as an important context for recovery from mental health problems, this is contrasted with indoor mental health environments which are felt by some to be set up in ways that reinforce their symptoms and identity. Other important factors are the level of peer support found on the programme. The report highlights how a natural environment, in a socially supportive context, offers an alternative to the familiar routines and hierarchies of client's experiences of mental health services. In the right conditions, a natural environment supports the development of different and healthier identities, with the potential to aid recovery from psychological distress. Nature seems to play a role in this process, and this is explored in a discussion of the research.

Practice

In prescribing nature, Patricia Hasbach discusses the pragmatics of conducting ecotherapy outdoors as a therapist within a one-to-one relationship. Beginning first with the intake interview, which, among other things, explores the client's history and relationship to nature, Hasbach talks about the role of imagery and metaphor in the ecotherapy process. Giving examples from practice, she discusses how, between weekly therapy sessions, homework can be assigned in order to promote the healing potential of nature. She gives particular attention to 'nature language' and how this can be used in the therapeutic process, and she discusses, as others have, some of the unique challenges that affect the therapeutic frame outdoors and the ethical implication of conducting ecotherapy.

Hayley Marshall's chapter outlines the roots of her understanding of nature-based psychotherapy from her own experience as a participant in therapy outdoors and from the perspective of transactional analysis and body psychotherapy. Drawing from both theory and case study examples, she positions the importance of the 'body' and embodied processes in nature-based therapy. Employing a range of contemporary psychotherapy theory, her chapter will be a welcome addition to the growing body of work trying to articulate how therapeutic processes can be understood in a natural environment.

Vanessa Jones, Brian Thompson and Julie Watson bring an important perspective from the National Health Service in the United Kingdom to show how nature is being integrated into service provision for recovery from an acute mental health crisis. The authors address the following question: How does a shared experience of being in nature support recovery from acute mental health crisis? Weaving together experiences of both facilitators and participants, the chapter describes how sessions were conducted, with a particular emphasis on mindfulness and art therapy processes. The chapter will be of immense interest to all those working in services in terms of understanding how ecotherapy can be carried out in statutory services.

Ronen Berger presents his version of ecotherapy called 'Nature Therapy', an approach that is firmly embedded within arts therapies and in particular drama therapy. Berger sees Nature Therapy as a unique approach both related to eco-therapy and ecopsychology, but a further development of these. He outlines the theoretical underpinnings of nature therapy as an approach that draws upon creative processes as a therapeutic method with nature positioned as a central partner in the process, and presents ideas and practices from shamanism and dramatherapy. Using case examples firmly embedded in practice, he illustrates the praxes and processes in relation to a hexagonal six-point model which incorporates the therapist–client–nature relationship with the group, art and the spiritual dimension on the six points of the star. Seeing Nature Therapy as a development of dramatherapy and other creative expressive therapies, his con-tribution firmly establishes the centrality of the link between ecotherapy and creative arts therapies.

Ecotherapy is not just about our relationship with the natural environment but also concerns our relationship with animals and their positive effect on our mental health. In chapter 14, Joe Hinds and Louise Ranger discuss equine-assisted therapy (EAT). Positioning EAT as a unique form of animal-assisted therapy, they outline some of the important epistemological issues that under-pin their understanding of this approach. Turning to the work of Prouty (2001), they show how his idea of pre-therapy may be seen as an important dimension to better understand how animals such as horses act as a therapeutic 'bridge' in determining psychological health. Human–animal relationships can provide a non-linguistic, cooperative connection that helps to define 'self' in reference to 'other'. These unique therapeutic associations also utilize transpersonal ideas to show how the relationship with a horse can provoke a sense of awe, enabling the horse to act as a transitional object to facilitate movement from one pattern of human relating and behaviour to another. The chapter represents an impor-tant step forward in developing knowledge about the therapeutic processes that come into play in this form of ecotherapy.

Recent decades have seen the growth of ecotherapy in different areas in the United Kingdom with the publishing of the Mind reports (Mind 2007; 2013a; 2013b), which set forth a version of ecotherapy linked to green exercise and horticultural therapy. In the United States, we have seen the promotion of eco-therapy as a new form of psychotherapy (Buzzell and Chalquist, 2009), and there is very interesting research coming out of Europe, in particular Scandinavia (Stigs-dotter and Grahn, 2003). Our aim in compiling and editing this book is to bring these emerging strands together to provide a snapshot of ecotherapy at this time in history. In outlining the theoretical, practice and research strands of ecotherapy, we wish to show the important aspects of an emerging, vibrant field of practice that will only grow in relation to mental health treatment and the unfolding environmental crisis. We hope you enjoy the book.

References

Abram, D. (1996) *The Spell of the Sensuous* (New York: Random House).

Bluhdorn, I. (2001) 'Reflexivity and Self-Referentiality: On the Normative Foundations of Ecological Communication', in C. B. Grant and D. McLaughlin (eds) *Language-Meaning-Social Construction Interdisciplinary Studies* (New York: Rodopi) pp. 181–201 (21).

Buzzell, L., and C. Chalquist (2009) *Ecotherapy: Healing with Nature in Mind* (San Francisco: Sierra Club Books).

Chalquist, C. (2013) 'Review of Ecopsychology: Science, Totems, and the Technological Species,' *Ecopsychology*, 5(1), 60–4

Clinebell, H. (1996) *Ecotherapy: Healing Ourselves, Healing the Earth* (Minneapolis, MN: Fortress Press).

Hasbach, P. H. (2012) 'Ecotherapy', in P. H. Kahn Jr. and P. H. Hasbach (eds) *Ecopsychology: Science, Totems, and the Technological Species* (Cambridge, MA: MIT Press) pp. 115–39.

Hegarty, J. (2010) 'Out of the Consulting Room and into the Woods? Experiences of Nature-Connectedness and Self-Healing', *European Journal of Ecopsychology*, 1, 64–84.

Jordan, M. (2009) 'Back to Nature', *Therapy Today*, 20(3), 26–8.

Jung, C. G. (1989) *Memories, Dreams, Reflections* (Knopf: Double Day).

Latour, R. (1993) *We Have Never Been Modern* (Hemel Hempstead: Harvester Wheatsheaf).

Macnaghten, P., and J. Urry (1998) *Contested Natures* (London: Sage).

Macy, J. (2009) 'The Greening of the Self', in L. Buzzell and C. Chalquist (eds) *Ecotherapy: Healing with Nature in Mind* (San Francisco: Sierra Club Books) pp. 238–45.

Metzner, R. (2009) 'Green Psychology, Shamanism, and Therapeutic Rituals', in L. Buzzell and C. Chalquist (eds) *Ecotherapy: Healing with Nature in Mind* (San Francisco: Sierra Club Books) pp. 256–61.

Mind (2007) *Ecotherapy: The Green Agenda for Mental Health* (London: Mind).

Mind (2013a) *Feel Better Outside, Feel Better Inside: Ecotherapy for Mental Wellbeing, Resilience and Recovery* (London: Mind).

Mind (2013b) *Making Sense of Ecotherapy* (London: Mind).

Prouty, G. F. (2001) 'The Practice of Pre-Therapy', *Journal of Contemporary Psychotherapy*, 31, 31–40.

Roszak, T. (1995) 'When Psyche Meets Gaia', in T. Roszak, M. E. Gomes and A. D. Kanner (eds) *Ecopsychology: Restoring the Earth, Healing the Mind* (San Francisco: Sierra Club Books) pp. 1–17.

Roszak, T., M. E. Gomes and A. D. Kanner (eds) (1995) *Ecopsychology: Restoring the Earth, Healing the Mind* (San Francisco: Sierra Club Books).

Sabini, M. (2008) *C. G. Jung on Nature, Technology, and Modern Life* (Berkeley, CA: North Atlantic Books).

Searles, H. (1960) *The Non-Human Environment in Normal Development and in Schizophrenia* (Madison, CT: International Universities Press).

Stigsdotter, U. A., and P. Grahn (2003) 'Experiencing a Garden: A Healing Garden for People Suffering from Burnout Diseases', *Journal of Therapeutic Horticulture*, XIV, 39–49.

Totton, N. (2011) *Wild Therapy: Undomesticating Inner and Outer Worlds* (PCCS Books: Ross-on-Wye).

PART I   THEORY

1

THEORETICAL AND EMPIRICAL FOUNDATIONS FOR ECOTHERAPY

Thomas J. Doherty

Introduction

This chapter explores some of the theoretical and empirical foundations for ecotherapy, which are not meant to be definitive, but rather to assist readers in reflecting on their own practice and to better appreciate and critique the ecotherapy approaches detailed in this volume. The goal is to create a conceptual ground for ecotherapy and to identify some overarching theory, assumptions and findings that act as a shared commons.

Hundreds of established psychotherapy and mental health counselling approaches (Prochaska and Norcross, 2009) promote differing visions of mental health and well-being. They use different tools to treat or prevent what, in their view, constitutes life problems or psychopathology; and they intervene at levels of scale from individual neurophysiology, thoughts and emotions to the structure of daily life, to the level of intimate and family relationships and on to group, community and population levels (Burns and Burns-Lundgren, 2015; Roth and Fonagy, 1996). So, once one becomes educated in this domain, it becomes clear that simply saying that a person does 'counselling' or 'psychotherapy' is not an adequate description because it begs the questions: What kind of psychotherapy and for whom? How is human psyche and agency conceived? On what standard of health and well-being is it based? What are its methods? How are outcomes measured?

So too with ecotherapy: the potential is great for approaches that apply existing therapeutic models in a natural ecological context and for the creation of others that constitute distinct innovations to therapy 'business as usual'. In addition to the questions posed above, an ecotherapist might ask: How does the therapy involve the interplay of social systems *and* natural systems? What is the role of the physical context (the built space of the consulting room or the local natural environment) in the therapy? In what way does the therapy address the 'client' or 'patient' as a human animal, a social primate of the species *homo sapiens*? How are other species recognized and involved in the therapy? How is relationship to community, bioregion or planet recognized? What is the role of environmental ethics in the therapy, and how are issues like global climate change or environmental justice addressed? How do these factors figure into the conception of health outcomes and the methods of the therapy, or not?

These profound questions draw attention to basic assumptions people share about psychotherapy. There is a strong element of consciousness-raising inherent in surfacing them. To assert that nature or environmental issues *do not* figure into therapy can be perfectly reasonable and ethical given the issue addressed – and need not imply that these issues are not important to health. But for our purposes, physical place, more-than-human nature and global environmental issues *do* figure into therapy and counselling, and for good reason. And although ecotherapy is still evolving in terms of variety and specialization, we can sketch out its theoretical and empirical underpinnings. This will allow for a more nuanced discussion of ecotherapy and set the stage for answering the question: What kind of ecotherapy do you do?

The Psychological Territory of Ecotherapy

To get a feel for the content of ecotherapy, consider the following questions, drawn from research questionnaires used in environmental psychology and sociology. Along with your intellectual responses, note the extent to which the questions elicit an emotional charge or a reaction. Also, notice how responding implicitly requires you to consider yourself in relation to others in your social group as well as others in society:

- 'We are approaching the limit of the number of people the earth can support.' Agree or disagree?

- 'Like a tree can be part of a forest, I feel embedded within the broader natural world.' Strongly disagree, neutral or strongly agree?

- 'I have done this: walked barefoot in a wild area; hunted, fished, trapped, raised and butchered my own meat; navigated by the sun or the stars...' Yes or no?

- Global warming is (a) caused mostly by human activities, (b) caused mostly by natural changes in the environment, (c) caused by some other means or (d) not actually happening.

- 'I am worried about risks to human health from nearby environmental pollution.' Agree or disagree?

- Please indicate how often you have done each of the following in the last year (i.e. never, rarely, sometimes, often, very often, non-applicable): composted food scraps, conserved gasoline by walking or bicycling, voted for a candidate who supported environmental issues and so on.

These survey items are meant to determine (i) whether respondents believe human activities are subject to or exempt from the natural order (NEP Scale: Dunlap, 2008); (ii) the extent to which someone perceives they are connected with nature (Connectedness To Nature Scale: Mayer and Franz, 2004); (iii) immersion and hands-on self-sufficiency in the outdoors, as in a hunter-gather context (Participation in Nature Scale: Scott, Amel and Manning, 2014); (iv) beliefs about human responsibility for global climate change (Global Warming's Six Americas Screening: Maibach et al., 2011); (v) emotions regarding felt impact of environmental changes (Environmental Distress Scale: Higginbotham et al., 2007); and (vi) the frequency of various conservation behaviours (Proenvironmental Behavior Scale: Schultz and Zelezny, 1998). Your responding, both emotional and intellectual, gives a flavour of the mental activity associated with environmental perception and how this is linked with identity, self-image, moral judgements about self and others, and expectations for responsible behaviour. It is in this realm of *ecological self in relation* – to one's own ideals, to other humans as they utilize natural resources for survival, to other species and habitats and to the planet Earth as a whole – that ecotherapy takes place.

Defining Ecotherapy

For the sake of our work, *ecotherapy* will be defined as 'psychotherapeutic activities (counselling, psychotherapy, social work, self-help, prevention, public health activities) undertaken with an ecological consciousness or intent'. These activities are considered *ecological* as they partake of natural ecology such as the local environment or the planetary biosphere, and not only the social ecology of human relationships and culture (Bronfenbrenner, 2005; Cook, 2012). Put in the language of conservation science, they concern coupled natural and human systems. Although the human sociocultural sphere, including the information technologies through which we can perceive global issues, is embedded in ecotherapy work, it is important to realize that the human need not be the basis or starting point of ecotherapeutic activities. In fact, a goal of many ecotherapies would be to bracket human culture and technologies, and look to the 'more-than-human' world (Abram, 1996) for a holistic and fundamental experience of identity, mental health and well-being.

Put another way, ecotherapy, in terms of its orientation and moral compass, can be seen as 'ecocentric' (i.e. focused on systems, wholes and interdependence, with humans being one part of the natural order). This is in comparison to the more normative and unacknowledged anthropocentric-biased nature of psychotherapy and counselling (i.e. human-centred and seeing all nature in terms of human ideas, uses and benefits). And as noted above, just as there is a great diversity in the form, content and scope of anthropocentric psychotherapy approaches, a similar potential for diversity exists in the ecopsychotherapeutic enterprise, both in theory and based on a survey of extant approaches.

Defining Ecotherapy

Psychotherapeutic activities (counselling, psychotherapy, social work, self-help, prevention, public health activities):

- Undertaken with an ecological consciousness or intent
- Often utilizing natural settings, activities or processes as an integral part of the therapeutic process
- Focusing on ecological aspects of self, identity and behaviour
- At various scales, from personal to planetary

Ecotherapy Activities and Scope

Ecotherapy often, but not necessarily, utilizes natural settings, activities, metaphors and processes as an ingredient of therapy. These can include conducting therapeutic conversations outdoors or using walking, gardening, or structured challenge and adventure. Ecotherapy may also involve bringing sense of place and other species into the therapeutic process (e.g. having a daily outdoor retreat space, engaging in animal-assisted therapy or simply considering the rights and well-being of other species and natural systems as a part of therapeutic goals). At its most basic, ecotherapy welcomes ecological aspects of self, identity and behaviour into the psychotherapeutic arena. Depending on the recipient(s) of the therapy, this ecological self may include direct or vicarious experience of natural or technological disasters, concerns about environmental toxins or degradation, or considerations of personal responsibility for larger global issues like climate change.

Most ecotherapy remains private and concerns the private sphere, just like traditional anthropocentric psychotherapies. However, like some anthropocentric therapies that are explicitly political in nature (e.g. feminist or liberation-based therapies), some ecotherapy approaches operate as a form of social and environmental activism – a sort of environmentalist therapy – and utilize individual therapeutic experiences to resolve a cultural-level split from wild nature in developed societies that is seen to impact health and identity and to drive ecologically destructive behaviours.

Cultural Competence and Ecotherapy

Before moving forward, a caveat is important. Despite intuition and evidence that adding a natural ecological dimension to psychotherapy and counselling is a healthy progression, would-be ecotherapists need to be prepared for scepticism and resistance, both from other mental health providers and from the public. Some scepticism is to be expected of any new intervention and can be addressed by presenting clear rationale, evidence and outcomes for ecotherapy. However, the consciousness-raising aspect of ecotherapy can also activate cultural stereotypes about environmentalism and draw the discussion into often-polarized environmental debates. Whether someone may intellectually and functionally link the concepts of psychology, psychotherapy and nature has much to do with their environmental world view, which in turn is informed by their cultural background, education and personal experience. So, in much the same way that cultural competency is essential to any psychotherapy (Sue, Zane, Hall and Berger, 2009), ecotherapists need to be culturally competent about the environmental world views of those they serve, their colleagues and their communities. This is one rationale for including findings on environmental beliefs and attitudes drawn from environmental and conservation psychology as a theoretical and empirical touchstone for ecotherapy.

To give a personal example, writing as an able-bodied, heterosexual white male in the Pacific Northwest of the United States, my ecotherapeutic work more easily partakes of regional values and a commonly held, self-actualizing 'Go West' narrative in US culture (Nash, 1992). Your region may be more or less receptive in terms of programmes, community uptake and institutional support, and have different cultural influences such as northern European countries versus Asian countries (Kellert, 1993). Given your diverse personhood, and your social and cultural milieu, you may be able to be more or less 'out' with your ecotherapy philosophy. But you can be confident there are resources available to ground your practice in a coherent theoretical and empirical structure.

The Evolution of Ecotherapy

Ecotherapy as a discrete endeavour, in the form of explicit environmental or ecological initiatives in counselling and psychotherapy, coalesced in the last decades of the twentieth century (Burns, 1998; Clinebell, 1996; Conn, 1998; Howard, 1993; Macy and Young-Brown, 1998; Roszak, Gomes and Kanner, 1995; Swanson, 1995). These advances, in turn, drew from many contemporary and historic sources, notably the nineteenth- and twentieth-century conservation and environmental movements (Adelson, Engell, Ranalli and Van Anglen, 2008; Gottlieb, 2005) and associated work in the peace, nuclear disarmament and environmental justice movements (Bullard, Johnson, King and Torres, 2014; Macy, 1983). Ecotherapy is also influenced by environmental spirituality of various kinds (Badiner, 1990; Berry, 1988), ecofeminism (Mies and Shiva, 1993; Plumwood, 1993), deep ecology (Drengson, Devall and Schroll, 2011), early ecopsychology theorizing (Roszak, 1978; Shepard, 1982), and work on environmental literacy (Orr, 1991; Thomashow, 1995).

In recent years, there's been a flowering of ecotherapy initiatives of increasing sophistication and specialization. Theoretical innovations at the turn of the millennium (Fisher, 2002, 2012; Kidner, 2001; Weber-Nicholsen, 2001) set the stage for broad-based surveys of ecotherapy practice and subculture (Buzzell and Chalquist, 2009). More recently, unique integrations by scholars and practitioners (Hasbach, 2012; Jordan, 2015; Totton, 2011) and development of targeted therapies have continued this trend, for example, coping with climate change (Randall, 2009); addressing trauma in military veterans (Vella, Milligan and Bennett, 2013); providing outdoor therapies for adolescents (Gass, Gillis and Russell, 2012); and observing modern-day rites of passage (Plotkin, 2003). In the evolution of ecotherapy, one can discern a creative tension between grassroots innovations and institutional, research-based initiatives and integration of additional therapy perspectives (e.g. psychodynamic, cognitive-behavioural, mindfulness-based) into the gestalt, humanistic and transpersonal frameworks that were prominent in earlier waves of ecotherapy.

There are a number of parallel initiatives in mental and physical healthcare and social services that can be considered ecotherapeutic. These include environmental social work, horticultural therapy, animal-assisted therapies, and disaster relief (Blazina, Boyraz and Shen-Miller, 2011; Gray, Coates and Hetherington, 2012; Haller and Kramer, 2006; Jungerson et al., 2013). Differences between ecotherapy and these parallel initiatives are more often an artefact of the disciplinary silo in which they have developed than in the goals, practices or outcomes. Ecotherapists will find common ground in terms of actual practices by aligning with professionals in these areas.

As a counter to the apparent newness and novelty of ecotherapy, it's important to note that outdoor therapeutic activities, for example in the form of therapeutic camps, have been present in the United States and in other countries since the 1860s (White, 2012), and therapeutic conversations while walking outdoors were a common practice in early days of the psychoanalytic movement (Reik, 1948). From the perspective of Western cultural history and environmental philosophies, the impulse towards holistic and therapeutic approaches to humans' relationship with nature and wilderness are perennial (Oelschlaeger, 1991). Most of today's modern ecotherapies can be meaningfully understood as responses to changes in Western culture (e.g. a desacralized nature, urbanization, increased use of machines and technology) that date to the Enlightenment and the Industrial Revolution (Merchant, 1980).

Empirical and Theoretical Basis in Environmentally Focused Psychology

While ecotherapy as a field is rather new and relatively untested in many domains, there are a number of long standing environmental initiatives in psychology that provide theoretical constructs and empirical findings useful to the practicing ecotherapist. At times, locating these requires some effort and scholarly investigation. While original studies may not have been explicitly designed with psychotherapy in mind, findings on environmental topics that impact on human health and well-being, crowding, noise, the effects of information technology, impacts of natural disasters (Bechtel and Churchman, 2002), will have obvious bearing on the creation of therapeutic contexts. Other studies, such as on the effective design of wildlife conservation programmes or ways to reduce barriers to pro-environment behaviour (Clayton and Myers, 2009), provide guidance on how to support environmental engagement on the part of individuals and communities. On a deeper level, environmental psychology research provides insights on basic perceptions of nature and the natural environment and the development of environmental world views.

There is great diversity among psychology-environment approaches in terms of epistemology, methodology and goals. The categories below (e.g. environmental psychology and ecopsychology) while useful in terms of conducting a literature review, are also somewhat arbitrary as these areas overlap and individual researchers and practitioners do not always hew to these labels. Various theoretical and practical debates among environmental psychology and ecotherapy scholars will broaden the personal and professional perspectives of would-be ecotherapists: certainly Thomas Doherty's interviews with Robert Greenway, Sherri Weber-Nicholsen, Joseph Reser (2009), Michael Cohen (2010), Andy Fisher, Riley Dunlap (2011) Peter Kahn and Patricia Hasbach (2012), have aided this process.

There is a rich history of study of the dynamic interchange between humans and their environmental milieu, both built and natural, and how this relates to both basic psychological processes and the amelioration of social problems. This area coalesced into the subfield of 'environmental psychology' in the late 1960s and early 1970s (Ittelson, Proshansky, Rivlin and Winkel, 1974). More recently, environmental psychology of the spatial and built environment has continued to grow and evolve in terms of focus and research methods (Gifford, 2007) and interweave a more explicit conservation mission (Clayton, 2012).

Some areas of environmental psychology that are of particular interest to ecotherapists are Stokols et al.'s (2009) theory and findings regarding contemporary polyfunctional environments (i.e. spaces that combine home, work and social settings and are linked through instantaneous global information technologies) and how these influence global environmental consciousness and mood and well-being. Also, research on links between clinical and environmental psychology, for example in terms of aetiology and treatment of anxiety disorders (Anthony and Watkins, 2002) and on the effective design of healthcare settings and psychotherapists' offices (Devlin, 2014), has practical significance. Finally, environmental psychology has much to offer in terms of understanding the various aspects of global climate change as an existential reality, and in terms of disaster impacts, and mitigation and adaptation responses (Doherty, 2015; Reser and Swim, 2011).

Ecotherapy is probably most associated with taking therapy 'outdoors' (Jordan and Marshall, 2010). Indeed, findings on the benefits of greenery and natural settings for psychological health and well-being through stress reduction, improved cognitive and emotional functioning, and the development of identity, efficacy and meaning, are some of the strongest in the social sciences (Kaplan and Kaplan, 1989). This knowledge has been applied in the design of buildings and workspaces, healing gardens in hospitals, and in community-wide greening programmes (Frumkin, 2012; Hartig and Marcus, 2006; Ulrich et al., 2008). As I have argued, knowledge of the therapeutic effects of nearby and wild nature can be seen as a form of basic 'mental health literacy' in terms of self-help strategies and potential for psychological treatments (see Jorm, 2012, cited in Doherty and Chen, 2016).

Conservation psychology coalesced as an interdisciplinary, 'crisis discipline' modelled after conservation biology, in which social scientists partnered with natural resource and wildlife conservation colleagues (Saunders, 2003). Conservation psychology theory and research is particularly useful to ecotherapy given its explicit focus and research findings on environmental identity (Clayton, 2003) and the effects urban 'nearby' nature, human-wildlife interactions and the psychological basis for care of other species, for instance in terms of fostering the public education and conservation efforts of zoos and aquariums and in terms of managing wild lands (Clayton and Myers, 2009).

Conservation psychology also provides examples of effective conservation behaviour change programmes and detailed studies of barriers and incentives to pro-environmental behaviours in complex, real-world contexts (McKenzie-Mohr, Lee, Schultz and Kottler, 2011). This includes the role of attention and mindfulness in making pro-environmental behavioural choices (Amel, Manning and Scott, 2009). Given that the factors that promote successful conservation or sustainability programmes are often difficult to determine and counterintuitive (Nolan et al., 2008), the empirical studies of successful conservation programmes are very important for ecotherapists who seek to influence behaviour change or to promote programmes that have a higher likelihood of success.

In contrast to the more conventional disciplinary approaches associated with environmental and conservation psychology, ecopsychology can be seen as a transdisciplinary area that critiques normative, anthropocentric psychology in general where more-than-human nature remains effectively absent. This includes a critique of other environmental psychology approaches that operate on a reductive, experimental basis and downplay experiential and therapeutic aspects of nature connection and lack a critical focus on systems of power and issues of social and environmental justice. In contrast, ecopsychology theorists seek to promote a more embodied, ethical interdependence with the natural world (Roszak, 1992/2001). While again quite diverse in terms of perspectives and approaches, most ecopsychology work can be characterized as holistic, departing from the basic Cartesian split associated with Western science and envisioning the human psyche and psychological processes as more fundamentally embedded in natural and wild systems (Kahn and Hasbach, 2012; and Bragg's 1996 concept of 'ecological self'). Ecopsychology theorizing tends to be explicitly political, drawing from critical social theory and feminism to address issues of power, ideology and economic processes that drive humans' exploitation of other peoples, species and planetary resources (Fisher, 2012). Ecopsychologists also tend to adopt a more explicit stance as therapeutic environmental activists, often working in grassroots settings (Macy and Young Brown, 1998).

With its validation of the emotional impacts of environmental issues and normalization of environmental fears and anxieties, ecopsychology can be seen as helping to create ecotherapy as an endeavour. These areas are highly overlapped and for some practitioners, ecotherapy would be seen as an applied form of ecopsychology (Buzzell and Chalquist, 2009). However, given the potential variety of ecotherapy settings and activities, philosophically diverse approaches to the theoretical and empirical basis of ecotherapy, and multiculturally diverse practitioners, it's more useful to see ecopsychology as a key theoretical and practical contributor to ecotherapy, but to keep some conceptual openness between these areas.

Theoretical Synthesis: Identity, Self, Consciousness and Setting

The environmentally focused schools of psychology described above provide measurable theoretical constructs that help us to understand the synergy of physical-environmental, social-behavioural and embodied-experiential phenomena that come into play in ecotherapy. From a non-reductive perspective, the cognitive and intellectual realm of beliefs, attitudes and attributions about the self and world (Clayton, 2003) is continually influenced by actual experience of being in the world (Bragg, 1996). Embodied experiences of ecological self are intimately influenced by the quality of one's moment-to-moment consciousness and focus of attention such as mindfulness, sense of flow, attention to patterns in nearby nature, or alternatively, immersion in communications technology or other human-centric stimuli (Amel, Manning and Scott, 2009; Stokols et al., 2009). Identity, self and consciousness cannot be meaningfully separated from the design of the physical setting, whether built or natural, and whether restorative or stressful (Kaplan, Kaplan and Ryan, 1998).

For example, a relaxing walk in a safe, forested park setting will provide opportunities to attend to natural views and stimuli (soft fascination) and facilitate an experience of ecologically embedded self that will influence one's cognitive appraisal of their identity and mood, and thoughts about the world at large. Conversely, a high-intensity behavioural setting exhibiting hard fascination (e.g. driving in rush-hour traffic), particularly a poly-functional setting with continuous access to global information technology, will provide a different set of stimuli to attend to and a different quality of consciousness and physiological arousal. This in turn is likely to be experienced as a different sense of self and to give rise to different thoughts about one's identity and one's sense of the world and their place in it. All of these factors – cognitive appraisals of identity, sense of embodied self, focused awareness and attention, and qualities of setting – can be utilized in the creation of ecotherapy interventions (see Figure 1.1).

Ecotherapy Research

The study of ecotherapy can be approached in a number of ways, ranging from positivist/biomedical approaches that focus on symptom reduction, to more systems-focused biopsychosocial approaches; to humanistic, meaning-making approaches; to constructivist/critical approaches that recognize the role of cultural discourses and power in the social construction of ecopsychological problems (Marks and Yardley, 2004). Ecotherapy programmes will have differing

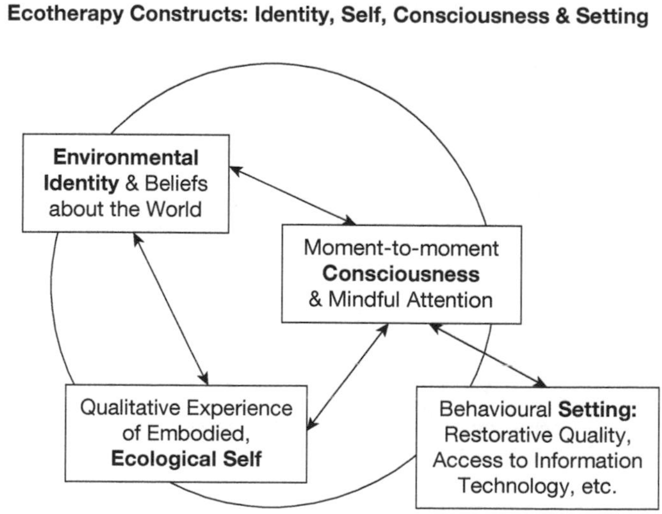

Ecotherapy Constructs: Identity, Self, Consciousness & Setting

Environmental **Identity** & Beliefs about the World

Moment-to-moment **Consciousness** & Mindful Attention

Qualitative Experience of Embodied, **Ecological Self**

Behavioural **Setting:** Restorative Quality, Access to Information Technology, etc.

Figure 1.1 Key ecotherapy constructs.

standards of evidence depending on their rationale and target goals. For example, expressive 'despair and empowerment' approaches (Macy and Young-Brown, 1998) will have more qualitative and subjective outcomes than interventions designed to address symptoms (Faber-Taylor and Kuo, 2009) that lend themselves to more quantitative methods.

Evidence-based Ecotherapy Programmes. As interest, funding and systematic study have increased, the evidence base for ecotherapy has become more substantial. Practitioners are now fortunate to have some well-developed models to learn from (Doherty and Chen, 2016). Academic research programmes that combine theory building, controlled study and intervention (see Landscape and Human Health Laboratory: http://lhhl.illinois.edu/) provide robust templates to build on, and have spurred their own interventions, such as outdoor-based treatment for children experiencing attention deficit disorder symptoms, (Faber-Taylor and Kuo, 2009). Private and public sector programmes have spawned ongoing research programmes as well. These include longitudinal outcome studies completed by the Outdoor Behavioral Healthcare Industry Research Cooperative (http://obhic.com/research.html) sponsored by a consortium of residential wilderness therapy programmes in the United States and Canada. Forestry Scotland's Branching Out programme, a community mental health programme that utilizes outdoor experiences, bushcraft and nature awareness, is also an exemplar. On the individual level, the construct of eco-wellness – the subjective experience of wellness through one's perceived connection with nature – has found empirical support in counselling settings. A perception of eco-wellness is mediated by factors such as access to restorative

Figure 1.2 Ecowellness.
Source: Adapted from R. F. Myers, J. E. Lewis and J. T. White (2015) 'Construction and Initial Validation of the Reese Ecowellness Inventory', *International Journal for the Advancement of Counselling*, 37, 124–42.

settings, and sense of safety, efficacy, spirituality and community connectedness (Reese and Myers, 2012; Reese, Myers, Lewis and Willse, 2015).

Theoretical and Empirical Issues Unique to Ecotherapy

Competency in ecotherapy requires a nuanced understanding of commonly used terms such as 'nature' or 'natural'. While these terms can provide a useful shorthand for the out-of-doors or for objects or processes with minimal influence of humans (or explicitly valued for non-human attributes), this distinction can also present a false dualism that obscures the inherent naturalness of all human cultures and endeavours. From a perspective of environmental and conservation psychology (Clayton and Myers, 2009), it is helpful to think of a spectrum from *domestic nature* such as plants in the home, to *nearby nature* such as parks and gardens, to *managed nature* such as tree farms and agricultural areas, to *wild nature* – native plants and animals, wilderness areas that are remote, challenging, or purposely left undeveloped; and 'wild' processes in the human body (Cryan and Dinan, 2012). From the perspective of environmental philosophy and history, ideas of 'nature', 'wilderness' and 'the environment' are also social and cultural constructions whose meanings vary greatly based on the social context (Cronon, 1995; Soule and Lease, 1995). Conceptualizing nature has practical implications. When hypothesizing about ecotherapy outcomes, it is important to be clear about what aspects of 'nature' you intend to access and utilize, how these are to be operationalized, and in service of what therapeutic goal. Consider for example, doing so-called wilderness therapy. A place may be subjectively experienced as 'wild' given its remoteness, level of challenge or visible presence of other species. This can be assessed through a qualitative interview. A setting may also be considered wild based on its legal designation, or quantitative assessments of its size, number of visitors, or diversity of its ecosystem.

Working with Systems and Scale

An important ecological skill for ecotherapists is '*thinking at scale*' the ability to track interdependent issues and phenomenon at different levels of local and global context, and to recognize the emotional and ethical ramifications. This can include understanding how '*distant suffering*' (Boltanski, 1999) associated with events at great physical remove can be personally experienced (Stokols et al., 2009). In the short term, this awareness can be disorienting and overwhelming. However, with patience and perseverance, simultaneously cultivating connections with local place and planetary awareness can also be comforting, a positive synergy of consciousness and dedication to daily efforts and local action.

Assessing Psychopathology in an Ecotherapy Context

Expertise in assessment and diagnosis of psychopathology and psychiatric disorders and use of diagnostic criteria is beyond the scope of this chapter. But this constitutes a necessary practical and ethical component of doing ecotherapy work. Some individuals seeking ecotherapy may be experiencing significant distress or impairment or suffering from psychiatric disorders. Others may be quite 'well' in terms of their general life functioning. Making a functional distinction between the concerns of someone who would be seen as normatively healthy by their cultural group but who is also suffering distress or concern regarding environmental issues, and another person who is impacted by a pre-existing interpersonal trauma, psychiatric disorder, or psychosocial adjustment process that in turn makes them susceptible to environmental distress, requires some clinical sophistication. In practice, these situations are rarely clear-cut. Would-be ecotherapists are encouraged to make use of their existing training regarding psychopathology and psychodiagnosis. In fact, no special diagnostic criteria are needed to treat ecotherapeutic issues. For example, existing criteria for adjustment, anxiety and depression disorders can be applied to problems associated with the natural environment – both acute and secondary.

In terms of natural disasters or climate change, causal pathways for psychopathology or psychiatric impairment are relatively clear-cut. Geophysical effects such as flooding, heat waves, droughts, and extreme weather events increase the likelihood of injury, trauma and anxiety-related responses in individuals and communities, and over time, the prevalence of chronic and severe psychological problems (see Doherty, 2015). Indirect or vicarious mental health impacts of environmental issues are more difficult to assess and diagnose compared to acute disaster impacts. These tend to be gradual, diffuse, and contingent on other aspects of a person's life functioning such as their exposure to media and information technology (see the discussion of the information-saturated polyfunctional environments in the environmental psychology section above) and their general level of environmental literacy.

In their treatment, ecotherapists are forced to make a difficult philosophical distinction between normal and expected worry about ecological threats and pathological worry that impacts their client's or patient's life functioning. Ecological worrying in and of itself does not correlate with pathology but rather with proenvironmental attitudes and positive personality traits such as altruism (Verplanken and Roy, 2013). Anecdotes of 'eco-anxiety' symptoms in the popular press (Nobel, 2007) including anxiety or panic, irritability, sleeplessness and malaise, signal the presence of diagnosable or sub-threshold disorders of various kinds. Only a comprehensive diagnostic history and interview can sort these issues out with specific individuals.

Creative Tensions in Ecotherapy

The practice of ecotherapy becomes a radical endeavour when it calls into question assumptions of what philosophers might call the 'world in force', the normative anthropocentric-technological world of so-called developed human societies. In particular, ecotherapy questions seemingly obvious dichotomies in psychotherapy (and in general culture) between built and natural, inner and outer, global and local, wild and domesticated, backcountry and front country. Ecotherapy not only blurs distinctions between these concepts but also upends their assumed hierarchies and therapeutic values. This has philosophical and practical implications. For example:

A major insight of ecotherapy is that what are commonly seen as mental processes located 'in the head' (thoughts, emotions, behavioural impulses) are actually ecological products of environmental interactions. There is no psyche and no therapy without the physical setting. Ecological psychology in its physical-spatial framing (rather than its social and anthropocentric variations) has long conceived of human psychological processes as transactional, based on a systemic embeddedness in the physical environment, and taking form as patterns of action that continually attune people to that environment as an integrated behaviour-setting (Heft, 2012). From the perspective of ecological psychology, certain settings provide affordances – physical properties of the environment that shape consciousness and behaviour. These spatial-systemic properties can also be understood from a phenomenological perspective and approached in the language of ecopsychology as 'turning the psyche inside out' (Fisher, 2012). This spatial-ecological thinking can also take on an evolutionary turn. When climbing a tree, finding a convenient branch that neatly fits one's hand is no accident. The human hand has been evolved to climb and has been shaped by such branches over millennia.

Ecotherapy involves practitioners who work in urban settings and those who act as guides or expedition leaders in more (un)managed or wild settings. Having done both types of work, I would encourage practitioners not draw too strict a line between the *backcountry* and the *front-country*. Approached from the perspective of physical challenge and risk management, a backcountry setting may be seen as more difficult than an urban setting. In some senses this is true. However, working out of doors and away from more mainstream settings offers greater space and freedom for doing ecologically focused and nature-based techniques without perceived stigma. Conversely, while front country activities may offer more infrastructure and convenience, they can also highlight the novel, political nature of ecotherapy with practices that question the therapeutic status quo. For example, trying to institute even the most benign ecotherapeutic initiative (e.g. a healthy plant or a window in every consulting office) in an urban, anthropocentric practice location can require laborious efforts to overcome scepticism; justify and seek support for the activity; and deal with the resources of the facility.

The Development of the Ecotherapist: Inside Out and Outside In

Rather than resolve these creative tensions in any essentialism about ecotherapy, I recommend that practitioners be mindful how their practice constitutes a synthesis of these dialectics and how this evolves during their career. I have observed in my own practice, and in the activities of others, a developmental trajectory in terms of ecotherapeutic practice that contains a tension between the indoors and outdoors and the level of risk and exposure in the activities (i.e. between sedentary, low-risk activities in nearby nature, such as doing walking sessions with clients, versus more physically active, challenging adventure activities requiring technical skills, specialized gear and explicit risk-management thinking, such as overnight outdoor retreats). Curiously, this trajectory can go in *either direction*: one can begin with office-style activities and then venture outwards into more complex and challenging scenarios as they become empowered; or one can transition into an office-based practice from a career of doing high adventure activities (due to lifestyle changes). For a complementary perspective, see Kempton and Holland (2003) for an interesting study of the life development of environmental advocates.

Putting It All Together

I have respect for inside and outside realms. My evolution as an ecotherapist, up until now, has gone more in an 'outside-in' direction. My conceptual baseline for ecotherapy was established during multi-week 'wilderness therapy' backcountry expeditioning in the western United States, in the late 1980s and early 1990s, and witnessing the standardization of grass roots backcountry outfitter and therapy programmes into the outdoor recreation and 'outdoor behavioural healthcare' industries. The benefits of this shift included shared knowledge and resources, quality control and improved risk management. The losses included the passing of idiosyncratic regional programmes and homogenization of wildness therapy models. My growing edge has included the urban delivery of ecotherapy, teaching the science and craft of ecotherapy and figuring out how to make a living doing this work in a personally and environmentally sustainable manner.

In my own work as an ecotherapist, I use a constructivist-developmental approach that fosters consciousness-raising and exploration of one's life history vis-à-vis nature (broadly, in the client's own cultural understanding) and sense of physical and regional place, and how these influence environmental identity and diversity. I find that this tends to organically segue into a discovery of personal agency and curiosity about experimenting with new behaviours. This creates a need for a more precise assessment of readiness for change and deployment of conservation behaviour change strategies. Immersion in the world of action creates experience (i.e. new knowledge, setbacks and successes) that then can be reflected on, in an ongoing cycle of growth (Kempton and Holland, 2003). I particularly enjoy doing this ecotherapy work in groups where the added complexity and synergy of different environmental identities and world views comes into play. (I imagine a similar enjoyment on the part of therapists who specialize in work with other species.) Finally, I enjoy the challenge of risk management – risk in the sense of emotional risk as well as physical or practical risks. Rather than perceiving this as a burden, I see this as a signal that the therapeutic work I'm doing is truly real and adventurous and not simply abstract or removed from the joys and dangers of the physical and natural world. I wish you well on your own ecotherapy journey.

References

Abram, D. (1996) *The Spell of the Sensuous* (New York: Pantheon).

Adelson, G., J. Engell, B. Ranalli and K. P. Van Anglen (2008) *Environment* (New Haven, CT: Yale University Press).

Amel, E. L., C. M. Manning and B. A. Scott (2009) 'Mindfulness and Sustainable Behavior: Pondering Attention and Awareness as Means for Increasing Green Behavior', *Ecopsychology*, 1, 14–25.

Anthony, K. H., and N. J. Watkins (2002) 'Exploring Pathology: Relationship Between Clinical and Environmental Psychology', in R. B. Bechtel and A. Churchman (eds) *Handbook of Environmental Psychology* (New York: John Wiley & Sons).

Badiner, A. H. (1990) *Dharma Gaia* (Berkeley, CA: Parallax Press).

Bechtel, R. B., and A. Churchman (2002) *Handbook of Environmental Psychology* (New York: John Wiley & Sons).

Berry, T. (1988) *The Dream of the Earth* (San Francisco: Sierra Club Books).

Blazina, C., G. Boyraz and D. Shen-Miller (2011) *The Psychology of the Human-Animal Bond: A Resource for Clinicians and Researchers* (New York: Springer Science & Business Media).

Boltanski, L. (1999) *Distant Suffering* (Cambridge: Cambridge University Press).

Bragg, E. A. (1996) 'Towards Ecological Self: Deep Ecology Meets Constructionist Self-Theory', *Journal of Environmental Psychology*, 16, 93–108.

Bronfenbrenner, U. (2005) *Making Human Beings Human: Bioecological Perspectives on Human Development* (Thousand Oaks, CA: Sage Publications).

Bullard, R. D., G. S. Johnson, D. W. King and A. O. Torres (2014) *Environmental Justice Milestones and Accomplishments: 1964–2014* (Houston: Texas Southern University Press).

Burns, G. W. (1998) *Nature-Guided Therapy* (New York: Taylor & Francis).

Burns, T., and E. Burns-Lundgren (2015) *Psychotherapy: A Very Short Introduction* (Oxford: Oxford University Press).

Buzzell, L., and C. Chalquist (2009) *Ecotherapy* (San Francisco: Sierra Club Press).

Clayton, S., and G. Myers (2009) *Conservation Psychology: Understanding and Promoting Human Care for Nature* (Cambridge, MA: MIT Press).

Clayton, S. (2003) 'Environmental Identity: A Conceptual and Operational Definition, in S. Clayton and S. Opotow (eds) *Identity and the Natural Environment: The Psychological Significance of Nature* (Cambridge, MA: MIT Press) pp. 45–65.

Clayton, S. D. (2012) *The Oxford Handbook of Environmental and Conservation Psychology* (New York: Oxford University Press).

Clinebell, H. (1996) *Ecotherapy* (Minneapolis, MN: Fortress Press).

Conn, S. (1998) 'Living in the Earth: Ecopsychology, Health and Psychotherapy', *Humanistic Psychologist*, 26, 179–98.

Cook, E. P. (2012) *Understanding People in Context: The Ecological Perspective in Counseling* (Alexandria, VA: American Counseling Association).

Cronon, W. (1995) 'The Trouble with Wilderness; or, Getting Back to the Wrong Nature', in W. Cronon (ed.) *Uncommon Ground: Rethinking the Human Place in Nature* (New York: W. W. Norton) pp. 69–90.

Cryan, J. F., and T. G. Dinan (2012) 'Mind-altering Microorganisms: The Impact of the Gut Microbiota on Brain and Behaviour', *Nature Reviews Neuroscience*, 13, 701–12.

Devlin, A. S. (2014) *Transforming the Doctor's Office: Principles from Evidence-based Design* (New York: Routledge).

Doherty, T. J. (2015) 'Mental Health Impacts', in B. S. Levy and J. Patz (eds) *Climate Change and Public Health* (New York: Oxford University Press).

Doherty, T. J. (2012) 'Ecopsychology Roundtable: Patricia Hasbach and Peter Kahn', *Ecopsychology*, 4, 1–9.

Doherty, T. J. (2011) 'Riley Dunlap: The *Ecopsychology* Interview', *Ecopsychology*, 3, 219–26.

Doherty, T. J. (2011) 'Andy Fisher: The *Ecopsychology* Interview', *Ecopsychology*, 3, 167–73.

Doherty, T. J. (2010) 'Michael Cohen: The *Ecopsychology* Interview', *Ecopsychology*, 2, 53–57.

Doherty, T. J. (2009a) 'Robert Greenway: The *Ecopsychology* Interview', *Ecopsychology*, 1, 47–52.

Doherty, T. J. (2009b) 'Shierry Weber Nicholsen: The *Ecopsychology* Interview', *Ecopsychology*, 1, 110–17.

Doherty, T. J. (2009c) 'Joseph Reser: The *Ecopsychology* Interview', *Ecopsychology*, 1, 57–63.

Doherty, T. J. and A. Chen (2016) 'Improving Human Functioning: Ecotherapy and Environmental Health Approaches', in R. Gifford (ed.) *Research Methods in Environmental Psychology* (West Sussex, UK: John Wiley & Sons), pp. 323–43.

Drengson, A., B. Devall and M. A. Schroll (2011) 'The Deep Ecology Movement: Origins, Development, and Future Prospects (Towards a Transpersonal Ecosophy)', *International Journal of Transpersonal Studies*, 30, 101–17.

Dunlap, R. E. (2008) 'The NEP Scale: From Marginality to Worldwide Use', *Journal of Environmental Education*, 40, 3–18.

Faber Taylor, A., and F. E. Kuo (2009) 'Children with Attention Deficits Concentrate Better after Walk in the Park', *Journal of Attention Disorders*, 12, 402–9.

Fisher, A. (2002) *Radical Ecopsychology: Psychology in the Service of Life* (Albany NY: State University of New York Press)

Fisher, A. (2012) *Radical Ecopsychology: Psychology in the Service of Life*, 2nd edn (Albany, NY: State University of New York Press).

Frumkin, H. (2012) 'Building the Science Base: Ecopsychology Meets Clinical Epidemiology', in P. H. Kahn and P. H. Hasbach (eds) *Ecopsychology: Science, Totems, and the Technological Species* (Cambridge, MA: MIT Press) pp. 141–72.

Gass, M. A., H. L. Gillis and K. C. Russell (2012) *Adventure Therapy: Theory, Research and Practice* (New York: Routledge).

Gifford, R. (2007) *Environmental Psychology* (Colville, WA: Optimal Books).

Gottlieb, R. (2005) *Forcing the Spring* (Washington, DC: Island Press).

Gray, M., J. Coates and T. Hetherington (2012) *Environmental Social Work* (New York: Routledge).

Haller, R. L., and C. L. Kramer (2006) *Horticultural Therapy Methods: Making Connections in Health Care, Human Service, and Community Programs* (Philadelphia, PA: Haworth Press).

Hartig, T., and C. C. Marcus (2006) 'Healing Gardens: Places for Nature in Health Care', *Lancet*, 368, S36–7.

Hasbach, P. (2012) 'Ecotherapy', in P. H. Kahn and P. H. Hasbach (eds) *Ecopsychology: Science, Totems, and the Technological Species* (Cambridge, MA: MIT Press) pp. 115–40.

Heft, H. (2012) 'Foundations of an Ecological Approach to Psychology', in S. D. Clayton (ed.) *The Oxford Handbook of Environmental and Conservation Psychology* (New York: Oxford University Press) pp. 11–40.

Higginbotham, N., L. Connor, G. Albrecht, S. Freeman and K. Agho (2007) 'Validation of an Environmental Distress Scale', *Ecohealth*, 3, 245–54.

Howard, G. (1993) 'Special Issue on Ecocounseling Psychology', *The Counseling Psychologist*, 21, 4.

Ittelson, W. H., H. M. Proshansky, L. G. Rivlin and G. H. Winkel (1974) *An Introduction to Environmental Psychology* (New York: Holt, Rhinehart and Winston).

Jordan, M. (2015) *Therapy and Nature* (London: Routledge).

Jordan, M., and H. Marshall (2010) 'Taking Counselling and Psychotherapy Outside: Destruction or Enrichment of the Therapeutic Frame?' *European Journal of Psychotherapy & Counselling*, 12, 345–59.

Jungerson, T. S., S. Daily, J. Uhernik, C. M. Smith et al. (2013) 'All Trauma Is Not the Same', *Counseling Today*, http://ct.counseling.org/2013/03/all-trauma-is-not-the-same/.

Kahn, P. H., and P. H. Hasbach (2012) *Ecopsychology: Science, Totems, and the Technological Species* (Cambridge, MA: MIT Press).

Kaplan, R., and S. Kaplan (1989) *The Experience of Nature: A Psychological Perspective* (Cambridge, MA: Cambridge University Press).

Kaplan, R., S. Kaplan and R. L. Ryan (1998) *With People in Mind: Design and Management of Everyday Nature* (Washington, DC: Island Press).

Kellert, S. (1993) 'Attitudes, Knowledge, and Behavior Toward Wildlife Among the Industrial Superpowers: United States, Japan and Germany', *Journal of Social Issues*, 49, 53–69.

Kempton, W., and D. C. Holland (2003) 'Identity and Sustained Environmental Practice', in S. Clayton and S. Opotow (eds) *Identity and the Natural Environment* (Cambridge, MA: MIT Press) pp. 317–41.

Kidner, D. W. (2001) *Nature and Psyche* (Albany, NY: State University of New York Press).

Macy, J. R. (1983) *Despair and Personal Power in the Nuclear Age* (Philadelphia, PA: New Society).

Macy, J., and M. Young Brown (1998) *Coming Back to Life: Practices to Reconnect Our Lives, Our World* (Gabriola Island, BC: New Society).

Maibach, E. W., A. Leiserowitz, C. Roser-Renouf, C. K. Mertz and K. Akerlof (2011) Global Warming's Six Americas Screening Tools: Survey Instruments; Instructions for Coding and Data Treatment; and Statistical Program Scripts. Yale University and George Mason University, Yale Project on Climate Change Communication, New Haven, CT, http://climatechangecommunication.org/SixAmericasManual.cfm.

Marks, D. F., and L. Yardley (2004) *Research Methods for Clinical and Health Psychology* (London: Sage Publications).

Mayer, F. S., and C. M. Frantz (2004) 'The Connectedness to Nature Scale: A Measure of Individuals' Feeling in Community with Nature', *Journal of Environmental Psychology*, 24, 503–15.

McKenzie-Mohr, D. M, N. R. Lee, P. W. Schultz and P. A. Kottler (2011) *Social Marketing to Protect the Environment: What Works* (Thousand Oaks, CA: Sage).

Merchant, C. (1980) *The Death of Nature* (San Francisco: Harper and Row).

Mies, M., and V. Shiva (1993) *Ecofeminism* (London: Zed Books).

Nash, R. (1992) *Wilderness and the American Mind* (New Haven, CT: Yale University Press).

Nobel, J. (2007, April 9) 'Eco-anxiety: Something Else to Worry About' [electronic version]. *The Philadelphia Enquirer*.

Nolan, J. M., P. W. Schultz, R. B. Cialdini, N. J. Goldstein and V. Griskevicius (2008) 'Normative Social Influence Is Underdetected', *Personality and Social Psychology Bulletin*, 34, 913–23.

Oelschlaeger, M. (1991) *The Idea of Wilderness* (New Haven, CT: Yale University Press).

Orr, D. (1991) *Ecological Literacy* (Albany, NY: State University of New York Press).

Plotkin, B. (2003) *Soulcraft* (Novato, CA: New World Library).

Plumwood, V. (1993) *Feminism and the Mastery over Nature* (New York: Routledge).

Prochaska, J. O., and J. C. Norcross (2009) *Systems of Psychotherapy* (Belmont, CA: Brooks/Cole).

Randall, R. (2009) 'Loss and Climate Change: The Cost of Parallel Narratives', *Ecopsychology*, 3, 118–29.

Reese, R. F., and J. E. Myers (2012) 'EcoWellness: The Missing Factor in Holistic Wellness Models', *Journal of Counseling and Development*, 90, 400–6.

Reese, R. F., J. E. Myers, T. F. Lewis and J. T. Willse (2015) 'Construction and Initial Validation of the Reese Ecowellness Inventory', *International Journal for the Advancement of Counselling*, 36, 1–19.

Reik, T. (1948) *Listening with the Third Ear: The Inner Experience of a Psychoanalyst* (New York: Grove Press).

Reser, J. P., and J. K. Swim (2011) 'Adapting to and Coping with the Threat and Impacts of Climate Change', *American Psychologist*, 66, 277–89.

Roszak, T. (1978) *Person/Planet* (Garden City, NY: Anchor Press).

Roszak, T. (1992/2001) *The Voice of the Earth* (Grand Rapids, MI: Phanes).

Roszak, T., M. E. Gomes and A. D. Kanner (1995) *Ecopsychology: Restoring the Earth, Healing the Mind* (San Francisco: Sierra Club Books).

Roth, A., and P. Fonagy (1996) *What Works for Whom? A Critical Review of Psychotherapy Research* (New York: Guilford Press).

Saunders, C. (2003) 'The Emerging Field of Conservation Psychology', *Human Ecology Review*, 10, 137–49.

Schultz, P. W., and L. C. Zelezny (1998) 'Values and Proenvironmental Behaviors: A Five-Country Survey', *Journal of Cross-Cultural Psychology*, 29, 540–58.

Scott, B. A., E. L. Amel and C. M. Manning (2014) In and of the Wilderness: Ecological Connection Through Participation in Nature', *Ecopsychology*, 6, 81–91.

Shepard, P. (1982) *Nature and Madness* (Athens, GA: University of Georgia Press).

Soule, M. E., and G. Lease (1995) *Reinventing Nature? Responses to Postmodern Deconstruction* (Washington, DC: Island Press).

Stokols, D., S. Misra, M. G. Runnerstrom and J. A. Hipp (2009) 'Psychology in an Age of Ecological Crisis: From Personal Angst to Collective Action', *American Psychologist*, 64, 181–93.

Sue, S., N. Zane, G. C. N. Hall and L. K. Berger (2009) 'The Case for Cultural Competency in Psychotherapeutic Interventions', *Annual Review of Psychology*, 60, 525–48.

Swanson, J. (1995) 'The Call for Gestalt's Contribution to Ecopsychology: Figuring in the Environmental Field', *Gestalt Journal*, 18, 47–85.

Thomashow, M. (1995) *Ecological Identity* (Cambridge, MA. MIT Press).

Totton, N. (2011) *Wild Therapy* (Ross-on-Wye, UK: PCCS Books).

Ulrich, R. S., C. Zimring, X. Zhu, J. DuBose, H. Seo, Y. Choi, X. Quan and A. Joseph (2008) *A Review of the Research Literature on Evidence-based Healthcare Design*, http://edinnovation.com.au/documents/attachments/58-hcleader-5-litreviewwp.pdf.

Vella, E. J., B. Milligan and J. L. Bennett (2013) 'Participation in Outdoor Recreation Program Predicts Improved Psychosocial Well-Being Among Veterans with Post-Traumatic Stress Disorder: A Pilot Study', *Military Medicine*, 178, 254–60.

Verplanken, B., and D. Roy (2013) '"My Worries Are Rational, Climate Change Is Not": Habitual Ecological Worrying Is an Adaptive Response', *PLoS ONE* 8(9) e74708.

Weber-Nicholsen, S. (2001) *The Love of Nature at the End of the World* (Cambridge, MA: MIT Press).

White, W. (2012) 'A History of Adventure Therapy', in M. A. Gass, H. L. Gillis and K. C. Russell (eds) *Adventure Therapy: Theory, Research, and Practice* (New York: Routledge) pp. 19–46.

2

NATURE-BASED PRACTICE: A BUDDHIST PSYCHOTHERAPY PERSPECTIVE

Caroline Brazier

Introduction

The journey from the consulting room into natural surroundings creates a challenge for the therapist. Working outdoors transgresses many of the norms of conventional therapeutic practice and inevitably invites different boundaries of time and space and a different style of therapeutic relationship.

This chapter explores one model of working out of doors, namely other-centred approach, a Buddhist-based therapy. In this context, it also reviews the practice of mindfulness as a methodology which may be drawn on in ecotherapy. As the therapeutic relationship makes the transition from consulting room to field, new ways of working become possible. It proposes a model of therapeutic alliance which is grounded in a process of mindful accompaniment in which therapist and client 'go forth' into a new and unpredictable environment, using this experience as a shared resource through which to explore personal and universal process.

Varieties of Therapeutic Experience in Nature-based Practice

Interest in nature-based therapies has grown over the past decade or so; however, the field remains fluid and embryonic. Although there seems increasing awareness among public bodies that being out of doors is good for mental health (Faculty of Public Health in association with Natural England, 2010), nature-based therapeutic work varies greatly in its style and depth.

To take one example, Mind, the UK-based charity which works for better mental health, has promoted ecotherapy across its services and has been a significant contributor to the field for some years now. Mind produced major reports in 2007 and 2013 (Mind, 2007, 2013) which cited numerous university research studies and government proposals that pointed to the benefits of out-door activity in fostering good mental health. The Mind reports illustrate a range of projects, including, recently, social and therapeutic horticulture, envi-ronmental conservation, nature art and craft, green exercise and care farming (Mind, 2013). These activities generally seem intended to increase practical interaction with the natural world and usually involve service users working together in groups led by a variety of mental health professionals. The reports demonstrate the scale of interest in this work, entailing nationwide projects, doing outdoor, though not necessarily nature-based, work with large numbers of people.

The activities described in the Mind reports would not generally be classified as psychotherapy or counselling, but the sorts of relationships between workers and service users which these activities give rise to are therapeutic in outcome. They are relevant to our discussion here, as we will see, because they involve the establishment of therapeutic conditions which support change.

Although mental health workers are providing practical access to the out-doors, other practitioners from counselling and psychotherapy professions are also exploring ways of moving therapeutic work with individuals and groups out of the consulting room and into the outdoors. These practitioners draw on a variety of psychotherapeutic schools (Rust and Totton, 2011) and integrate their conceptual frameworks in different ways. Underpinning theory may draw on psychodynamic theory, Jungian concepts of archetypes and myth, behav-ioural approaches, humanistic and even shamanic thinking.

Mindfulness and Practice in Nature

The mindfulness movement, spearheaded by Jon Kabat-Zinn (1990) and others (Segal, Williams and Teasdale, 2002), has developed substantially over the past decade. Defined as 'paying attention in a particular way: on purpose, in the present moment, and non-judgmentally' (Kabat-Zinn, 1994, p. 4), the practice of mindfulness is now applied in many therapeutic and related contexts. Mind-fulness is primarily concerned with developing awareness of immediate phe-nomena and changing people's experience through daily practice and through exercises that develop attention. Mindfulness practices contribute to environ-mentally based therapies by sharpening awareness and offering tools for grounding and embodied connection.

The practice of mindfulness, as commonly portrayed in secular settings, has come under scrutiny from the Buddhist community. A number of writers are currently questioning whether the therapeutic working model applied in most programmes of that name draws sufficiently on the roots of the teaching (Bazanno, 2014), or whether understanding of the practice can be deepened by revisiting the original sources (Brazier, 2013a). The key Buddhist text on the

subject is the *Satipatthana Sutta*.[1] This text describes a practice in which attention is focused on four areas: body, reaction, mind and dhamma (basic elements). This can be seen as a progressive process in which the practitioner starts
by initially investigating body experience and then, as this stage is mastered,
moves on to observing the body's tendency to reactivity, then to inquiring into
the mind's structures and, finally, to the fundamental nature of things (Analayo,
2003).

Mindfulness teaching, following the *Satipatthana*, commonly begins with a
focus on the body. This requires bringing attention to the body when sitting,
walking, breathing and so on. These exercises teach awareness in the present
moment. As we will see below, I make considerable use of body scans and
grounding exercises in working out of doors, often using them at the start of
sessions to create a foundation for other work. Mindfulness exercises also focus
on detailed observation of ordinary things which would otherwise be overlooked. By slowing the person down and concentrating attention, things are
seen which would otherwise be missed. This too is foundational for therapeutic
work and has obvious relevance to working in nature.

In the original text, as he observes the breath or movement or mind phenomenon, on each occasion the practitioner is told to bring awareness to the
dependently originated nature of the object of attention and to its impermanence. These two observations refer to the Buddhist conception that all things
come into being subject to conditions, and all things are subject to ending and
decay. The things we observe are transient, interdependent phenomena. This
aspect of the mindfulness teaching, which is less emphasized in secular contexts, links the practice to awareness of the existential nature of human experience, which is also very relevant to working out of doors.

Engaging with the natural world, impermanence is everywhere. We see dead
animals on the path or watch leaves fall in autumn, but we also watch the arrival
of swallows in spring and young plants emerging on rotting logs. From the
cycle of decay, new growth arises. Mindfulness is not just about finding calm; it
is also concerned with gaining insight into the fundamental nature of existence.
Working in nature, such observations can be particularly acute.

In addition to the immediate observation of body activity, the first section of
the *Satipatthana Sutta* includes references to two particular meditations which
further develop the themes of dependent origination and impermanence. The
first of these meditations is the contemplation of the elements. The elements in
Buddhism are earth, air, fire, water and space. Practitioners reflect on each of
the five elements in turn, recognizing how together they make up their body
and also make up all the things in their environment. They and their surroundings both depend upon the same elements for their material existence. The
elements meditation creates a framework for thinking about work in the outdoors. It leads to a less personalized, more appreciative view of experience and,
because it points towards the interconnectedness of all material things, has

been used to raise ecological awareness by highlighting the mutual depend-ence between humans and the life of the planet.

The other meditation in this section of the text is the reflection on the decomposition of a dead body. Commonly known as the charnel ground meditations, this practice was originally done by monks in ancient India, who went to the places where dead bodies were taken to be burned, to meditate. These somewhat gruesome reflections were intended to help the meditator sharpen awareness of his own impermanence. Although ecotherapy work does not usually involve reflecting on human corpses, examples of death and decay can be seen everywhere in the countryside and may be used as the focus for work.

Both the meditation on the elements and the charnel ground meditations can be directly adapted as group or individual exercises (Brazier, 2011). They are not generally taught on mindfulness courses, but these practices are part of the teaching of mindfulness as it appears in the Buddhist texts, and illustrate how the practice is concerned with developing insight into the basic nature of things rather than simply finding peaceful mind-states.

Mindfulness and Grounded Presence

Although mindfulness practices are concerned with deepening insight, they also involve improving the quality of attention by helping to develop grounded-ness and non-judgemental awareness. Mindfulness can be helpful to both thera-pist and client. It manifests in:

- the therapist's own quality of mindfulness;

- mindfulness developed by the client as a result of indirect communication either through modelling or through activities which naturally invite more awareness; and

- direct teaching of mindfulness exercises.

In meditation, the practitioner gives intense objective attention to the subjec-tive, observing thought patterns, moment by moment, with analytic rigour. Inter-nal and external become meaningless concepts as all mental and physical processes are scrutinized with the same intensity. The mind watches itself and everything else with equal attentiveness. The therapist's mindfulness helps her to develop clarity and sharpness in giving attention to the client's material, and to be a solid presence in the work. Therapy can be seen as a kind of meditation for two. As the therapist gives intense, mindful attention to the interpersonal process, the client learns to do likewise and becomes less reactive to things and more interested in their felt quality. Together therapist and client attune to each other's process.

Therapy relies upon the therapist's way of being. In the Tariki ecotherapy training,[2] the first practice which we teach is embodied presence. We use grounding and body awareness exercises as a basis for developing empathic resonance with others. Through embodied awareness, the student learns to hold the psychological space in a calm and focused way. Broad, body-based attention is directed to the client, his or her perceptual world, and the physical space in which the work is taking place. This attention is clear, but non-directive. The therapist waits for the client to set the lead.

Embodied presence is particularly important in leading ecotherapy activities because working out of doors raises issues of psychological containment. Without the physical boundary of the therapy room, the work is in danger of becoming scattered and lacking depth, or of feeling unheld and becoming uncontained for the client. Inasmuch as the therapist brings this kind of presence to the work, he or she creates the therapeutic container.

By anchoring the therapeutic container in the therapist's presence rather than a physical space, the therapeutic work is not necessarily confined within one location. It can move as the therapist moves. Just as a baby monkey feels safe travelling with the troop so long as his mother is a constant presence for him, the client will feel held while aware of the therapist's proximity.

Mindfulness can be transmitted through unconscious mimicry of the therapist. As the client experiences the quality of presence which the therapist embodies, he may start to become more settled and mindful, developing a locus of trust and stability within himself. Gradually, individuals or groups will find their own containment and become less dependent on the therapist's presence. As this happens, solo work becomes more appropriate.

Buddhist Psychology and Therapeutic Work

Mindfulness practice has grown up within Buddhism, a tradition which is generally recognized as psychological in its approach. Its intent is therefore linked to that of Buddhist practice as a whole and is ultimately concerned with liberation of the mind.

Buddhist psychology sees ordinary mental process as a conditioned phenomenon. It is a product of past experience, circumstances, culture and so on. The world view is also distorted by the perceptual anomalies brought about by personal biases of this kind. These anomalies are created by the mind's tendency to seek out things which are familiar or comforting, and to create illusions where familiarity is not to be found. Ordinary perception is described as *avidya*. This literally means 'not seeing' or 'ignore-ance'.

People exist within a psychological bubble of conditioned perceptions created in response to fear. People feel a sense of existential threat because their lives are finite and uncertain. This threat, called *dukkha*, is commonly translated

as 'affliction' and consists of things like sickness, old age, death and disappointment, as well as the uncertain nature of the psychological bubble itself.

The real world becomes a screen upon which personally meaningful stories
are imposed, of which the roots may be in the personal past or in collective
mythology. These stories give colouration to perception. They can enrich life,
but mostly they create distorted views, cutting the person off from reality and
creating a limited perception of things. Buddhism offers practices such as mindfulness to take the practitioner beyond ignorance. These practices are about
achieving clarity and waking up to the world as it is rather than as we would like
it to be.

The mind is conditioned by a variety of factors including past experiences,
present circumstances and the cultural background. The conditioned mind-
state gives a sense of protection because it creates an illusion of continuity,
giving a semblance of control and solidity to the personal world. It also forms
the basis for identity. But while the personal bubble may be protective, it is also
isolating. It prevents relationships from being real. Other people, creatures and
objects are viewed through a veneer of projected self-material and not seen
authentically. They are not experienced as having innate existence, but are
viewed instead for their utility.

The clinging which drives the selective attention that creates the self-bubble
is either made up of positive attraction or of negative aversion, commonly
referred to as greed- and hate-type responses. These feed tendencies towards
consumption on the one hand and alienation on the other. They are the foundation of self-building because identity is basically a matter of identification with
some things and differentiation from others. In the human relationship with the
environment, greed and hate responses underlie many of the global problems
which we currently face. Recognizing how these mental processes distort perception in small, everyday situations can therefore not only affect an individual's
psychological well-being but also give insight into how larger human problems
are conditioned. Recognizing the drives towards consumption may give some
indications for controlling it.

Other-centred Approach and Nature-based Therapy

In my therapeutic work, I draw on a Buddhist model of psychotherapy known as
other-centred approach (Brazier, 2009). Given their common roots, this model,
which is grounded in the Buddhist psychological understanding outlined above,
fits well with a mindfulness-based method. Other-centred therapy particularly
explores the ways that the client's relationship with his or her personal world is
coloured by identifications and projections. It also explores relationship with the
other-than-self, looking at ways to improve relationships and bring more
authenticity into perception and interactions. In many cases, the relationship to

the 'other' is investigated in terms of human interactions, but the model also lends itself to looking at the relationship with the natural environment.

Other-centred methodology addresses the isolation and alienation of the conditioned mind through three functions:

- Establishing the therapeutic container through embodied presence, which involves grounded-ness, mindful accompaniment and authentic relationship

- Inquiring into the conditioned mind and its manifestation in the world view

- Inquiring into reality and working to clarify the experience of others

Each of these areas is relevant to working out of doors (Brazier, 2009).

The first area of methodology is concerned with establishing the therapeutic relationship as a container. As we have already seen, mindfulness of body process is foundational to therapeutic work of this kind (Brazier, 2011). Developing embodied presence particularly takes the form of grounding and body awareness exercises. It also involves the development of empathic skills and creating a collaborative way of working as embodied presence is the combination of grounded-ness and a particular quality of relationship.

The therapeutic relationship in other-centred approach is conceived of as outwardly orientated and described as triangular. Together therapist and client explore the psychological field, which might include the way that the client perceives things, his or her personal world view and the actual experiences which both therapist and client encounter through the work together. The therapeutic relationship is one of accompaniment, and this feature is consolidated when therapy moves out of doors. Here therapist and client have the potential to share the real experience of walking together and relating to wild places, side by side.

Working in a collaborative way, therapist and client investigate the ways in which the client distorts experience through projection and expectation. They also explore, as far as possible, the reality of situations and seek an objective view of people, places and objects. The concept of empathy is extended so that therapist and client try to develop more empathy for the 'others' of the client's world, moving from a simplistic initial assessment based on personal agendas to a more complex view which takes into account the multiple conditions operating in any situation. This shift from a personally embedded position to one in which the client is less attached to one viewpoint creates space for reappraisal in his or her perception of difficult relationships or situations and lowers the sense of personal threat.

Out of doors, this attitude of inquiry becomes investigative and curious. Trees, walls and meadows are more evidently real than the stories and memories which are recounted in the therapy room. They do not have their own agendas in the way that other humans do, so are usually neutral subjects against which to explore projections. Although natural features may carry associations, these can be recognized and deconstructed or used as creative inspiration. Nature is capable of surprising us out of assumptions. At the same time, the development of empathy for the other can be extended through creative work out of doors. Natural materials may be invited to 'find a voice' as the client finds new ways to 'ask them what they would like to be'. Of course, such exercises are imaginative and projective, but they access a different aspect of relating to nature from that commonly adopted.

Conditioned Mind-States and Therapy

Changing external conditions changes mind-states, and changing the mind-state changes the world view. Habits of perception are persistent, and some people tend towards negative ways of thinking. On a wet morning, a person may experience everything more negatively than on a sunny one. On the other hand, if I am in a bad mood, I may not even notice the sunshine until it is pointed out. Changing one's surroundings can, however, refocus attention and create new patterns of perception. If it remains sunny, I may start to feel better, and my perception of everything around me will change too. This is why being out of doors tends to improve people's mental health. Exposing people to different environmental conditions creates new mental and behavioural patterns which tend to be self-replicating.

Buddhist psychology sees mental states as arising in relation to a variety of conditions (Jones, 2011). This suggests that developing more positive awareness through mindfulness practices and changing the physical conditions of people's lives by taking them out into nature can provide a route to improving well-being. It therefore makes sense for Buddhist therapies to concern themselves with creating wholesome living conditions and encouraging access to healthy environments as much as with therapist–client interactions. For this reason, other-centred work sits well alongside practical interventions such as community work and mental health projects. Practical changes to a person's circumstances form one important route to change. Combined with more overtly psychological talking therapy, such changes can be extremely powerful. Ecotherapy work combines practical exposure to environmental conditions with psychologically orientated therapeutic interventions, so it has the capacity to work at a number of levels.

Reality is seen as the teacher in other-centred method, and the therapist will tend to make interventions which sharpen awareness of the various factors operating in any given situation. A fundamental question in other-centred work is 'Is it true?' Although this may not always be asked directly, through collaborative inquiry the implicit questioning of habitual interpretations of reality will tend to initiate a search for greater authenticity (Brazier, 2009). As the client is exposed to the experience of the wild, whether in wind, sun or storm, the physical experience of weather and terrain impose themselves on the senses. With this immediacy, a direct encounter with nature, though still mediated through reactions, will still tend to bring about healthier and less personally enmeshed experience.

Triangularity in the Therapeutic Relationship

Other-centred approach views the therapeutic relationship as triangular (Brazier, 2009). The relationship consists of three elements: the therapist, the client and the client's world. This conception of the therapeutic relationship as a triad rather than a dyad is important because, as we have seen, it proposes that the interpersonal process, the dialogue between therapist and client, is primarily a collaborative inquiry into the nature of the third element, that is, the client's perceptual world. The interaction is process led and focuses on how the client perceives others.

In conventional therapy, the client's others are largely present as objects of the imagination and the mind-sense. The therapist comes to know these 'others' by psychologically coming alongside the client and, through empathic resonance, developing a sense of his or her world view. By exploring this world view together, the client's perception of others gradually comes into question and changes. Because the world view and the identity are mutually conditioning, changes in the way things are viewed impact on the sense of self and affect behavioural patterns.

In nature-based therapy, the triangular quality of relationship is particularly prominent because the natural world is strongly present to both therapist and client. This renders the third element of the triangle complex. The environment is a real presence rather than a psychological phenomenon, but both client and therapist have perceptions of it which differ from each other's and from the actuality, if such a thing could be known. The presence of a real environment allows for a much more explicit inquiry into the gap between both the therapist's and the client's conditioned views of and reality.

Triangularity in the therapeutic relationship creates a dynamic between therapist and client which tends towards being collaborative and equalizing. This is sometimes referred to as 'fellow feeling'. This does not mean fudging boundaries or confusing projection with actuality. The distinction between empathy and identification is important in any therapeutic work, and this means recognizing when personal perspectives are contaminating one's ability to understand the client's world (Rogers, 1980). At the same time, a sense of commonality provides an important condition for the work. Face-to-face encounter is relatively uncommon out of doors. The side-by-side working is common and naturally gives rise to a less formal style of relationship in which open discussion flows more easily.

Differences of Power and Boundaries in Working Outdoors

Outdoor work often demands longer time periods than conventional therapy. The style of interaction is generally more fluid, and levels of intensity vary according to the activity. This in itself inevitably affects the relationship style of the work, whatever the therapeutic orientation of the therapist. A residential or long-term group session will probably include light moments, jokes or, in some cases, teasing, which would not be suitable in the therapy room. Time may be divided into 'working time' and 'downtime' or may be less clearly differentiated. Whatever the contract, however, incidents which happen during downtime cannot be ignored during group processes.

One outcome of this is that the therapist will inevitably reveal more personal process to the group than would be apparent in the consulting room. Her reactions to situations cannot be hidden, and she may sometimes be caught feeling uncomfortable or off guard. Perhaps the therapist is less fit than some of the other group members and gets out of breath on a hill or is visibly disconcerted by unanticipated events. Far from being a blank screen, her human limits and strengths become visible. These more intimate connections tend to normalize relations, but they do not prevent transference occurring. Sometimes they moderate it. The therapist may be seen as a fellow traveller or friend more than as an expert, or she may be expected to have all the answers. This can lead to complex issues and power dynamics.

The way that sessions are structured also affects the relationship between the therapist and participants as well as any transference dynamics. Although exercises in ecotherapy groups are generally practical and low key, when combined with therapy, the way that these are led may be interpreted as authoritarian or didactic, and this may amplify transference issues. The therapist may also be seen in an 'expert' role. Much depends upon personal style, but one can certainly see examples of people working in the field who have acquired a strong following based on personal charisma. The introduction of spiritual activities or shamanic practices, may, for some clients, and even some therapists, exacerbate this problem as they buy into spiritual transference issues and risk elevating the therapist to a guru-like status which is clearly problematic.

Despite the fluidity of outdoor work, the therapist retains responsibility for observing his own mental and physical states, those of the client or group members, and also keeping awareness of the surrounding terrain and activity in hand. This multidimensional awareness requires focus and mindfulness. Part of this involves maintaining the therapeutic boundary. In an earlier article (Brazier, 2013b), I discussed the complications surrounding the therapeutic boundary in outdoor therapies. Working in the therapy room, it is usual practice to offer time-limited sessions and to ensure a contained, private space. Standards are governed by codes of practice and by the norms developed within the profession. Working in the natural environment, time frames are generally less easily controlled; privacy may be intruded on by the unanticipated arrival of third parties or by unpredictable events, and the style of relationship may be affected by many uncontrollable factors.

In the article cited above, I concluded that there were two sources of therapeutic containment operating in nature-based therapies. Firstly, as we have already seen, the therapist herself provides a source of containment. She is able to give a robust response if things become uncertain, and by her quality of presence and personal boundaries she creates a solid reference point which holds the group process. Her presence also brings to focus the therapeutic agenda, reminding participants to be reflective. With these qualities available, the group can be fluid and mobile, moving from place to place. The therapist's personal boundaries and solidity anchor the group and the work.

Secondly, the natural environment offers containment. This happens at two levels. Firstly, particular working spaces may be chosen because they are intimate and enclosed and thus provide a natural sense of containment. Reading the landscape in such a way as to select suitable home spaces which offer this sense of security is a skill which the therapist and group masters. Secondly, at a more profound level, a sense of containment may come from a deep engagement with the natural environment wherever this occurs. Through grounding exercises and encounter with nature in many places and ways, confidence develops. The earth is found to be trustworthy and solid, even when, at a more immediate level, things become uncomfortable or local environments are spoiled. Connecting with the wild, people discover intrinsic reliability of life and of the earth.

One can think of these two boundary elements through the image of a small boat far out to sea. The facilitator might be thought of as the anchor, and the natural world as the ocean on which the boat can sail. With these resources, the client or the group develops internal resources and resilience, and these people gradually acquire their own sense of containment.

Conclusion

The move from therapy room to the outdoors brings with it both challenges and opportunities. Exploring a Buddhist-based, other-centred methodology, in this chapter I have examined some different aspects of therapeutic work which are enabled in this context and have also noted some challenges.

Buddhist practice is primarily a phenomenological investigation of mental process. Some therapeutic applications of Buddhist thought have been popularized in mindfulness teaching, and others are being developed through several different psychotherapeutic models. These approaches are now being used in the field of ecopsychology and ecotherapy in various ways. I have shared some of my own experiences in this chapter and have also reflected on some general principles which can be applied in this process, drawn from mindfulness teaching, Buddhist psychology, ecotherapy practice, group theory and other-centred therapy.

What has emerged is a picture of the complexity which this work represents. Working out of door is in its infancy, and ecotherapy is a broad field which can incorporate therapies that are diverse in style and theoretical underpinnings. We can observe that Buddhist psychology offers a unique integration and a depth understanding of human process and its moment-by-moment reinforcement. Buddhist models of therapy already combine environmental and behavioural approaches, an understanding of cognitive processing and theories of conditioned mind which combine well with a psychodynamic perspective. With this diversity within the model, the approach can provide a useful vehicle for exploring the field of nature-based therapies and aid in creating new integrations. In addition to this, Buddhist psychology rests within a paradigm which is based on a view of the self as a constructed and often problematic phenomenon. In a world where ecological threat is perceived as a daily reality, it would seem that a model of therapy which brings into question assumptions of the importance of personal entitlement and autonomy is needed. As environmentally based therapists, we cannot ignore this moral challenge.

References

Analayo (2003) *Satipatthana* (Cambridge: Windhorse).

Bazzano, M. (2014) *After Mindfulness* (Basingstoke, UK: Palgrave Macmillan).

Brazier, C. (2009) *Other-Centred Therapy: Buddhist Psychology in Action* (Hampshire: O-Books).

Brazier, C. (2011) *Acorns Among the grass* (Hampshire: Earth Books).

Brazier, C. (2013a) 'Roots of Mindfulness', *European Journal of Psychotherapy & Counselling*, 15, 127–38.

Brazier, C. (2013b) 'Sacred Space: Different Boundaries in Environmentally Based Therapies', BACP *Thresholds*, Autumn.

Faculty of Public Health in association with Natural England (2010) *Great Outdoors: How Our Natural Health Service Uses Green Space to Improve Wellbeing Briefing Statement*.

Jones, D. (2011) *This Being, That Becomes: The Buddha's Teaching on Conditionality* (Cambridge: Windhorse).

Kabat-Zinn, J. (1990) *Full Catastrophe Living: Using the Wisdom of Your Body and Mind to Face Stress, Pain, and Illness* (Crystal Lake, IL: Delta).

Kabat-Zinn, J. (1994) *Wherever You Go, There You Are: Mindfulness Meditation in Everyday Life* (New York: Hyperion).

Mind (2007) *The Green Agenda for Mental Health*.

Mind (2013) *Feeling Better Outside, Feeling Better Inside: Ecotherapy for Mental Wellbeing, Resilience and Recovery*.

Rogers, C. (1980) *A Way of Being* (Boston: Houghton Mifflin).

Rust, M. J., and N. Totton (2011) *Vital Signs: Psychological Responses to Ecological Crisis* (London: Karnac).

Segal, V., M. Williams and J. Teasdale (2002) *Mindfulness-Based Cognitive Therapy for Depression* (New York: Guilford Press).

Notes

1 This sutta appears twice in the Buddhist canon, at Majjhima Nikaya 10 and Digha Nikaya 22.
2 Ten Directions Ecotherapy Training Programme offered by Tariki Trust.

3

EUDEMONIC PHILOSOPHY AND HUMAN(ISTIC)–NATURE RELATIONSHIPS

Joe Hinds

Introduction

Orientated within a broad humanistic account of therapy, the present chapter focuses on how the natural environment is able to provide optimal conditions to elicit a eudemonic awakening; this is preceded by a summary explanation of eudemonia. Importantly, existential and transpersonal modes of understanding are examined in order to locate people's experiencing while engaged with nature. Of particular interest is the *quality* of reported emotional states as indicators of the transformative effect of nature on the human condition. Throughout, a simplistic interpretation of eudemonia is used, one that relates to a psychotherapeutic approach and that resonates strongly with nature-based experiences. Overall, the present chapter is intended to show that nature presents important opportunities that might contribute towards a eudemonic life developed through relational, reflexive and emotional mechanisms. Experiential accounts are presented to strengthen the argument for the inclusion of a eudemonic philosophy within nature-based therapies.

Eudemonia *(greek - good spirit)*

The Greek philosopher Aristotle defined eudemonia (literally, 'good spirit') as well-being brought about by realizing and attaining what is worth having in one's life and 'living in truth to oneself' (Norton, 1976, p. 216) in accordance with reason and contemplation (Huta, 2013). It is further described as a moral or virtuous living (e.g. exemplifying kindness, courage and honesty), one that stands in contrast to hedonic happiness, which is, essentially, the pursuit of pleasure and the avoidance of pain (Huta, 2013). Moreover, eudemonia acknowledges effort and agency in value-based activities that are engaged in because they contribute to a purposeful existence and to a 'good life': a life that benefits (and, importantly, does not harm) others. Eudemonia is not achieved through momentary pleasure (hedonism), but is something that is developed over the life course – a good life *lived* well by developing, exercising and extending our human capacities (e.g. Ryff, 2013).

Although definitive 'lists' of various virtues thought to 'improve' individual well-being have been suggested (e.g. Seligman, Steen, Park and Peterson, 2005), these may be seen as rather prescriptive and, portrayed in terms of excellence, rather idealistic (Woolfolk and Wasserman, 2005); moreover, there are 'manifold intangibles that make life worth living' (Haybron, 2008, ix). The freedom to choose a path towards authenticity and responsibility is, within humanistic talking therapies, the individual's (e.g. Strasser and Clarke, 2013), and indeed, this choice and subsequent behaviours are in themselves meaningful (Guignon, 2002).

Importantly, the discovery of the 'true self', or *daimon*, that which is *intrinsically* worthy, cannot be entirely *extrinsically* driven (Vernon, 2008). Drawing on Rollo May's (1969) interpretation, the daimon is a 'fundamental, archetypal function of human experience' (p. 123) that represents a 'unique pattern of sensibilities and powers which constitute the individual as a self in relation to [the] world' (p.125). The daimon is usually experienced as a 'blind' urge to assert, affirm and perpetuate the 'self'. However, by being conscious of its presence and receptive to its totality, the daimon can be personally informative, directive and creative. Eudemonic 'well-being' is achieved by being in harmony with one's daimon (May, 1969). Perhaps paradoxically, however, eudemonia develops from undertaking a pursuit that has some significance *outside* of the individual, one that is able to elicit an awareness and acceptance of a holistic understanding of one's self and one's place in the world (Vernon, 2008). This way of being may not contribute to or involve 'happiness' per se, although undoubtedly there are prudential benefits; rather, it contributes to the development of values, worth and meaning in one's life (Vernon, 2008).

Although some authors have made a distinction between eudemonic acting and feeling (Huta, 2013), the present view posits that truly eudemonic states, despite Aristotle's emphasis on reasoning, are characterized by the convergence of contemplative, emotional and behavioural 'parts' of the self, prompting 'the fulfilment of human nature' and leading of a 'full life' (Haybron, 2008, p. 35). The union of the physical, intellectual and emotional with an acceptance of finitude (see below), to inform a value-based common good, has been expressed previously as *wisdom* (Kohut, 1966; Sternberg, 1998). Although beyond the scope of the present chapter, this convergence with eudemonia warrants elucidation.

Although there have been efforts to 'accurately' understand and apply eudemonic concepts in the modern world, for historical and cultural reasons this has led to differing interpretations (Vernon, 2008). The contemporary psychological understanding of eudemonia, born from an individualistic, atomistic and capitalist culture (Midgely, 2003), remains a less than holistic interpretation of what may be beneficial to human functioning and potential, with some indicating as problematic the absence of negative emotional states (Woolfolk, 2002). Indeed, it is the integration of various aspects of the self (e.g. 'good' and 'bad') into our self-structure that allows for the possibility of living generatively and authentically in relation to the world (May, 1969). A considered critique of a traditional eudemonia rejects some of its explicit and implicit tenets arguing, for instance, for a collectivist rather than an individualist perspective (e.g. Tantum, 2014). Although Aristotle held contemplation of one's place in the world and the subsequent discovery of meaning in life to be essential (Vernon, 2008), it is important to consider eudemonia as being 'less about navel gazing and more about understanding one's relation to the world' (Hamilton, 2013, p. 486). Additionally, there is a need for recognition of the 'obliging social and physical context[s] to help shape the way we live' (Haybron, 2008, p. 255). Exposure to the natural environment has been shown to be a valuable conduit for engendering at least some degree of human psychological benefit and potential (Annerstedt and Währborg, 2011; Weinstein, Przybylski and Ryan, 2009).

Existentialism

Aspects of eudemonia have been present in humanistic and existential accounts of the human condition in relatively recent history, including works by Nietzsche, Rogers and Maslow (Haybron, 2008; Ryff, 2013), together with more contemporary writings (e.g. Passmore and Howell, 2014a; Schroll, Rowan and Robinson, 2011). The idea that despair can be a catalyst for constructive action is embedded within existential philosophy (e.g. May, 1981). Indeed, the natural world can evoke existential anxieties through the perception of it as threatening, disgusting and uncertain, and may make salient to people their mortality (Kellert, 2002; Koole and van den Berg, 2005). Certainly, embodied and challenging experiences in nature can contribute to a reconfiguration of people's world view (Marshall, this volume; Skalski and Hardy, 2013; Vernon, 2008), mirroring the process of relationship with our environment (*Umwelt*) and the paradoxical acceptance of death in order to live (van Deurzen, 2013; cf. Pienaar, 2011). Moments of breakdown, replete with negative emotions, may be opportunities for therapeutic *breakthrough* that enable the self to develop through the integration of its various conscious and unconscious strands (Bollas, 2013). A holistic and authentic notion of human functioning and eudemonia might therefore *include* those emotional states that are often portrayed as negative (Woolfolk, 2002). Expressed differently, 'humanity's inherent negativity is the source for its development, where those contradictions which result in crisis and which are resolved lead to higher levels of Being' (Buss, 1976, p. 9).

So although evidence suggests that nature affords people the opportunity to recover from depleted cognitive capacities (e.g. van den Berg, Hartig and Staats, 2007) and for prevention against more affective conditions such as stress and anxiety (e.g. Maller, Townsend, Pryor, Brown and St Leger, 2005), the degree to which these experiences lead to the development of a eudemonic awakening is debatable. Orr (1993), among many, has suggested that the reacquaintance of humans with nature is necessary to regain what it means to be *wholly* human. Although it is possible to develop a meaningful sense of self-in-relation-to-the-world through emotional engagement with nature, without suffering (Milton, 2002), finding harmony and meaning in and through nature has often been accompanied by fear and arduousness (Frankl, 1959; Fredrickson and Anderson, 1999; Hinds and Sparks, 2011).

Eudemonia and Nature

A growing body of evidence suggests that experiences associated with being in or engaged with nature induce a relatively unique group of emotional responses and states that may be aligned to the concept of eudemonia, particularly if a sense of connection (relatedness) to nature is considered (Davis and Gatersleben, 2013; Passmore and Howell, 2014a; Trigwell, Francis and Bagot, 2014; see also Zelenski and Nisbet, 2014). Research has indicated that activities motivated by eudemonic ideals tend to elicit feeling states of awe, inspiration and a sense of connection with a greater whole (Huta and Ryan, 2010). For instance, developing a meaningful relationship with nature through gardening may be an important precursor to experiencing eudemonia (Webber, Hinds and Camic, 2015).

Eigner (2001) suggests that the well-being associated with an embodied immersion in the natural environment may be a qualitatively different, 'higher quality' well-being compared to more hedonically construed well-being. Participants active in various voluntary environmental protective behaviours, such as the maintenance of local natural environments, have reported that the natural environment produced 'an amazing feeling of happiness', an 'inner sort of calm' and feelings of being 'really satisfied', more relaxed and more like themselves (Eigner, 2001, pp. 191–92). Participants exposed to natural environments in other studies have reported experiencing feelings of union with nature, joy, a sense of wonder and peace of mind (Jacob and Brinkerhoff, 1999) and, after being introduced to a woodland environment, a sense of union with nature and tranquillity (Kjellgren and Buhrkall, 2010). Indeed, Kaplan and Kaplan (1989) suggest that over time, contact with nature leads to 'deep reflection', or what might also be referred to as mindfulness; this has been found within a cohort of smallholders (Jacob and Brinkerhoff, 1999), described here as a process whereby

[t]he anxieties of the future have space to recede to the background, and the past's residual fears can be replaced by peace of mind. The world for one moment appears whole and the mind moves towards a stillness. [...] One's being, then, is not seen as separate, apart from a world outside of consciousness; rather one, if only for an instant, appears to be drawn into the ongoing stream of a perceived universal reality, with the potential for finding tranquillity, union and wholeness. (Jacob, 1997, p. 84)

There are also examples of mixed emotional responses reported by people in nature (Hinds and Sparks, 2011). MacFarlane (2003) cites John Dennis's 1688 description of crossing the Italian Alps as 'a delightful horrour, a terrible joy' (p. 73), and empirical works have found that a large minority of respondents reported experiencing simultaneous states including, for example, elevated awareness and perception, and feelings of awe, respect, fear *and* happiness (van den Berg and ter Heijne, 2005). Moreover, these emotional states resonate with notions that Maslow had regarding the actualized person for whom the appreciation for the 'basic goods of life', such as nature, are likely to be experienced with feelings of 'awe, pleasure, [and] wonder', (Maslow, 1956, p. 177). Schneider (2003) proposes that experiencing awe equates to the human capacity 'for the thrill and anxiety of living [...] humility and boldness, reverence and wonder', (p. 135) which in turn allows for personal and interpersonal openness and dialogue.

Transpersonal Relating and Contemplation

As these deeply relational nature-based experiences seem to suggest, the natural environment is able to evoke relatively unique emotional and spiritual or self-transcendent experiences (Morrison, 2009; Totton, 2011; Williams and Harvey, 2001) including eudemonic-like states such as contemplation and awe (Hinds and Sparks, 2011). Akin to Maslow's later writings regarding the transpersonal (Koltko-Rivera, 1998), self-transcendence may be characterized as a transpersonal identification with entities beyond the individual, such as a deep connection with nature (e.g. Kirk, Eaves and Martin, 1999). For instance, Fredrickson and Anderson (1999) discovered that direct and prolonged wilderness experiences elicited profound emotions such as awe, a deep sense of peace and an emotional connectedness to the natural environment that, at times, for some individuals, verged on the spiritual and therefore may be aligned with and indicative of a spiritual eudemonia (van Dierendonck and Mohan, 2006).

Through the nurturance of a transpersonal relationship (Schroll et al., 2011), one that demonstrates a deep sense of meaningful connection (Abram, 1996; Ashley, 2008), the natural environment can be a catalyst for a spiritual awakening. Indeed, the concept of eudemonia was conceived during a time when transcendent meaning was abundant (Haybron, 2008); the Greeks of Aristotle's time revered the earth as a living goddess, expressing their awe, wonder and gratitude to her (Midgely, 2003). Crucially, that which was taken for granted during Aristotle's time, namely a belief in a transcendent 'other', is largely missing in contemporary Western society (Vernon, 2008).

Nature, in these circumstances, may be conceived as 'intimate other'; the third entity within an outdoor therapeutic encounter, one in which people can explore in an embodied, multisensory and sensuous way, a here-and-now experiencing (Adams, 2010). Others have stressed the importance of exposure to the natural environment to build a sense of self that is orientated around a transpersonal relatedness (Jordan, 2009). For instance, people's encounters with mountains have resulted in them experiencing their selves honestly, unguardedly and wholeheartedly by being aware of a transcendent 'higher reality' described variously as 'infinity, eternity, ecstasy, reverence, salvation, [and] humility' (Lester, 2004, p. 96). Moreover, the mountains come to represent not just a good place but all that is 'noble, real, unselfish, and unselfconscious in life' (Lester, 2004, p. 93). Climbers also talked of 'a mysterious harmony' and 'a purpose larger than myself' (Lester, 2004, p. 96), complementing other research focused on white-water rafting (Arnould and Price, 1993), extreme sports (Brymer and Gray, 2009), forest encounters (Williams and Harvey, 2001) and wilderness experiences (Hinds, 2011).

Central to the ecotherapy understanding of healing trauma is the idea of developing a relationship with the natural world, a relationship which, in the modern western and scientific world, has been seen in dualistic terms (Davis, 2011; Macy, 2009). Engagement with the transpersonal blurs the boundaries of self and other in a 'co-existence of opposites', permitting the simultaneous sense of 'self' and 'other' and (often held to be) opposite and intense emotions (Clarkson, 2002, p. 148). Moreover, the ability to accept and synthesize these dichotomies is an important part of the process of personal growth and development (Weeks and L'Abate, 1982). This degree of experiencing requires holistic and reciprocal patterns of connectivity (strong relationality) rather than individual or atomistic relationality (Wiggins, Ostenson and Wendt, 2013). Direct contact with nature may lead to a non-dualistic identification which is sometimes a confusing and paradoxical place where opposing emotions can co-occur and there is a blurring of 'self' and 'other' (Ashley, 2008; see also Braud, 2001).

Clear and unambiguous feedback from an embodied and multisensory experience where one may even feel discomfort, pain and tiredness (Reser and Scherl, 1988) can be a powerful challenge to the status quo and has the potential to generate new insights about the self in relation to the world, effectively 'dislodging' or 'decentring' the self-concept (Clarkson, 2012). The external environment impacts the internal (and vice versa), providing opportunities for different perspectives on the self, the immediate environment and the interaction between them (Reser and Scherl, 1988). This person–environmental 'dialogue' seems to foster contemplative states (Davis, 2011) via an emotional embodied experiencing (Abram, 1996; see also Bohart, 2011). These opinions seem to echo sentiments of philosophers such as Emerson: 'The lover of nature is he whose inward and outward senses are truly adjusted to each other' (1836/1982, p. 38); and Muir: 'I only went out for a walk, and finally concluded to stay out till sundown, for going out, I found, was really going in' (1966, p. 439).

Ethics

An important cornerstone of the eudemonic tradition is the idea of living a moral or ethical life. Modern life characterized by pervasive information technology tends to obscure a 'robust sense of reality' (Borgmann, 1999, p.15). Attempts to fill the modern crisis of meaning, the 'existential vacuum' (Frankl, 1959), with modern consumer trappings and other inauthentic ways tend to have detrimental effects on well-being (Boyle, 2003; Hamilton, 2004). Recently, eudemonia has been wedded to proposed ethical guidelines reconceived to address current issues of environmental sustainability (Richards, 2013). Others have found that living a simpler life in conjunction with the natural environment mitigates the negative effects of modern living and promotes an environmental consciousness (Brown and Kasser, 2005; Kasser, 2009). Additionally, immersion in natural environments seems to increase people's intrinsic value for community, intimacy and personal growth (Weinstein et al., 2009). Importantly, there is a corpus of research and informed opinion now to suggest that nature experiences, in many forms, may promote an environmental ethic (Collado, Staats and Corraliza, 2013; Kellert, 1993; Shapiro, 1995). From a therapeutic position, healing individual trauma in the wild may liberate people's attention so that they can 'reconnect with their innate love and care for the other-than-human' (Totton, 2011, p. 213; see also Greenway, 2009).

Summary

It has been recognized that it requires 'direct encounters with nature [...] for deeper emotional responses and spiritual understandings' (Koger and Winter, 2010, p. 315). Moreover, the meanings we require to make sense of the world come not entirely from the words we use, but rather meaning 'sprouts in the very depths of the sensory world, in the heat of meeting, encounter, [and] participation' (Abram, 1996, p. 75). Thus therapy outdoors may be considered *intro*

a relatively unique therapeutic intervention with the potential to elicit profound insight and change and to awaken a gestalt of human functioning and being in order to live eudemonically. It is therefore proposed that an embodied emotional immersion within a (sometimes physically as well as psychologically challenging) natural environment may elicit contemplative and transformative 'moments' that, although not resulting in the immediate uptake of a virtuous life (whatever that entails), do initiate a process of self-realization that fosters a better appreciation of one's place in the world.

With that in mind, I close with a poem presented to me voluntarily by a participant during a 12-day wilderness experience in northern Scotland. Although this collective experience has been reported elsewhere (Hinds, 2011), the following individual verbatim extract has not. It was an impromptu writing and is, I feel, an apt example of the eudemonic awakening which may be elicited from immersion in nature. Moreover, the poet had found the strength for the first time to confront and disclose personal trauma without an explicit therapeutic intervention, thus adding emphasis to the author's words and the transformative experience of the natural environment.

> On the edge of the world, at the edge of the land,
> Standing facing the sea, I look down to my hand
> It's brown with the wind, the sun and the rain,
> It's wrinkled and lined with sand, ingrained
> It's lined with a life that I thought I knew best,
> All my hopes and my fears and a sum of the rest
> I look up to the sea and take a sniff of air.
> As the waves crash in, I'm remembering where
> I grew up and who I've been,
> Who I've touched and what I've seen.
> How I've cried and laughed and joked,
> What I thought and what I spoke.
> A gull soars past, flying high,
> Which takes my eyes towards the sky,
> There clouds billow in, pushed along by the wind,
> a mix of whites, greys and blues,
> And when the sun sets, a hint of rouge.
> I've been here before, on the edge of the world,
> Standing facing the sea, calling out without words,
> Looking towards a curved horizon,
> Something for me to rest my eyes on.
> Somewhere for me to relax and remember,
> A place for then, for now, forever.
> Now I know where my boundaries lie
> Where the waves touch the sky.

References

Abram, D. (1996) *The Spell of the Sensuous* (New York: Random House).

Adams, W. W. (2010) 'Bashō's Therapy for Narcissus: Nature as Intimate Other and Transpersonal Self', *Journal of Humanistic Psychology*, 50, 38–64.

Annerstedt, M., and P. Währborg (2011) 'Nature-assisted Therapy: Systematic Review of Controlled and Observational Studies', *Scandinavian Journal of Public Health*, 39, 371–88.

Arnould, E. J., and L. L. Price (1993) 'River Magic: Extraordinary Experience and the Extended Service Encounter', *Journal of Consumer Research*, 20, 24–45.

Ashley, P. (2008) 'Toward an Understanding and Definition of Wilderness Spirituality', *Australian Geographer*, 38, 53–69.

Bohart, A. C. (2011) 'A Meditation on the Nature of Self-Healing and Personality Change in Psychotherapy Based on Gendlin's Theory of Experiencing', *The Humanistic Psychologist*, 29, 249–79.

Bollas, C. (2013) *Catch Them Before They Fall* (London: Routledge).

Borgmann, A. (1999) *Holding on to Reality: The Nature of Information at the Turn of the Millennium* (Chicago: University of Chicago Press).

Boyle, D. (2003) *Authenticity: Brands, Fakes, Spin, and the Lust for Real Life* (London: Harper Perennial).

Braud, W. (2001) 'Experiencing Tears of Wonder-Joy: Seeing with the Heart's Eye', *The Journal of Transpersonal Psychology*, 33, 99–111.

Brown, K. W., and T. Kasser (2005) 'Are Psychological and Ecological Well-being Compatible? The Role of Values, Mindfulness, and Lifestyle', *Social Indicators Research*, 74, 349–68.

Brymer, E., and T. Gray (2009) 'Dancing with Nature: Rhythm and Harmony in Extreme Sports Participation', *Journal of Adventure Education and Outdoor Learning*, 9, 135–49.

Buss A. R. (1976) 'Development of Dialectics and Development of Humanistic Psychology', *Human Development*, 19, 248–60.

Clarkson, P. (2002) *The Transpersonal Relationship in Psychotherapy* (London: Whurr).

Collado, S., H. Staats and J. A. Corraliza (2013) 'Experiencing Nature in Children's Summer Camps: Affective, Cognitive and Behavioural Consequences', *Journal of Environmental Psychology*, 33, 37–44.

Davis, J. V. (2011) 'Ecopsychology, Transpersonal Psychology, and Nonduality', *International Journal of Transpersonal Studies*, 30, 137–47.

Davis, N., and B. Gatersleben (2013) 'Transcendent Experiences in Wild and Manicured Settings: The Influence of the Trait "Connectedness to Nature"', *Ecospsychology*, 5, 92–102.

Eigner, S. (2001) 'The Relationship Between "Protecting the Environment" as a Dominant Life Goal and Subjective Well-being', in P. Schmuck and K. M. Sheldon (eds) *Life Goals and Well-Being: Towards a Positive Psychology of Human Striving* (Göttingen: Hogrefe and Huber) pp. 182–201.

Emerson, R. W. (1836/1982) 'Nature', in L. Ziff (ed.) *Nature and Selected Essays* (New York: Penguin Books) pp. 35–82.

Frankl, V. E. (1959) *Man's Search for Meaning* (London: Random House).

Fredrickson, L. M., and D. H. Anderson (1999) 'A Qualitative Exploration of the Wilderness Experience as a Source of Spiritual Inspiration', *Journal of Environmental Psychology*, 19, 21–39.

Greenway, R. (2009) 'The Wilderness Experience as Therapy: We've Been Here Before', in L. Buzzell and C. Chalquist (eds) *Ecotherapy: Healing with Nature in Mind* (San Francisco: Sierra Club Books) pp. 132–9.

Guignon, C. (2002) 'Hermeneutics, Authenticity, and the Aims of Psychology', *Journal of Theoretical and Philosophical Psychology*, 22, 83–102.

Hamilton, C. (2004) *Growth Fetish* (London: Pluto Press).

Hamilton, R. (2013) 'The Frustrations of Virtue: The Myth of Moral Neutrality in Psychotherapy', *Journal of Evaluation in Clinical Practice*, 19, 485–92.

Haybron, D. M. (2008) *The Pursuit of Unhappiness: The Elusive Psychology of Well-Being* (Oxford: Oxford University Press).

Hinds, J. (2011) 'Exploring the Psychological Rewards of a Wilderness Experience: An Interpretive Phenomenological Analysis,' *The Humanistic Psychologist*, 39, 189–205.

Hinds, J., and P. Sparks (2011) 'The Affective Quality of Human-Natural Environment Relationships', *Evolutionary Psychology*, 9, 451–69.

Huta, V. (2013) 'Eudaimonia', in S. David, I. Boniwell and A. C. Ayers (eds) *Oxford Handbook of Happiness* (Oxford: Oxford University Press) pp. 201–13.

Huta, V., and R. M. Ryan (2010) 'Pursuing Pleasure or Virtue: The Differential and Overlapping Well-Being Benefits of Hedonic and Eudaimonic Motives', *Journal of Happiness Studies*, 11, 735–62.

Jacob, J. (1997) *New Pioneers: The Back-to-the-Land Movement and the Search for a Sustainable Future* (University Park, PA: Penn State University Press).

Jacob, J. C., and M. B. Brinkerhoff (1999) 'Mindfulness and Subjective Well-being in the Sustainability Movement: A Further Elaboration of Multiple Discrepancies Theory', *Social Indicators Research*, 46, 341–68.

Jordan, M. (2009) Nature and Self: An Ambivalent Attachment? *Ecopsychology*, 1, 26–31.

Kaplan, R., and S. Kaplan (1989) *The Experience of Nature: A Psychological Perspective* (Cambridge. Cambridge University Press).

Kasser, T. (2009) 'Psychological Need Satisfaction, Personal Well-Being, and Ecological Sustainability', *Ecopsychology*, 1, 175–80.

Kellert, S. R. (1993) 'The Biological Basis for Human Values of Nature', in S. R. Kellert and E. O. Wilson (eds) *The Biophilia Hypothesis* (Washington, DC: Island Press) pp. 42–69.

Kellert, S. R. (2002) 'Experiencing Nature: Affective, Cognitive, and Evaluative Development in Children', in P. H. Kahn Jr. and S. R. Kellert (eds) *Children and Nature: Psychological, Sociocultural and Evolutionary Investigations* (Cambridge, MA: The MIT Press) pp. 117–51.

Kirk, K. M., L. J. Eaves and N. G. Martin (1999) 'Self-Transcendence as a Measure of Spirituality in a Sample of Older Australian Twins', *Twin Research*, 2, 81–7.

Kjellgren, A., and H. Buhrkall (2010) 'A Comparison of the Restorative Effect of a Natural Environment with That of a Simulated Natural Environment', *Journal of Environmental Psychology, 30,* 464–72.

Koger, S. M., and D. D. Winter (2010) *The Psychology of Environmental Problems*, 3rd edn (New York: Psychology Press).

Kohut, H. (1966) 'Forms and Transformations of Narcissism', *Journal of the American Psychoanalytical Association*, 14, 243–72.

Koltko-Rivera, M. E. (1998) 'Maslow's "Transhumanism": Was Transpersonal Psychology Conceived as "a Psychology Without People in It"?', *Journal of Humanistic Psychology*, 38, 71–80.

Koole, S. L., and A. E. van den Berg (2005) 'Lost in the Wilderness: Terror Management, Action Orientation, and Nature Evaluation', *Journal of Personality and Social Psychology*, 88, 1014–28.

Lester, J. (2004) Spirit, Identity, and Self in Mountaineering', *Journal of Humanistic Psychology*, 44, 86–100.

MacFarlane, R. (2003) *Mountains of the Mind: A History of Fascination* (London: Granta Books).

Macy, J. (2009) 'The Greening of the Self', in L. Buzzell and C. Chalquist (eds) *Ecotherapy: Healing with Nature in Mind* (San Francisco: Sierra Club Books) pp. 238–45.

Maller, C., M. Townsend, A. Pryor, P. Brown and L. St Leger (2005) 'Healthy Nature Healthy People: "Contact with Nature" as an Upstream Health Promotion Intervention for Populations', *Health Promotion International*, 21, 45–54.

Maslow, A. H. (1956) 'Self-actualising People: A Study of Psychological Health', in C. E. Moustakas and S. R. Jayaswal (eds) *The Self: Explorations in Personal Growth* (New York: Harper and Row) pp. 160–94.

May, R. (1969) *Love and Will* (New York: W. W. Norton and Company).

May, R. (1981) *Freedom and Destiny* (New York: W. W. Norton and Company).

Midgely, M. (2003) *The Myths We Live By* (London: Routledge).

Milton, K. (2002) *Loving Nature: Towards an Ecology of Emotion* (London: Routledge).

Morrison, A. L. (2009) 'Embodying Sentience', in L. Buzzell and C. Chalquist (eds) *Ecotherapy: Healing with Nature in Mind* (San Francisco: Sierra Club Books) pp. 104–10.

Muir, J. (1966) L. M. Wolfe (ed.) *John of the Mountains: The Unpublished Journals of John Muir* (Wisconsin: The University of Wisconsin Press).

Norton, D. L. (1976) *Personal Destinies: A Philosophy of Ethical Individualism* (Princeton, NJ: Princeton University Press).

Orr, D. W. (1993) 'Love It or Lose It: The Coming Biophilia Revolution', in S. R. Kellert and E. O. Wilson (eds) *The Biophilia Hypothesis* (Washington, DC: Island Press) pp. 415–38.

Passmore, H-A., and A. J. Howell (2014a) 'Eco-Existential Positive Psychology: Experiences in Nature, Existential Anxieties, and Well-Being', *The Humanistic Psychologist*, 42, 370–88.

Passmore, H-A., and A. J. Howell (2014b) 'Nature Involvement Increases Hedonic and Eudaimonic Well-Being: A Two-Week Experimental Study', *Ecopsychology*, 6, 148–54.

Pienaar, M. (2011) 'An Eco-Existential Understanding of Time and Psychological Defences: Threats to the Environment and Implications for Psychotherapy', *Ecopsychology*, 3, 25–39.

Reser, J. P., and L. M. Scherl (1988) 'Clear and Unambiguous Feedback: A Transactional and Motivational Analysis of Environmental Challenge and Self-Encounter', *Journal of Environmental Psychology*, 8, 269–86.

Richards, D. G. (2013) 'Eudaimonia, Economics and the Environment: What Do the Hellenistic Thinkers Have to Teach Economists About 'the Good Life?' *Ethics and the Environment*, 18, 33–53.

Ryff, C. D. (2013) 'Psychological Well-Being Revisited: Advances in the Science and Practice of Eudaimonia', *Psychotherapy and Psychosomatics*, 83, 10–28.

Schneider, K. J. (2003) 'The Fluid Center: An Awe-Based Challenge to Humanity', *Journal of Humanistic Psychology*, 43, 133–45.

Schroll, M. A., J. Rowan and O. Robinson (2011) 'Clearing up Rollo May's Views of Transpersonal Psychology and Acknowledging May as an Early Supporter of Ecopsychology', *International Journal of Transpersonal Studies*, 30, 120–36.

Seligman, M. E. P., T. A. Steen, N. Park and C. Peterson (2005) 'Positive Psychology Progress: Empirical Validation of Interventions', *American Psychologist*, 60, 410–21.

Shapiro, E. (1995) 'Restoring Habitats, Communities, and Souls', in T. Roszak, M. E. Gomes and A. D. Kanner (eds) *Ecopsychology: Restoring the Earth, Healing the Mind* (San Francisco: Sierra Club Books) pp. 224–39.

Skalski, J. E., and S. A. Hardy (2013) 'Disintegration, New Consciousness, and Discontinuous Transformation: A Qualitative Investigation of Quantum Change', *The Humanistic Psychologist*, 41, 159–77.

Sternberg, R. J. (1998) 'A Balance Theory of Wisdom', *Review of General Psychology*, 2, 347–65.

Strasser, A., and M. Clarke (2013) 'The Challenge of Ethics and the Call to Responsibility', in E. van Deurzen and S. Iacovou (eds) *Existential Perspectives on Relationship Therapy* (Basingstoke, UK: Palgrave Macmillan) pp. 122–33.

Tantum, D. (2014) *Emotional Well-being and Mental Health* (London: Sage).

Totton, N. (2011) *Wild Therapy: Undomesticating Inner and Outer Worlds* (PCCS Books: Ross-on-Wye).

Trigwell, J. L., A. J. P. Francis and K. L. Bagot (2014) 'Nature Connectedness and Eudaimonic Well-Being: Spirituality as a Potential Mediator', *Ecopsychology*, 6, 241–51.

van den Berg, A. E., T. Hartig and H. Staats (2007) 'Preference for Nature in Urbanised Societies: Stress, Restoration, and the Pursuit of Sustainability', *Journal of Social Issues*, 63, 79–96.

van den Berg, A. E., and M. ter Heijne (2005) 'Fear Versus Fascination: An Exploration of Emotional Threats to Natural Threats', *Journal of Environmental Psychology*, 25, 261–72.

van Deurzen, E. (2013) 'The Challenge of Human Relations and Relationship Therapy: To Live and to Love', in E. van Deurzen and S. Iacovou (eds) *Existential Perspectives on Relationship Therapy* (Basingstoke, UK: Palgrave Macmillan) pp. 15–31.

van Dierendonck, D., and K. Mohan (2006) 'Some Thoughts on Spirituality and Eudaimonic Well-Being', *Mental Health, Religion and Culture*, 9, 227–38.

Vernon, M. (2008) *Wellbeing* (Stocksfield, UK: Acumen).

Webber, J., J. Hinds and P. M. Camic (2015) 'The Well-Being of Allotment Gardeners: A Mixed Methodological Study', *Ecopsychology*, 7, 29–37.

Weeks, G. R., and L. L'Abate (1982) *Paradoxical Psychotherapy: Theory and Practice with Individuals, Couples, and Families* (New York: Brunner/Mazel).

Weinstein, N., A. K. Przybylski and R. M. Ryan (2009) 'Can Nature Make Us More Caring? Effects of Immersion in Nature on Intrinsic Aspirations and Generosity', *Personality and Social Psychology Bulletin*, 35, 1315–29.

Wiggins, B. J., J. A. Ostenson and D. C. Wendt (2013) 'The Relational Foundations of Conservation Psychology', *Ecopsychology*, 4, 209–15.

Williams, K., and D. Harvey (2001) 'Transcendent Experience in Forest Environments', *Journal of Environmental Psychology*, 21, 249–60.

Woolfolk, R. L. (2002) 'The Power of Negative Thinking: Truth, Melancholia, and the Tragic Sense of Life', *Journal of Theoretical and Philosophical Psychology*, 22, 19–27.

Woolfolk, R. L., and R. H. Wasserman (2005) 'Count No One Happy: Eudaimonia and Positive Psychology', *Journal of Theoretical and Philosophical Psychology*, 25, 81–90.

Zelenski, J. M., and E. K. Nisbet (2014) 'Happiness and Feeling Connected: The Distinct Role of Nature Relatedness', *Environment and Behavior*, 46, 3–23.

4

ECOTHERAPY AS PSYCHOTHERAPY – TOWARDS AN ECOPSYCHOTHERAPY

Martin Jordan

Introduction

This chapter explores the relationship between ecotherapy and therapeutic process. Starting with a review of the current ideas in ecotherapy, I consider ecotherapy and its relationship to occupational and horticultural therapies. I then briefly outline my definition of psychotherapy and ideas that underpin the therapeutic relationship, including transference and countertransference, with a particular emphasis on therapeutic space in relation to the ideas of Winnicott and forms of developmental vitality drawing upon Stern. Next I examine how the client–therapist–nature matrix works therapeutically, looking at the different variables within this context, and then conclude with an outline of ecopsychotherapy and therapeutic process in a natural environment.

Current understanding in the practice of ecotherapy positions contact with nature as having positive psychological benefits, with a number of research papers and articles supporting this (see Chalquist, 2009; Mind, 2013a, 2007). Ecotherapy has developed along two potentially divergent, and at times confusing, lines. In the United Kingdom, following from the original Mind report (Mind, 2007) ecotherapy developed as a form of horticultural therapy, green exercise, conservation and land management work, and finally as an amalgamation of these processes. In attempting to develop an agenda for green mental healthcare in the National Health Service, the marketing department at Mind labelled a report 'Ecotherapy' (Mind, 2007) in order to communicate a diverse range of activities whose central point of convergence was some form of contact and activity within nature. The term *ecotherapy* in the United Kingdom has a strong association with these practices and ideas. At the same time, Linda Buzzell and her colleague Craig Chalquist were developing their own definition and practice of ecotherapy, and making more explicit links to both ecopsychology (Roszak et al., 1995) and psychotherapy (Buzzell and Chalquist, 2009). They propose that ecotherapy forms a challenge to traditional ideas within psychotherapy that locate therapy as conducted within an indoor environment abstracted from the context of nature and the outside world. *Ecotherapy* is used as an umbrella term for nature-based methods of physical and psychological healing. Buzzell and Chalquist (2009) propose that ecotherapy represents a new form of psychotherapy that acknowledges the vital role of nature and addresses the human–nature relationship. However, a recent information booklet by Mind (2013b) on ecotherapy includes the more traditional idea of therapy in its definition:

> Ecotherapy (in its strict sense) is about building a relationship with nature, so that personal wellbeing is considered equally alongside the health of the environment. Sessions usually include some type of formal therapy such as cognitive behaviour therapy (CBT) or counselling. (Mind, 2013b, p. 5)

However, it is clear, given a review of the majority of ecotherapy projects underway in the United Kingdom, that one-to-one counselling or psychotherapy doesn't happen in most programmes, with a few notable exceptions (see Linden and Grut, 2002). Clinebell (1996) first coined the term *ecotherapy*, positing a form of 'ecological spirituality' whereby our holistic relationship with nature encompasses both nature's ability to nurture us, through our contact with natural places and spaces, and our ability to reciprocate this healing connection through our ability to nurture nature. In this sense, ecotherapy has always shared a close relationship to ecopsychology (Roszak et al., 1995), placing human–nature relationships within a reciprocal healing (and disconnected and destructive) relationship with nature. Clinebell (1996, p. xxi) makes a distinction, preferring to use the term *ecotherapy* over *ecopsychology*, stating that ecopsychology is about the psyche and the 'greening of psychology', whereas ecotherapy focuses on the total mind–body–spirit–relationship organism. Hasbach (2012) disagrees with the notion that by just going out into nature for a walk we are engaged in ecotherapy, and defines ecotherapy as a new modality of therapy that enlarges the traditional scope of treatment to include the human–nature relationship (Hasbach, 2012, p. 116). As a result of this confusion, I want to define what I mean by psychotherapy and begin to link this to psychotherapeutic work in nature.

Defining Psychotherapy

I will explore what constitutes psychotherapy in terms of knowledge, how I understand this, how it is represented in my practice and how this shifts as I take my practice outdoors into natural environments. There is no one definition of psychotherapy or psychotherapeutic process, but competing ideas based on different models of distress and understanding of how the psyche works.

The etymology of the word *psychotherapy* comes from the ancient Greek *psyche* meaning 'soul or spirit', and *therapy*, 'to nurse or cure'. The aim of counselling and psychotherapy from this definition is healing for the soul, reflecting what it might mean to heal or cure somebody. Rogers (1957) focuses on the conditions necessary for therapeutic personality change, positing the idea of a 'core self' as central to the psyche. Freud (1912) also talks about personality change when he states, 'Where id was, ego shall be,' placing a structural model of mind that interacts and is a contributing factor in the client's difficulties. Both theories rely on modernist notions of a bounded, stable and static interiority, which exists predominantly independently of others and the contexts it exists within. Although both approaches posit seeds of a relational self which is further developed in the theories of relational psychotherapy (Mitchell, 1988), I believe they both still rely on modernist foundational premises which situate a core decontextualized, ahistorical self. Recent developments in the growth of cognitive behavioural therapy, especially as it is positioned in the NHS, would support this idea of a rationalized, decontextualized understanding of distress, whereby mental functioning is deemed the sole domain of a person's interior psychological world, independent of any social or cultural factors.

Recent postmodern attempts to reimagine therapeutic practice have focused on a self that is dialogic and socially constructed, placing emphasis on the narrative construction of problems and distress (Brown and Scott, 2007; McLeod, 1997; White and Epston, 1990). Postmodern therapies have also attempted to democratize the power dynamics between therapist and client by attempting to involve clients much more fully in understanding the nature of the construction of their problem (Anderson and Goolishian, 1992), challenging the expert status of the therapist. There are also echoes of these ideas in Ronen Berger's work on nature therapy (Berger, 2006: Berger and McLeod, 2006), whereby nature shifts the power dynamics between therapist and client, providing a more democratic space for therapy.

Counselling and psychotherapy cannot fully alleviate the symptoms unless they can treat the cause (the political and historical constellations that shape the era), and yet that cause is the exact subject psychology is not allowed to address. In this sense, we can see how the critiques put forward by ecopsychology and ecotherapy, of dominant social norms which are inherently destructive to the environment and also destructive to the human race, are attempting to place counselling and psychotherapy within a wider cultural and political sphere where nature and the environment play a central role in mental health and well-being. Elsewhere I have written about the relationship in developing an ecological self and the role of psychotherapy in this process (Jordan, 2012). I will outline some of these ideas here and discuss how they relate to psychotherapy.

This starting point of understanding human–nature relations leaves us with the problem of how subjective interiors and objective material exteriors come into some form of communication. The question arises as to whether it is useful to think in these terms, as they set up the very binary dualisms which psycho-therapy in natural environments might seek to overcome. If we view the Carte-sian self as an invention of the enlightenment which drove modernism down the very path which separated things out in order to get a better view of them, reconciling them, or finding spaces where we can view interiors and exteriors without setting up the same binary dualisms which positioned us in the first place, is quite a challenge. So, for example, to experience the therapeutic potential of a natural environment, we have two choices: to fall back on interi-ors, for example in terms of how we might feel and what psychological and historical frames we bring in our contact with nature, as well as how we under-stand what symbols and metaphors resonate with our personal emotional nar-rative; or, alternatively, we can move outwards, contacting the environment through our senses, exploring how our bodies feel in this process and what visual and sensory stimulus we encounter.

The question arises of where and how to focus in psychotherapeutic work in nature. Does the therapist focus solely on the interior of the client and the normative relational dynamics such as the client's developmental history and experience of relationships in this, locating distress as a predominantly inter-nal experience? Or should the therapist focus on this sensate experience of the natural world, and what the client is experiencing in the moment of encounter with the natural world, by provoking and exploring contact with the natural world? The two approaches have different potential therapeutic effects and rely on different theoretical lineages in order to understand emo-tional distress.

The relational turn in psychotherapy has positioned the subjects in complex relational processes between bodies and environments. Mitchell (1988) argues that there is no 'object' in a psychologically meaningful sense without some sense of oneself in relationship to it. There is therefore no 'self' in a psychologically meaningful sense in isolation outside of a matrix of relations (1988, p. 33). Mitch-ell proposes that in developing a sense of self, the human being is faced with the difficulty of the temporality and complexity of our conscious existence. Mitchell sees human consciousness as operating in time and in a continual flux, a stream of thoughts, feelings, sensations and desires; from a relational perspective, the self is a temporal and spatial entity in a process of continual movement.

Key to helping bring change in these distortions of self is the relationship that can be formed with the therapist. The relational perspective draws upon a variety of ideas that are not purely related to one particular school in counselling and psychotherapy. Central tenants of the approach are the idea that psycho-logical phenomena develop within a broad field of relationships, both past and present, and that experience within the therapeutic encounter is continually and mutually shaped by both participants (Bridges, 1999). This approach draws upon ideas from self-psychology, psychodynamic developmental psychology and intersubjectivity theory.

There are some central components of the therapeutic relationship that manifest as a process of the therapeutic encounter. Transference was initially identified by Freud (1912) as a pattern in the client's life of relating to both the therapist and others, which originates from early experience with caregivers, predominantly the child's parents. Transference issues manifest in the process of therapy in terms of how the client feels towards the therapist and his or her needs and conflicts. Often these issues can manifest around the frame of therapy in terms of timing of sessions, whether the client arrives late and finds it difficult to end the therapy and how the client feels about the therapist's breaks and holidays. What also emerges, as the later school of object relations develops and moves away from Freudian drive theory, is the process of countertransference. This is understood as the therapist's emotional reaction to the client's transference issues (Heimann, 1950). The emotions the therapist experiences during the therapy sessions become central to understanding the emotional material of the client, which is sometimes held out of awareness, or unconsciously. In this sense, the intersubjective space between therapist and client contains the affective material that is central to understanding and conducting counselling and psychotherapy. Gill (1982) emphasizes the importance of re-experiencing in the therapeutic process, believing that because the client's problems are caused experientially, they will be transformed experientially and cannot be reasoned away intellectually. Therefore the therapy process becomes one where the client can feel safe and held enough to re-experience some of the initial emotional difficulties that brought him or her to therapy in the first place. Therefore the 'space' within which therapy takes place is very important for the emotional work that occurs, and it is here I turn next.

The Emotional Space of Therapy

Winnicott (1958) outlines the importance of emotional space in early infant development. In his theory of transitional phenomena and transitional objects, he identifies the centrality of the growing relationship to interior emotional and exterior emotional spaces for the baby. This process, undertaken in relation to the mother and the outer world, is where the baby is attempting to negotiate the relationship between the 'me' and the 'not me'. Winnicott sees the transitional phenomena that the baby is using as a way of the infant making sense of objects that are not part of the infant's body, yet are not fully recognized as belonging to external reality. He introduces the idea of 'transitional space', a space between the dyad of inner and outer. Winnicott posits this space as a kind of 'third space':

> [T]here is the third part of the life of a human being, a part that we cannot ignore, an intermediate area of experiencing, to which inner reality and external life both

contribute. It is an area which is not challenged, because no claim is made on its behalf except that it shall exist a resting-place for the individual engaged in the perpetual human task of keeping inner and outer reality separate yet inter-related. (Winnicott, 1958, p. 230)

By introducing the idea of the space between the objective and subjective world of the infant as a transitional space, he positions the infant as an active participant in having to negotiate this sense of the subjective and objective. He sees play as the vehicle through which the transitional space functions to both join and separate baby and mother. Winnicott falls back onto the interior of the infant, stating how external objects are appropriated and used in the service of emotional development, and used in defence against anxiety and depressive states. Transitional objects in their symbolic form represent the 'external' breast – the good enough 'mother', who makes active adaptation to the infant's needs and helps the infant to negotiate the emotional upheavals of early emotional development (Winnicott, 1958).

Counselling and psychotherapy, from a psychodynamic perspective, have always taken precedence over the holding environment as the space within which affect can be understood and contained (Bion, 1970). The holding environment and containment of the client's emotional states have become synonymous with the room: the indoor, comfortable, safe and warm space. This in turn has become synonymous with safe, ethical counselling and psychotherapy practice (Casement, 1992).

The importance of the transitional space that Winnicott (1958) posits allows for the concept of emotional space which can exist between internal and external, subjective and objective, mother and infant. This helps us start to imagine other forms of emotionality which can exist within and between geographical and relational 'spaces', and between mind and nature. The idea that space can have an emotional effect has been taken up within the field of emotional geography.

Emotional Geography

In recent years, geography has taken an 'emotional turn' (Bondi et al., 2005; Smith et al., 2009), locating the importance of emotions in relation to places and spaces and exploring how affect positions the perceiver and place in a reciprocal feedback loop. Bondi et al. (2005) state that the importance of places and their symbolic importance stems from their emotional associations and the resultant feelings they inspire. Emotional geography attempts to understand emotion as experiential and conceptual, and how it is mediated and articulated in a socio-spatial way rather than as a purely interiorized subjective mental state. Bondi et al. (2005) argue for a non-objectifying view of emotions as relational flows, fluxes or currents, in between people and places rather than 'things' or 'objects'; in doing this, they want to position emotions 'spatially'. This relationship between affect and space is an important aspect of understanding the rationale for taking therapeutic work outdoors and why, for some people, specific natural spaces have a particular emotional effect. This was one aspect of what was happening therapeutically outdoors that I hoped the research might illuminate further.

Bondi and Fewell (2003) see counselling as working at a 'spatial temporal' interface which transgresses normal boundaries of care; in particular, issues of confidentiality and ethical boundaries are reimagined simultaneously as being both concrete and specific, fluid and illusory. This dualism between what is real, material, concrete space and what is imagined, fantasy, symbolic space is played out in the counselling relationship via the contradictory positions of counsellor and client attempting to maintain what Bondi and Fewell (2003) call a non-hierarchical and relational practice while also engaging with the positioning of their clients, which are neither fixed nor easy to change. In relation to boundaries, counselling attempts to offer a clearly demarcated time and space which is safe and confidential, protecting clients from relationships with the counsellor outside of the counselling relationship. In this sense, Bondi and Fewell argue spatio-temporal boundaries mark a separation between 'ordinary life' and the space of counselling, in which deeply private anxieties and concerns can be addressed. One of the most prominent spatial metaphors of counselling is the space between inside and outside. In their research, Bondi and Fewell argue that counsellors conceptualize the interface between client and practitioner as a dynamic space within which these exteriorizations and interiorizations can be explored, thereby redefining the space and boundary between inner and outer realities (Bondi and Fewell, 2003, p. 540).

Case Example

Micky was a trainee therapist. His previous experiences of therapy had been difficult. He had either experienced the therapist as too cold or distant, or had felt that the therapist had 'invaded' his mind, and he felt at times suffocated. This experience was mirrored in other intimate relationships with partners, where he would oscillate between feeling desperately needy or would reject people when he felt he was getting too close or the relationship was getting serious. At assessment, Micky talked about his family history. His mother and father's marriage had been unstable and very argumentative. His father would regularly walk out, leaving Micky with his depressed mother, and he would feel overwhelmed by her despair and neediness. Micky had grown up with a poor sense of himself, quite often adapting himself to others' needs and wishes in order to be liked.

▶

Initially, the therapy was very difficult, and Micky would quite often cancel sessions or try to change the time of therapy. The therapist felt it was very difficult to connect with Micky and form a working therapeutic relationship. There were long pauses and silences in the subsequent sessions, and Micky reported feeling very ambivalent about therapy. When the therapist suggested that the therapy wasn't working and that maybe Micky wanted to end it, Micky became very angry with the therapist, accusing him of being both unprofessional and not committed to the relationship. Rather than reacting to this anger, the therapist explored it with Micky and suggested they might meet outdoors and walk together as the sessions indoors felt so difficult; he proposed that they try this approach to see how it felt.

They met in some woodland and walked and talked as they moved through the woods, stopping to notice things on the way. In the outdoor session, Micky talked more about how he felt, and the session went well. Micky said he found the woods containing and holding, and he could relax more in the sessions. Micky also reported that he found it 'much easier' to talk without the room and the eye contact of the therapist; that somehow he felt safer with the therapist while they were walking.

In subsequent sessions, when they again met in woodland locations and walked and talked, the therapist also found it easier to tune into Micky on an embodied level and make contact with him more easily than they had done indoors. The therapist reported in supervision that he found it much easier to regulate his emotional responses to Micky when they met outdoors. As the sessions progressed Micky was more able to be in contact with the therapist, turning up on time and not cancelling sessions. He began to be more able to stay in touch with painful feelings while moving and feeling contained by the trees – and, eventually, the therapist – outdoors.

Nature as a 'Third' Space for Psychotherapy

When we traditionally think of the therapeutic relationship, we think of the dyad between the therapist and client as being the central vehicle through which the therapy happens. However, recent developments, particularly within relational psychoanalysis, have posited a third space created between therapist and client, a meeting of the two subjectivities, both conscious and unconscious, which both create this shared third area (Ogden, 2004a). Benjamin (2009) sees this third space as an essential containing space where both therapist and client can survive the failures and ruptures inevitable in the therapeutic encounter. Benjamin (2009) sees the third space as providing the psychic ground for regulation of both parties and a vital space which enables both therapist and client to bring this regulation into conscious awareness and to be utilized in the therapeutic dyad.

For psychotherapy in nature, I propose that nature acts as a third space for the therapeutic dyad to inhabit in a concrete and material sense, as well as both consciously and unconsciously. Research undertaken by the author (Jordan,

2014a) found that a significant number of therapists who had taken their therapeutic practice outdoors into natural spaces had a long personal history of using
nature as a space for affect regulation and well-being. For some, complex family
dynamics in early childhood meant that they had formed a relationship with
natural spaces that provided them with comfort and affect regulation, something that was much more complex and less available to access in their human
relationships as they were growing up. Nature, as well as providing a space for
clients to affect-regulate during the therapeutic encounter outdoors, also provides a regulatory space for therapists, thus enabling them to metabolize difficult emotional material, particularly when this is in the form of projective
identification and more powerful unconscious material related to abuse and
trauma. The third space of nature is very important to both parties.

I have proposed elsewhere that nature is a 'vital' space (Jordan, 2014b), and
it is precisely this vitality in its living and vibrant qualities that is so important to
the therapeutic process outdoors. Therapy expands to include both the therapeutic dyad and the third space of nature, which either forms a backdrop to the
therapy or situates itself in the foreground of the work, taking the form of powerful metaphors and symbols. Although discredited within contemporary scientific understanding of biology and ecology, 'vitalism' (Driesch, 1914), the idea
that there is a living force in matter, has found a resurgence in social scientific
thinking. Bennett (2004) has advocated a contemporary form of vitalism, proposing that we can account for matter in terms of the affect it has on humans,
what she terms 'thing power'. Rather than a dead material space, things acquire
power in terms of their ability to hold matter and energy in the spaces between
inert matter and vital energy, between animate and inanimate 'and where all
things to some degree live on both sides' (Bennett, 2004, p. 352). For psychotherapy, Stern (2010) defines vitality as a manifestation of being alive and essential to human experience, something distinct from known physical, chemical
and mental forces. Drawing from the original ideas of vitalism as a dynamic
teleology, a moving unfolding and relational force of becoming, vitality is positioned as a constant sense of movement which maintains our sense of being
alive. Nature therefore becomes a space that gives the therapeutic encounter a
different kind of vitality and aliveness, thus aiding the therapeutic process.

Concluding Comments – The Therapist–client–
nature Matrix

The relationship between therapist, client and nature is of central importance to
understanding the psychotherapeutic processes of ecotherapy. A number of
interesting things emerge, not only around the relationship to nature but also
as concerns the effect on the therapist–client relationship. For some the outdoors and natural space act as an intermediary in what some clients experience

as an intense process. In this way, we can see the outdoor natural space, how it allows therapist and client to walk alongside each other and not have such direct eye to eye contact, as a less threatening way of doing therapy. In this we can understand why nature acts as a 'third space', a safer transitional space for the intensity of the therapeutic encounter. Nature can act as another form of object relation which allows both client and therapist to find ways to relate to one another. Recent research by Iantorno (2013) found that clients using nature as a therapeutic space were seeking to either regulate difficult emotions or to strengthen and revitalize themselves through contact with nature.

A central idea in emotional geography is that different geographic spaces have an effect on emotions and that different outdoor locations can have an effect on feelings and on the therapeutic relationship. The idea that it is the room alone that provides a safe container for therapeutic work is challenged by utilizing nature as a therapeutic space essential for some clients to feel safe. The transitional space created outdoors can mean that for some clients who have difficult early experiences, an outdoor natural space feels less threatening, allowing the client to make emotional contact with the therapist more easily. Some clients find the intensity of contact created in a room environment diffi-cult and need a different kind of space in order to feel safe enough in the thera-peutic relationship.

In his research into nature therapy, Berger (2006) discusses the idea of nature as a 'co-therapist' in the process of nature-based therapy. It is through the pres-ence of the natural world that the therapeutic process is facilitated; nature in this sense acts as another presence which both guides and provokes therapeutic process. Within psychotherapeutic work, it is important to not lose sight of the centrality of the therapeutic relationship between therapist and client, which must be part of the assemblage of relationships between therapist, client and the outdoor natural space. This is an important distinction in different approaches to ecotherapy and especially when ecotherapy becomes psychotherapy.

In this sense, the client and therapist relationship is essential for processing and understanding difficult feelings. This sits alongside the importance of nature as a 'vital' space for therapy, where both therapist and client can regulate their emotional responses to each other and feel held by nature as embodying and representing a transitional space. This has been under-theorized to date in eco-therapy, and this chapter is an attempt to address this gap in thinking and understanding.

References

Anderson, H., and H. Goolishian (1992) 'The Client Is the Expert: A Not-Knowing Approach to Therapy', in S. McNamee, and K. Bergen (eds) *Therapy as Social Construction* (Newbury Park, CA: Sage) pp. 25–39.

Benjamin, J. (2009) 'A Relational Psychoanalysis Perspective on the Necessity of Acknowledging Failure in Order to Restore the Facilitating and Containing Features of the Intersubjective Relationship (the Shared Third)', *International Journal of Psychoanalysis*, 90, 441–50.

Bennett, J. (2004) 'The Force of Things: Steps Toward an Ecology of Matter', *Political Theory*, 32(3), 347–72.

Berger, R. (2006) 'Beyond Words: Nature-Therapy in Action', *Journal of Critical Psychology, Counseling and Psychotherapy*, 6(4), 195–9.

Berger, R., and J. McLeod (2006) 'Incorporating Nature into Therapy: A Framework for Practice', *Journal of Systemic Therapies*, 25(2), 80–94.

Bion, W. R. (1970) *Attention and Interpretation: A Scientific Approach to Insight in Psychoanalysis and groups* (London: Tavistock Publications).

Bondi, L., and J. Fewell (2003) 'Unlocking the Cage Door: The Spatiality of Counselling', *Social and Cultural Geography*, 4(4), 527–47.

Bondi, L., J. Davidson and M. Smith (2005) 'Introduction: Geography's "Emotional Turn"', in J. Davidson, L. Bondi and M. Smith (eds) *Emotional Geographies* (Aldershot: Ashgate).

Bridges, N. A. (1999) 'Psychodynamic Perspective on Therapeutic Boundaries: Creative Clinical Possibilities', *Journal of Psychotherapy Research and Practice*, 8(4), 292–300.

Brown, C., and T. Augusta-Scott (2007) *Narrative Therapy: Making Meaning, Making Lives* (London: Sage).

Buzzell, L., and C. Chalquist (2009) *Ecotherapy: Healing with Nature in Mind* (San Francisco: Sierra Club Books).

Casement, P. (1992) *On Learning from the Patient* (Hove: Guilford Press).

Chalquist, C. (2009) 'A Look at the Ecotherapy Research Evidence', *Ecopsychology*, 1, (2), 1–10.

Clinebell, H. (1996) *Ecotherapy: Healing Ourselves, Healing the Earth* (London: Fortress).

Driesch, H. (1914) *The History and Theory of Vitalism* (Trans C. K. Ogden) (London: Macmillan).

Freud, S. (1912/1958) 'Recommendations to Physicians Practising Psychoanalysis', *Standard Edition*, 12, 109–20 (London: Hogarth Press).

Gill, M. (1982) *Analysis of Transference: Volume 1 Theory and Technique* (Madison: International Universities Press).

Hasbach, P. (2012) 'Ecotherapy', in P. Kahn and P. Hasbach (eds) *Ecopsychology: Science, Totems and the Technological Species* (London: MIT Press).

Heimann, P. (1950) 'On Counter-Transference', *International Journal of Psychoanalysis*, 31, 81–4.

Iantorno, R. (2013) *Encounters with Nature: A Heuristic Inquiry into the Experience of Connecting with Nature Through Metaphor in Integrative Psychotherapy*. Unpublished MSc thesis, The Sherwood Psychotherapy Training Institute/Coventry University.

Jordan, M. (2012) 'Did Lacan Go Camping? Psychotherapy in Search of an Ecological Self', in M. J. Rust and N. Totton (eds) *Vital Signs: Psychological Responses to the Ecological Crisis* (London: Karnac).

Jordan, M. (2014a) 'Taking Therapy Outside: A Narrative Inquiry into Counselling and Psychotherapy in Outdoor Natural Spaces', unpublished PhD thesis, University of Brighton.

Jordan, M. (2014b) *Nature and Therapy: Understanding Counselling and Psychotherapy in Outdoor Spaces* (London: Routledge).

Linden, S., and J. Grut (2002) *The Healing Fields: Working with Psychotherapy and Nature to Rebuild Shattered Lives* (London: Francis Lincoln).

McLeod, J. (1997) *Narrative and Psychotherapy* (London: Sage).

Mind (2007) *Ecotherapy: The Green agenda for Mental Health* (London: Mind).

Mind (2013a) *Feel Better Outside, Feel Better Inside: Ecotherapy for Mental Wellbeing, Resilience and Recovery* (London: Mind).

Mind (2013b) *Making Sense of Ecotherapy* (London: Mind).

Mitchell, S. (1988) *Relational Concepts in Psychoanalysis: An Integration* (Cambridge, MA: Harvard University Press).

Ogden, T. (2004a) 'On Holding and Containing, Being and Dreaming', *International Journal of Psychoanalysis*, 85, 1349–64.

Ogden, T. (2004b) 'The Analytic Third: Implications for Psychoanalytic Theory and Technique', *The Psychoanalytic Quarterly*, 53(1), 167–95.

Rogers, C. R. (1957) 'The Necessary and Sufficient Conditions for Therapeutic Personality Change', *Journal of Consulting Psychology*, 21, 95–103.

Roszak, T., M. Gomes and A. Kanner (1995) *Ecopsychology: Restoring the Earth, Healing the Mind* (London: Sierra Club).

Smith, M., J. Davidson, L. Cameron and L. Bondi (2009) *Emotion, Place and Culture* (Aldershot: Ashgate).

Stern, D. N. (2010) *Forms of Vitality: Exploring Dynamic Experience in Psychology, the Arts, Psychotherapy, and Development* (New York: Oxford University Press).

White, M., and D. Epston (1990) *Narrative Means to Therapeutic Ends* (New York: W.W. Norton).

Winnicott, D. (1958) *Collected Papers: Through Paediatrics to Psycho-Analysis* (London: Tavistock).

5

THE MANY ECOTHERAPIES

Linda Buzzell

Introduction

Ecopsychology is the study of the relationship between the human psyche (body–mind–soul–spirit) and the rest of nature. Ecotherapy (also called applied or clinical ecopsychology) focuses on healing that dangerously dysfunctional relationship. Because humans are an integral – and increasingly destructive – part of nature, many ecotherapists now look beyond how humans can merely 'use' nature to feel better psychologically and physically, and increasingly stress a reciprocal circle of healing that must tend to the needs of humans *and* the rest of nature. Both are hugely ambitious endeavours, especially at this make-or-break moment of human and ecological history on our home planet.

Level 1 and Level 2 Ecotherapies

The terms I use to describe these different approaches to ecotherapy are Level 1 (human-focused ecotherapies and results-oriented nature-based therapies) and Level 2 (whole-systems ecotherapies). And of course it's not always clear at what level we are operating at any given moment or where along the scale between the two we find ourselves.

Broadly speaking, Level 1 can be described as human-centred nature therapy (using nature and nature connection to improve human mental and physical health; taking one's daily vitamin N to avoid Nature Deficit Disorder, etc.). The good news at Level 1 for humans and human-tending clinicians is that a rapidly growing body of research supports the effectiveness of many Level 1 ecotherapies – enough for many nature-based therapies to qualify as 'evidence-based medicine' (Louv, 2011; Pretty, Peacock, Sellens and Griffin, 2005; Mind, 2013; Selhub, 2012). This has led to an increase in the demand for trained ecotherapists and a rise in various professional training programmes and symposia. The bad news is that the history of humans 'using' the rest of nature for whatever purpose is a cautionary tale, as such usage has destroyed the life sup-

port systems and ecosystems of countless species and now threatens the anni-
hilation of our own life support systems as well.

Level 1 ecotherapy is often based on a traditional Western world view that
values humanity well above the rest of nature. This allow us to adopt a dis-
tanced, 'objective' dominator position where 'using' other living beings or
inanimate 'natural resources' for whatever purposes requires no permission
or thought for the effects of that usage on the 'used' – a form of colonization or
slavery (Kidner, 2001).

This human-centred world view also includes the dysfunctional delusion that
there is a human self that can be safely disconnected from both healthy culture
and the rest of nature.

David Kidner's profoundly important book *Nature and Psyche: Radical Environmentalism and the Politics of Subjectivity* (Kidner, 2001) guides us in exploring
modern industrial culture's repressed subjective, challenging 'our taken-for-
granted ontology' and describing a dissociated 'industrialized [human] psyche'
that needs to relearn a 'flowing outward of the self into the world beyond, and
a resonance between "self" and "world" that places a question mark over their
separability' (Kidner, 2001, p. 166). He offers a timely reminder – especially for
those ecotherapists caught at Level 1 practice: 'The task we face … is not simply
to alleviate our individual discomforts, but also to recognize that these are
derived from the wider ontological split [between industrialism and the natural
order] that is tearing the world apart' (Kidner, 2007, p. 137).

Kidner's work (2001) may also encourage us to explore some of the tensions
between an impersonal, seemingly objective, scientific approach to measuring
the effects of various ecotherapies, and a more holistic understanding of the
larger ecology of distress. So, for example, the well-known University of Essex
ecotherapy research (Mind, 2013) that examined the effects on mood of walks
in green nature can be seen as supporting a Western empirical view of human
nature-connection activity that is grounded in a positivistic scientific understanding of how this connection with non-human nature affects our emotions
and how we can quantify these results – playing into a Level 1 understanding of
the value of ecotherapy but failing to look more deeply at the global malaise
caused by industrial growth and the effect this has on both subjectivity and the
outer world.

Level 2 ecotherapies focus on a Circle of Reciprocal Healing, a wider approach
rooted in the ecologically based, whole systems understanding that there can
be no true human health on a sick planet. Once we awaken from the delusion-
ary 'big lie' that humans and the human ego are somehow magically separate
from and superior to the rest of nature – and are therefore entitled to 'use' it as
mere resources without considering consequences – we discover the deeper
truth that we are all part of nature and embedded in the whole. This allows our
perspective to widen, and we can discover what John Seed calls 'the ecological
self' (2005).

Psychologist Sarah A. Conn raised the critical issue of reciprocity in her essay 'When the Earth Hurts, Who Responds?' (Conn, 1995) and again, with her late husband, psychologist Lane Conn, in 'Opening to the Other' (Conn and Conn, 2009):

> Individual health ... is connected to the health of other beings and to the health of the Earth as a whole ... Ecological health is the larger context of human health; they go together as outside-inside. Healthy human functioning in an ecopsychological context includes sustainable and mutually-enhancing relations not just at the intrapersonal level (within humans) or the interpersonal level (among humans) but also at the level of 'interbeing' (between humans and the non-human world).
>
> (Conn and Conn, 2009, p. 112)

Andy Fisher's *Radical Ecopsychology* (2013) also supports a second-level approach. 'A straightforward question I ask in sorting through the field of ecotherapy is: In what ways and to what extent does a given practice address the roots of the ecological crisis? This is a radical question.' Fisher recommends a deeper understanding of the parent discipline of ecopsychology itself, which might lead to 'radical praxes that offer "therapy" that is as much cultural and social as personal' (Fisher, 2013, p. 221).

So at Level 2, ecotherapy concerns itself not merely with the healing of a particular person or presenting problem or diagnosed illness, but with the larger healing of the human–nature relationship as it presents in a particular person or community or place at a particular historical moment. Level 2 ecotherapy often includes a cultivation of the sense of our extended ecological self, breaking down the artificial barriers between the health of an individual human or group and the health of the wider cultural, economic and environmental context. It involves respect, concern and even love for others and the Other (our extended ecological self, which may even include a spiritual component). The individual psyche then finds itself a seamless part of a much wider – even cosmic – whole.

With this in mind, before we ecotherapists and our clients begin to participate in any particular nature-connection healing process or activity, we might consciously choose a Level 2 approach to the interaction. Rather than rushing into one-sided, utilitarian relationships with any part of nature uncontrolled by the human ego, we could take a humbler and less narcissistic approach, as if engaging with an equal or superior being rather than an inanimate servant, slave or tool.

One simple example could involve slowing down and taking time to 'listen' to and empathize with the aspect of nature we are approaching before beginning any ecotherapeutic connection. We might also explore the ancient practice of asking permission from the particular aspect of the rest of nature we hope to connect with before barrelling into another's space and life. And we may feel called to express gratitude with gifts, reverence or reciprocal service (perhaps participating in the healing of a natural place or animal). At Level 2, we now deeply understand that what happens to the rest of nature happens to us – and vice versa. We are an integral part of nature, not separate or superior. The seeming 'other' whose presence brings healing is as worthy of care and tending as we ourselves. The boundary between self and 'nature' begins to dissolve.

One Ecotherapy Can Be Practised at Multiple Levels

Many ecotherapies – probably most – can be practised at either Level 1 or Level 2 or somewhere along the scale between them. Let's consider *animal-assisted therapy* (AAT), an increasingly popular healing modality. At its Level 1 extreme, AAT might involve something like the capture of wild dolphins for the purpose of providing 'dolphin therapy' to paying customers, without regard for the rights or comfort of the animal in question. Thankfully, many animal-assisted therapies are now moving in the direction of further reciprocity and care – Level 2. An example of the latter might be Return to Freedom, a horse sanctuary founded by Neda DeMayo in the Santa Ynez Valley, California, that rescues horses threatened with extermination and allows them to run free in natural herds in a natural habitat, interacting with each other and with humans as they choose.

> The healing effects spread beyond [DeMayo's] four-legged friends to people transformed by friendly encounters with wild horses. On the human side, the benefits have included higher self-esteem, increased trust in intuition and instinct, feeling more at home in one's body, and a sense of the spiritual arising from the natural, as during a walking meditation among a trusting herd. Something of the spirit of freedom epitomized by a galloping horse rubs off on us too.
>
> (DeMayo, 2009, p. 149)

Perhaps the key to this effect is the fact that the animals have a real choice about whom they will or won't associate with. So when a free animal chooses to make contact with a hurting or merely curious human, this is a special nature-connection moment that can be profoundly moving and even healing to the person involved. The evolving paradigm of pairing abused animals with nature-deprived or abused humans seems especially poignant and effective. Veterans with post-traumatic stress disorder (PTSD), for example, may find tending abused animals to be healing to both simultaneously (Bliss, 2009a, 2009b) – the Level 2 Circle of Reciprocal Healing at work. We might even expand AAT to include trans-species psychology, which challenges ecotherapists to overcome the inherent anthropocentrism of our field and suggests that only by striving for the well-being of other animals can we ensure our own well-being (Bradshaw, 2009).

Let's take a quick look at a couple of other well-known ecotherapy modalities to see how this evolution from Level 1 to Level 2 might work there as well. If we look at wilderness therapy, for instance, we can see a possible trajectory from the most mundane commercial survival 'outdoor challenges' for wayward teens to the far more sophisticated offerings of The School of Lost Borders or Animas Valley Institute (Plotkin, 2003), depth-oriented wilderness experiences that can even include what Bron Taylor (2010) calls 'dark green' spiritual experiences of profound oneness with the rest of nature.

Horticultural therapies, including garden and farm therapies, can also be practised at multiple levels, from the simplest school or community garden experience, where the focus might simply be on growing food for humans to eat, to a much more integrative and profound understanding of the reciprocal nature of subjective and objective ecosystem relationships.

The difference between Level 1 and Level 2 approaches to interacting with the rest of nature in a garden became viscerally apparent to me in the 1990s, when my husband and I moved to a small home with a more spacious (but sadly degraded) yard than we'd ever had in the city. We took the Permaculture Design Course for guidance, and over the years, with careful tending and working with the rest of nature rather than against it, this tiny piece of wider nature has become a wild-looking, permaculture-style backyard food forest full of intermingling plants that benefit humans, wildlife and the ecosystem as a whole. This physical blending of humans, 'relatives' and habitat transformed me and my therapy practice as well, as I discovered that nature's principles and practices could be applied not only to land care but people care as well.

For example, the first permaculture principle is 'observe and interact'. Initially, we applied this to garden care. Through listening to the land and observing carefully, we found ourselves breaking away from the traditional, human-and-machine-focused, monocrop and 'planting in rows' approaches and instead using biomimicry as we observed how nature grows her plants for maximum abundance. Quite without intending to, I also discovered how this principle could be applied to the human psyche as well. Through interacting daily with the newly restored natural environment outside our back door, now full of life and energy, I observed how being outdoors not only predictably lifted my mood but also melted away any anxiety or stress I might be feeling. This observation and interactive experience gradually transformed my psychotherapy practice into an ecotherapy practice, complete with an outdoor therapy 'office' where I was able to share the garden's healing effects with clients as well. My gratitude for this involves a reciprocal, committed tending of the place that changed my life.

Why Do Nature-connection Therapies Work?

The robust empirical evidence for the healing effectiveness of the various ecotherapies – at whatever level they're practised – raises the question of why almost any kind of nature connection – even mere pictures of nature on a wall – seems to provoke a measurable therapeutic response. My theory is that what Richard Louv calls Nature-Deficit Disorder (2008, 2011) is an ongoing condition suffered by much of modern humanity in industrial cultures around the world. Like captive tigers born and raised in a cramped zoo cage, we find ourselves going crazy in industrial society but often having no idea why we're unhappy, or what it is that we're really longing for. A rising percentage of today's unnaturally domesticated, 'cage-raised', screen-addicted or cubicle-enslaved humans have various symptoms equivalent to the tiger's endless pacing or frustrated, depressed lethargy. Research is showing us that even the tiniest exposure and reconnection to the habitat our species evolved in, and for, can produce unexpected healing and profound joy in body, mind and soul. I am reminded of the popular Internet videos of a herd of cows, confined for the winter to a barn and dried hay, that is allowed out in the spring onto a field of grass. All lethargy and plodding left behind, these adult cows find themselves cavorting and prancing with calf-like joy at the sight and taste of the succulent grass, the open air and the sunlight. We too are just such animals, which is perhaps why the many online videos of released animals find such wide audiences.

But One Size Doesn't Fit All

An important thing I learned when I began shifting my psychotherapy practice into an ecotherapy practice was that 'one size definitely doesn't fit all'. A nature-connection prescription like equine-assisted therapy that is highly effective with one person may be a complete dud with another. Taking a step back, I began to inquire more deeply into the history of my client(s)' relationships with the rest of nature. I asked, 'Have you felt a special connection with the rest of nature – including animals, plants or places – either in childhood or now?' Almost without exception, this query will open a very emotional conversation that allows me to better appreciate the uniqueness of each person's connection with the wider world. For example, I once raised this question with a therapist friend, who replied: 'Oh, ecotherapy. That's not for me. I'm a city kind of gal.' Knowing about the love she has for her companion animals, I asked, 'But what about your kitties?' She sighed and replied softly. 'Oh, my babies …' 'Well, that's your nature-connection ecotherapy,' I replied. 'Animal-assisted therapy.' Her cuddles with her beloved kitties have helped her through a devastating bereavement.

Experiences like this have convinced me to take more time helping clients explore and discover their preferred method of nature connection before prescribing any ecotherapy practice at either Level 1 or Level 2. I see this as an important first step in any ecotherapy treatment. Luckily for clinicians and those who come to us for help in healing, nature-connection practices come in many shapes and colours, offering a wide enough variety that almost every client can find a way to access nature's astonishing healing powers.

Multiple Ecotherapies, Multiple Populations, Multiple Methods of Nature Connection – Practised at Multiple Levels

Ecotherapy practitioners around the world are continuing to discover and develop a wide variety of creative and effective nature-connection healing practices that can be used at multiple levels to treat many different populations suffering from many different 'presenting problems'. I leave the examination of most of these to others more familiar with the modality in question and hope they will explore their possible evolution from an initial 'human use' perspective to a Level 2 reciprocal healing understanding.

Somatic

One that deserves a mention here, however, is somatic therapy. Reconnecting with the 'wild nature' in our own bodies can be a simple Level 1 process, where the focus is initially exclusively our own well-being (e.g. some of the more narcissistic Western yoga practices), but it can also – sometimes without any conscious effort on our part – begin to evolve to reciprocally connect us not only to the nature 'in here' but also to our extended body/mind 'out there'. Once we incorporate (literally) the Level 2 awareness that we too are part of nature, it becomes apparent that nature-connection healing can take place not only by going out to parks or wilderness but also through deeply reconnecting with our inner nature – the parts of our bodies, minds, souls and spirits that are less under the control of our sometimes-arrogant egos (although of course those very egos are also part of nature – just a much smaller part of it than they realize!). In many cultures, this idea of the body as a seamless part of wider nature is nothing new, of course. For thousands of years, traditional yogis have connected with their breath and the breath of the world; and Chinese healers have worked with the life energy they call chi. Any practice that connects us with our wild bodies can become a true ecotherapy.

Another source of connection with uncontrolled-by-the-human-ego nature lies within the psyche itself. Ecopsychotherapeutic processes can allow us to reconnect with the 'wilderness within'. Following in the footsteps of countless indigenous cultures, Freud and Jung explored free associations and dreams for enlightenment, guidance and healing. Modern practitioners of individual and community eco-dreamwork, like Stephen Aizenstat (2009), Lauren Z. Schneider (2009) and Meredith Sabini (2009), actively incubate dreams of and by the rest of nature, explore natural symbols and messages as they appear in dreams, and practise dream council work where 'wild mind' is allowed to speak to the collective. Ecotherapist Nick Totton's *Wild Therapy* (2010) is another great help in exploring this undomesticated, inner terrain and connecting individual psyche to wider Psyche. 'Therapy is by nature wild,' he says, 'but a lot of it at the moment is rather tame.' Totton's goal is 'to help shift the balance back towards wildness by showing how therapy can connect with ecological thinking, seeing each species, each being, each person inherently and profoundly linked to each other' (Totton, 2010, p. 1), definitely Level 2!

Ecotherapies That Treat Conditions Specific to Our Era

The depression that originates in our awareness of the destruction of the natural world is an emotion that potentially reconnects us to the earth, in which we share the suffering of the earth, recognizing that the world we inhabit is 'a world of wounds'. (Kidner, 2001, p. 37)

I don't want to end this brief tour of the multiple ecotherapies without addressing some of the most complex and challenging modalities. We live in perilous times. The huge, almost unprecedented historical shifts we are experiencing have many names: Joanna Macy's 'The Great Unraveling' (Macy and Johnstone, 2012); economist and former Harvard Business School professor David Korten's 'The Great Turning' (2006); social critic James Howard Kunstler's 'The Long Emergency' (2005); permaculture teacher Rob Hopkins' 'Transition' (2008); and author Carolyn Baker's 'Collapse' (2011). Whatever we call this era of rapid natural degradation, it is causing huge psychological trauma and distress in many humans (and other species) around the world. Some of the names ecotherapists use for the almost ubiquitous anxiety, depression, panic, heartbreak and dread (especially evident in young people worried about their future) include eco-anxiety, eco-grief, eco-trauma, solastalgia and even eco-despair.

In this critical situation, we cannot afford to remain stuck at Level 1, continuing to use and abuse the rest of nature for whatever purposes. Without a collective evolution to true whole systems thinking and reciprocity, our species may not survive much longer. Ecotherapists are now faced with the daunting task of helping our clients and communities not only process the challenging information and losses of our time but also shift consciousness towards a deeper understanding of the unity of life that will radically alter our behaviour towards the rest of nature.

Psychotherapist and ecotherapist Sarah Anne Edwards and I wrote an essay, 'The Waking Up Syndrome' (Edwards and Buzzell, 2009), that attempts to track the various states and stages people go through as they awaken to the full realization of our collective jeopardy, based on thanatologist Elizabeth Kubler-Ross's stages of death and dying (1969). Our hope is that by identifying and naming the various natural emotional reactions most of us will have to the ongoing eco-trauma of Kunstler's 'Long Emergency,' we and our clients can gain a compassionate understanding of our own and others' feelings and reactions, ultimately finding the personal and collective strength to go forward into constructive action, resilient adaptation and solutions.

Perhaps the 'darkest' ecotherapies directly address the possibility of total collapse. Former psychotherapist and history professor Carolyn Baker, author of *Navigating the Coming Chaos: A Handbook for Inner Transition* (Baker, 2011), now hosts a call-in radio show, *The Lifeboat Hour*, and her ecotherapy practice includes 'collapse coaching' to encourage, guide and comfort those in despair over our circumstances. And for decades, ecophilosopher and ecotherapist Joanna Macy and her colleagues have been leading 'From Despair to Empowerment' workshops that provide powerful guidance. Macy's book *Active Hope: How to Face the Mess We're in without Going Crazy* (Macy and Johnstone, 2012), co-authored with physician Chris Johnstone, offers a sensible way forward in these uniquely challenging times.

Community-based Ecotherapy Practices

Historically, psychotherapy has focused primarily on treating the individual human patient or client while ignoring not only the extended human social, cultural, economic and political context but also the environmental ground of all being. But as ecology and Level 2 ecopsychology teach us, everything is interconnected – and must be consciously reconnected in our minds by those of us who have been living under the delusion of separation.

David Kidner (2001) is again a wise guide on this as well as many other issues. He points out that to truly heal the current, woefully dysfunctional human–nature relationship, we must also heal the necessary conduit for all such interactions – modern human culture (especially Western industrial culture, with its reductionistic, instrumental, materialist philosophy and dualistic, anthropocentric and domination-focused language and ideas). Facilitating the transition and recovery from nature-destructive industrial culture is a hugely ambitious ecotherapy undertaking, but one that a number of influential theorists and practitioners like Andy Fisher (2013) feel is increasingly critical.

Various ecotherapies are evolving to help communities with this recovery, assisting with the practical, psychological and even spiritual healing of the ubiquitous alienation from the rest of nature and nature-based ways of living. Permaculture is one example of this and has proven to be highly attractive to young people needing a way to envision and practise a pleasurable and satisfying sustainable lifeway. Others focus on assisting in the creation of eco-villages, teaching council practice or facilitating community Transition. In fact, the Transition movement has spread around the globe and includes 'Heart and Soul of Transition' groups that address the psychological and spiritual side of The Great Turning (Macy and Johnstone, 2012). Many communities now follow ecotherapist Cecile Andrews' (2009) prescription of creating community circles with various purposes, including voluntary simplicity circles, sustainability book clubs and neighbourhood exchanges. Still others stress what ecopsychologist Craig

Chalquist and I call 'cultural ecoresilience', building personal and community strength, flexibility and trauma tolerance that facilitate bioregional mitigation and adaptation in the face of escalating environmental degradation and the serial, progressive economic and ecological catastrophes our behaviour has already set in motion.

We also need to radically expand our understanding of community and diversity, actively including all human cultures as well as the rest of nature. Community environmental justice work like that being done by environmental justice activists Carl Anthony and Paloma Pavel in Oakland, California, is inspirational for many ecotherapists. Authors of the Breakthrough Communities project of Earth House Center, they are building and modelling multiracial leadership for regional sustainable community. Anthony warns against what he perceives as an 'ecopsychological blind spot in the United States, due to its Eurocentric perspective, which has been based on the dominance paradigm. The "self" that ecopsychology needs to address, is a multicultural self, with many voices and many perspectives' (Anthony, 1996).

Ecospirituality

Some may feel that it is not within the purview of ecopsychology or ecotherapy to address the realm of spirituality, but it is impossible to ignore the fact that every successful human culture in every era – including our own – has a sense of and reverence for what it holds to be sacred, even if that 'god' is merely money, success, 'market fundamentalism' or faith in experimental science. In practice, ecotherapists quickly discover that an ineffable sense of the sacredness of nature within ourselves and our surroundings is a key factor in both mental health and the transition towards a life- and behaviour-changing sense of ecological selfhood that can include the wider cosmic Self.

The field of ecospirituality is expanding rapidly, both among those greening up traditional religions with 'creation care' practices and those who describe themselves as 'spiritual, but not religious'. In addition to perusing the work of Tielhard de Chardin, Thomas Berry and Brian Swimme, those interested may enjoy reading Bron Taylor's *Dark Green Religion: Nature Spirituality and the Planetary Future* (2010) and Llewellyn Vaughan-Lee's anthology *Spiritual Ecology: The Cry of the Earth* (2013).

The Goal of the Many Ecotherapies

All of the many Level 2 ecotherapies mentioned above – different from each other as they may seem – share the same aim and dream: to facilitate the healing of the tragically pathological relationship between the conscious human psyche, individually and in community, with the rest of nature. We and our ecotherapy clients and students may begin with Level 1 baby steps – discovering that growing a garden or petting a dog or hiking on a leafy trail can raise our spirits and calm our anxieties – but hopefully we will also be able to advance to a deeper understanding of the indivisible unity between our bodies, minds and deepest selves and the rest of the natural world. For it is this ancient oneness that offers the deepest healing possibilities, not only for ourselves but for our communities, cultures and the tragically wounded earth and its disappearing life forms.

This may seem a huge undertaking for ecotherapists – and certainly we cannot heal the earth by ourselves and thankfully are part of a much wider community facilitating The Great Turning – but perhaps for those of us whose calling includes psychotherapy, counselling, nature coaching and teaching, it can be the most urgent, exciting and rewarding work of our era.

References

Aizenstat, S. (2009) 'Dream Tending and Tending the World', in L. Buzzell and C. Chalquist (eds) *Ecotherapy: Healing with Nature in Mind* (San Francisco: Sierra Club Books) pp. 262–69.

Andrews, C. (2009) 'The Small Group as Ecotherapy: Building a Culture of Connection', in L. Buzzell and C. Chalquist (eds) *Ecotherapy: Healing with Nature in Mind* (San Francisco: Sierra Club Books) pp. 192–96.

Anthony, C. (1996) Ecopsychology with Carl Anthony, http://library.noetic.org/library/audio-lectures/carl-anthony-ecopsychology.

Baker, C. (2011) *Navigating the Coming Chaos: A Handbook for Inner Transition* (Bloomington, IN: iUniverse).

Bliss, S. (2009a, 2 February) Agrotherapy: How Farms Heal, http://www.commondreams.org/view/2009/02/02-5.

Bliss, S. (2009b) 'In Praise of Sweet Darkness', in L. Buzzell and C. Chalquist (eds) *Ecotherapy: Healing with Nature in Mind* (San Francisco: Sierra Club Books) pp. 174–84.

Bradshaw, G. A. (2009) 'Transformation through Service: Trans-species Psychology and Its Implications for Ecotherapy', in L. Buzzell and C. Chalquist (eds) *Ecotherapy: Healing with Nature in Mind* (San Francisco: Sierra Club Books) pp. 157–65.

Conn, L. K., and S. A. Conn (2009) 'Opening to the Other', in L. Buzzell and C. Chalquist (eds) *Ecotherapy: Healing with Nature in Mind* (San Francisco: Sierra Club Books) pp. 111–15.

Conn, S. A. (1995) 'When the Earth Hurts, Who Responds?', in T. Roszak, M. Gomes and A. Kanner (eds) *Ecopsychology: Restoring the Earth, Healing the Mind* (San Francisco: Sierra Club Books) pp. 156–71.

DeMayo, N. (2009) 'Horses, Humans and Healing', in L. Buzzell and C. Chalquist (eds) *Ecotherapy: Healing with Nature in Mind* (San Francisco: Sierra Club Books) pp. 149–56.

Edwards, S. A., and L. Buzzell (2009) 'The Waking Up Syndrome', in L. Buzzell and C. Chalquist (eds) *Ecotherapy: Healing with Nature in Mind* (San Francisco: Sierra Club Books) pp. 123–30.

Fisher, A. (2013) *Radical Ecopsychology: Psychology in the Service of Life* (Albany, NY: State University of New York Press).

Hopkins, R. (2008) *The Transition Handbook: From Oil Dependency to Local Resilience* (White River Junction, VT: Chelsea Green).

Kidner, D. (2001) *Nature and Psyche: Radical Environmentalism and the Politics of Subjectivity* (Albany, NY: State University of New York Press).

Kidner, D. (2007) 'Depression and the Natural World: Towards a Critical Ecology of Psychological Distress', *International Journal of Critical Psychology*, 19, 123–46.

Korten, D. C. (2006) *The Great Turning: From Empire to Earth Community* (San Francisco: Berrett-Koehler).

Kubler-Ross, E. (1969) *On Death and Dying: What the Dying Have to Teach Doctors, Nurses, Clergy and Their Own Families* (New York: Scribner).

Kunstler, J. H. (2005) *The Long Emergency: Surviving the End of Oil, Climate Change, and Other Converging Catastrophes of the Twenty-First Century* (New York: Atlantic Monthly Press).

Louv, R. (2008) *Last Child in the Woods: Saving Our Children from Nature-Deficit Disorder* (Chapel Hill, NC: Algonquin Books).

Louv, R. (2011) *The Nature Principle: Human Restoration and the End of Nature-Deficit Disorder* (Chapel Hill, NC: Algonquin Books).

Macy, J., and C. Johnstone (2012) *Active Hope: How to Face the Mess We're in without Going Crazy* (Novato, CA: New World Library).

Mind (2013) Feel Better Outside, Feel Better Inside: Ecotherapy for Mental Wellbeing, Resilience and Recovery (London: Mind), http://www.mind.org.uk/media/336359/Feel-better-outside-feel-better-inside-report.pdf?ctaId=/about-us/policies-issues/ecotherapy/slices/read-the-report/.

Plotkin, B. (2003) *Soulcraft: Crossing into the Mysteries of Nature and Psyche* (Novato, CA: New World Library).

Pretty, J., J. Peacock, M. Sellens and M. Griffin (2005) 'The Mental and Physical Health Outcomes of Green Exercise', *International Journal of Environmental Health Research*, 15, 319–37.

Sabini, M. (2009) 'Dreaming a New Paradigm', in L. Buzzell and C. Chalquist (eds) *Ecotherapy: Healing with Nature in Mind* (San Francisco: Sierra Club Books) pp. 211–18.

Schneider, L. Z. (2009) 'The Whale's Tale', in L. Buzzell and C. Chalquist (eds) *Ecotherapy: Healing with Nature in Mind* (San Francisco: Sierra Club Books) pp. 116–22.

Seed, J. (2005) 'The Ecological Self', *EarthLight Magazine*, 53, 14, http://www.earthlight.org/2005/essay53_johnseed.html.

Selhub, E. M. and A. C. Logan (2012) *Your Brain On Nature: The Science of Nature's Influence on Your Health, Happiness and Vitality* (Ontario: John Wiley & Sons).

Taylor, B. (2010) *Dark Green Religion: Nature Spirituality and the Planetary Future* (Berkeley, CA: University of California Press).

Thefunkyfarmer. (2012) 'Happy Cows Skipping out to Grass for the First Time', April. (Video file) https://www.youtube.com/watch?v=huT5__BqY_U.

Thewatchvideos63. (2013) 'Holland Dairy Cows Are Released to Pasture after a Long Winter.' (Video file) https://www.youtube.com/watch?v=rDvnUiO-LAk.

Totton, N. (2011) *Wild Therapy: Undomesticating Inner and Outer Worlds* (London: Karnac Books).

Vaughan-Lee, L. (2013) *Spiritual Ecology: The Cry of the Earth* (Point Reyes, CA: The Golden Sufi Center).

PART II   RESEARCH

6

WORKING WITH NATURE IN PALLIATIVE CARE

Deborah Kelly

Introduction

My 'way in' to working in and with nature was, in part, through my childhood love of the natural world: being in nature, the physical, sensory and imaginal experiences; lying in the summer grass, talking to trees, acknowledging the elementals, learning the folklore, knowing the freedom of the fields and skies; and alongside the extraordinary familiarity of my home lands, knowledge that some landscapes and weathers can be wild and dangerous, and some stories tell of the darkness of the earth, of journeys to the underworld and beyond.

Later, my interest deepened through a sense and exploration of sacred landscapes. Through Chinese medicine, and in particular the Five Phases theory (Kaptchuk, 1983), I learned how nature, health, the elements and the rhythm of the seasons are interlaced. As an integrative arts psychotherapist, nature became a place of creative exploration, through body and imagination, metaphor and myth.

Thus, for me, working with nature is many layered. It incorporates the experience of the moment, the sensuousness of the landscape, captured in reverie or full phenomenological contact. It can evoke a sense of the past, by way of personal memories and ancestral echoes of the land, felt in our bodies, or imagined through folk law and legend. Nature also offers a rich abundance of metaphors and poesies: of struggle and conquest, beauty and awe, life and death, stories of initiation, of journeying to other realms.

I work in landscapes of southern England, ancient woodland and rolling hills close to the sea. The landscapes evoke, for me, a benign beauty, and yet in wild weather the surging seas and noisome trees can be both exhilarating and formidable. Our relationship with nature can be a source of inspiration, exploration and revelation, yet it is not always comfortable. Nature is not always benign. To borrow from Richard Mabey, 'I am all for nature cures, but let them be profound and mysterious and terrible at times. We will be all the better for it' (Mabey, 2010, p. 196).

In this chapter, I focus on my work with palliative care groups in nature and in particular on research into the experience of practitioners in this field. This work began 15 years ago, inspired by Dr Michael Kearney's vision of an integrated approach to palliative care, which incorporated the advantages of modern medicine and symptom control, alongside holistic approaches that might address existential pain and suffering (Kearney, 1996, 2000).

A New Paradigm

Palliative medicine developed rapidly in the 1960s in response to the pioneering work of Cicely Saunders. Prior to this, medical interventions in end-of-life care were minimal. Although nursing and spiritual care was available, medicine had been concerned with cure rather than palliation. As doctors became more involved with the terminally ill, a huge improvement in symptom management and pain control was seen, alongside an acknowledgement of the interrelatedness of physical, emotional and spiritual distress. In 1987, palliative care was recognized as a new medical speciality in the United Kingdom. However, as the medical influence increased, there was concern among some practitioners that the original 'holistic focus of (palliative care) might be lost under the weight of the biomedical model' (Balfour Mount, cited in Kearney, 2000, p. viii) and that the new specialists in palliative care would be reduced to 'symptomologists' (Kearney, 1992). Kearney's concern was that while the advances in medicine were addressing the physical symptoms more efficiently, the medical model had no paradigm for attending to suffering, to the spiritual or existential domain of human experience.

The challenge to palliative medicine, articulated by Dr Kearney, was a dual commitment; to improve analytical and clinical skills while facilitating a personal experience of illness in an intuitive way, enabling patients to 'dive down into the experience of illness in a quest for healing' (1992, p. 46); an emotional or spiritual, if not physical, healing. This ability to facilitate experiences of depth corresponds to the skills required in depth psychology – moving from the surface experience, the abode of the ego, where language is literal and the mode of knowledge is scientific and rational, to the depth experience, where the mode of knowing is intuitive, and the language that of symbol and metaphor.

Kearney also challenged the palliative care practitioners to be committed to making a journey themselves from the surface to the deep, to know what it means to cross these inner boundaries (1992, p. 45). He argued for a new paradigm in palliative care, rooted in ancient Greece and based on a synthesis of Hippocratic medicine and Asklepian healing. There are over one hundred healing centres or shrines to Asklepius, the god of healing over the ancient world, the most famous being at Epidaurus and Kos. The temples were usually built in beautiful and significant landscapes, close to wells or springs. Here the 'invalid' was attended to through bathing, fasting, exercise, ritual and festivals. Plays and philosophical debate were also considered therapeutic and part of the preparation for the final rite of healing: the incubation of a dream. This took place in the 'abaton', a specially designated place, often a depression in the earth, where the invalid, close to the earth and the heart of the temple, would receive a healing dream. If Asklepius himself, or his snake, the bearer of earth wisdom, appeared in the dream, this was considered particularly significant. In this way, the Asklepian rites prepared the patient for an encounter with the divine: 'This was no visit to a doctor who simply administers medicine; it was an encounter with the naked event of healing itself' (Kerenyi, 1959, p. 34).

Kearney presents a comparison between Hippocratic medicine (our modern medicine) and Asklepian healing. He sees Hippocratic medicine as drawing on objective evidence and treating pain 'from without'. Asklepian healing draws on subjective evidence and is concerned with healing suffering 'from within' (Kearney, 2000). The Asklepian principles of attending to body, mind and soul, in preparation for healing to emerge 'from within', is an important influence on my work. The use of bodywork, imagination, reverie and ritual invites a journey into depth, into the chthonic aspects of nature and myth, facilitating a reconnection to the potential healing within. Even in palliative care, this healing can be a remembering, a reconnection that allows the person to die in peace.

Nature and Palliative Care

For the past 15 years, and supported by a local charity, we have been facilitating groups for people living with a life-threatening illness, usually in the palliative stage of treatment. They are held each week, usually in woodland, and are supportive and reflective rather than psychotherapeutic. However, the invitation for exploration is ever present, through reflection, meditation, ritual (walking a labyrinth, fire rituals) creative exploration and working with stories of the seasons. Nature has many avenues into the exploration of mortality and all that this engenders. Some ways are containing and supportive, such as the reconnection to Mother Earth; some are awesome and touch on the numinous; some follow Persephone into the underworld. All are potentially transformative.

For example, the natural world offers a sense of cyclical time rather than the linear trajectory governed by Chronos. Life and death ebb and flow through continual cycles of growth, decline and renewal. Nothing is lost. When there is a sense of time running out, an experience of beauty can expand a moment into eternity. As Rollo May writes, 'Beauty is eternity born into human existence' (May, 1985, p. 72). At the same time, a glimpse of the incalculable distance of the stars or the age of the universe can help place our lives in perspective.

A sense of interconnectedness, of being 'at one' with the natural world, can facilitate our search for meaning. If we can move away from Cartesian duality, we may experience becoming 'enwrapped in a world soul' (Tacey, 2009, p. 153). In this way, nature can take us beyond ego: 'an overcoming of self-hood, an adventure beyond the eclipsing mind' (O'Donoghue, 2013, p. 31). Nature also offers us a mirror, reflecting beauty and ugliness, health and disease. The growth on a tree may reflect the cancer inside; the ecological damage outside can mirror the physiological damage inside. Wild winds can match our rage; cold mists, our despair. Nature therapy may not always be about well-being; it needs also to resonate with our pain.

Research

In 2011, I undertook a heuristic pilot study of the experience of practitioners working in nature as part of ongoing doctoral research. One of Kearney's challenges was that although Hippocratic medicine required external knowledge and skills, an Asklepian approach calls for self-knowledge, a demand to face our own mortality, to be alongside suffering. This research was done in the hope that it would contribute to the issue of psychospiritual care provision in palliative care settings and the part nature may play in this.

In choosing a method of inquiry, I wanted to use a methodology that resonated with my therapeutic approach, to use nature, metaphor and imagination within the process. Writers on imaginal and transpersonal research (Angelo, 2005, 2010; Braud and Anderson, 1998, 2011; Romanyshyn, 2007) discuss an approach to research that is circular rather than linear. This process of researching, relooking and circling around a subject to view it from many perspectives and through many avenues stands in contrast to the linear process of empirical and quantitative research, inviting a creative approach not just in the collection of data but also in the dissemination. Likewise, Marie Angelo delivers an invitation to allow images to speak in academic research:

> I wanted to establish a practitioner vision, for which the method and grounds of knowledge, the epistemology, would be as imagistic as the content.
>
> (2005, p. 16)

This approach to research offers an opportunity to develop a broader, deeper, more expansive exploration, with imagination as an integral part of the process.

Moustakas's heuristic research (1990) presented a framework which could address both the inquiry into experience and a creative methodology. Moustakas identified six stages within the research process: initial engagement, immersion, incubation, illumination, explication and creative synthesis (1990). The research process demands the researcher to explore his or her internal experience and to remain connected to, and in relationship with, the subject of inquiry. Rather than observing the subject from a distance, heuristic inquiry leads the researcher into a deepening experience (an immersion), collecting data through self-dialogue, personal journals and self-inquiry; and incorporating opportunities for creative exploration. Similar to the holistic and intuitive preparation for the incubation of a healing dream, this process also follows a flow of engagement and immersion in preparation for the incubation, illumination and explication of a creative synthesis. As for the Asklepian invalid, it offers the researcher the opportunity to be 'visited by the gods.'

The research participants consisted of myself and two co-researchers, all of whom had facilitated or co-facilitated the group relevant to the inquiry. The two co-researchers were included to facilitate validation and to address a peripheral question concerned with the qualities and training needed to do this work. One co-researcher was a specialist palliative care nurse; the other, a complementary therapist. Because I had been trained in both these professions and was a psychotherapist, I hoped to elicit how our professional trainings might impact our experience. The question we aimed to explore was simply this: What is our experience of working in nature with palliative care groups? The method in practice involved semi-structured interviews, exploration through journal writing, creating images, reverie and being in nature.

From an initial phase of engagement with the material, several themes began to emerge, and the material began to be arranged accordingly. As they emerged, each theme was illustrated by a photographic image from nature, chosen by me and checked by the research participants for their suitability and resonance. These formed the creative synthesis: 24 images, alongside a poem, which emerged from contemplation of the data. The full record of the research can be found at www.wildmercury.co.uk. The main themes are presented here, all of which I consider to be completely interconnected:

- Nature as healing: being 'at ease', supported

- Nature as container: physical and emotional sense of a benevolence, sheltered, coming home

- Nature as a resource: of immediate experience; of metaphors, myths, stories

- Nature holding and reflecting the cycles of life and death, seasons, rhythm

- Depth of experience: listening more clearly, hearing more, sacred space, dropping into depth, shadowlands of death, fear

- Boundaries: professional/personal, death/life

There follows an expansion of some of these themes, with examples of researchers' (or research participants') comments indented.

Nature as Healing, Being at Ease, Supported

Being in nature was seen as a positive experience that gave a sense of being 'at ease', of 'breathing more easily', of grounded-ness.

> Whilst working in nature, the whole experience feels more natural. It feels easier to breathe, to relax and the words, stories, metaphors flows [sic] freely. I feel energy is coming through me, not from me, to support me.

> There is freedom. I need my shoes off! Need to feel in touch with the earth to be grounded.

> There is a sense of time slowing down, my body easing, my vision clearing.

This was extended to include experiences of 'feeling better' once connected to nature.

> When I came here today, I felt a lot tension ... now I feel more able. Being here is like a pause between breaths, to clarify what has been going on outside of here, so I feel able to go back.

> My eyes felt blurred yet when I heard the wind, my breath softened.

All three research participants had positive childhood experiences of being in nature, and connections were made between these and their current experiences. There was a sense of reconnection, which felt deeply benign and nurturing.

> I think it's to do with my upbringing of being in nature, of a love of being outdoors with grandpa, of loving the allotment and walks and being close to nature.

> I've gone back in time to my childhood dancing – being barefoot. Always being barefoot ... . Its [sic] about being at one with the sounds of the woodland, and being at one with nature and therefore feeling relaxed.

> I feel my feet on bare earth, soft, firm, delicious, dropping into memories and smells of wild childhoods, summer meadow, warm earth.

Nature as Container

This sense of being at home and at ease developed into the theme of 'container', which became another layer of therapeutic holding. Nature, the wood, the trees, the circle, seemed to amplify the sense of containment. This was experienced not only as having a supportive and positive impact on the researchers, but also that the group members felt 'held' by nature, which influenced the experiences of research participants in two ways: the therapeutic containment of the facilitators was amplified, and, possibly as a consequence, group members seemed to speak more deeply about their feelings and experiences, compared with other venues. In turn, the facilitators felt more able to be with group members in depth because they too felt 'held' by nature.

> I feel physically very safe, secure and at ease.

> My mother, mother earth, motherhood, nurturing and nourishing, I feel held and at home, giving and receiving. I know this place.

Nature as a Resource

From the sense of containment, to 'containing resources', nature was experienced as a huge source of therapeutic material. This seemed important and significant not just for me, who, as an art therapist, saw the 'resources' as an extension of my modality, but to the co-researchers who drew on this resource too. This resource was experienced in two different but interconnected ways: as an opportunity to use nature as a source of creative exploration – to create poetry, to meditate, to see the metaphors of death and rebirth as a vehicle for reflection; and also as a source of ancient wisdom.

> It means I am not alone. That I have this huge resource of beauty, metaphor, of cycles of life and death on which I can draw. It holds everything.

> If I get stuck, or if somebody talks of unsolvable problems, there's always a metaphor from nature, or there's a moment you can just sit with, and hear the birdsong, or the wind, and there are stories."

The stories were linked to a felt source of 'ancient wisdom, of knowledge': stories of the season, myths and folklore, and the sense of people having been here before us.

> Nature isn't just trees and seasons, it's about ancestors.

Not only was there a sense of the ancestral presence, but a more literal aspect of this came in the realisation that previous members of the group were also with us, literally in some cases, with their ashes scattered, but more generally through memories and rituals. The land offered an opportunity for planting trees 'in memoriam', for shared activities such as planting bulbs in the autumn, creating Mandalas and celebrating the festivals of the seasons.

> This ancient woodland, the dead are with us.

> It helps me deal with grief and bereavement, because the people who have died are also held in memories in the mandala, the labyrinth, in the woods, so that they take

their place in the present which is not overwhelming. Not denying their passage, but includes the positive aspects of loss.

The resources of nature were not only experienced as a therapeutic tool, to support facilitation, but were used by research participants to support them-selves, particularly in managing the deeper and shadow aspects of the experi-ence: fear, death, illness, tragedy, suffering. Stories of initiation and journeys to the underworld (Persephone, Chiron) were relevant to the facilitators as well as the group members in the sense of them having to 'go deeply' into their own fears about mortality and illness, about experiencing grief.

> For me, this sense of nature holding both life and destruction holds me in the present. Witnessing suffering, I can use nature to balance me, just by listening to the wind, or looking at the blue sky, brings in other realities alongside suffering. It stops me being overwhelmed.

> I hear a robin sing, persistent, sublime. Transcendent. A silver sliver of music, like a rope cast towards us from nature's heart, to stop us from drowning. We just need to reach out and hold it.

Nature Holding the Cycles of Life and Death, the Rhythm of the Seasons

This aspect is linked to the experience of using nature as a resource in its clear ability to reflect the cycle of life and death. The seasons also acted as a struc-ture to the exploratory work and therefore provided another sense of contain-ment. The research participants experienced this as positive and useful in the sense of their own place in the cycle of life and the cycle of the seasons, in teaching them about rhythm, pace and in reconnecting themselves with old rituals and festivals. There was a sense of unity in this, of shared experience, with the group members. However, there was also a sense of 'here we go again' as the year turned, people came and some died, and the facilitators were still here.

> Death a normal part of life. In a strange way supports me to feel calmer and I'm not exempt, so there is a common theme. I still have lots of questions of life and death, learning to trust the process and draw on nature … but – nothing new under the sun!

> Unlike the hospice, which holds, for me, accumulated death with no processing, here, people's deaths become compost for the people left behind – teaching wisdom. Stories, adding to the material for growth.

There is an exchange of energies, the breath breathing in ideas from nature-ripples on a pond, the flow of the waves, the wind in the trees, the sunlight and the shadow, the rain drops cleansing. The breath expelling worries, fears, concerns feeling. A natural cycle, an exchange of gases, pruning, coppicing, composting to enable new growth and blossoming.

Depth of Experience

Research participants talked of the experience of being able to see and hear more clearly when working in nature, of entering sacred space ...

Being here, you can see them more clearly, and hear them more clearly.

Feels easier to see people's souls!

And communicating without words

... and how people seem to drop into a deeper place more quickly.

I still feel moved by the way people tell their story and how they feel so easily here, how easy it seems in this environment for people to tell their story, to let go of their story ... reflect [on] how they feel.

From a sense of being grounded in nature, there was a sense of being able to 'go deeper'.

I feel grounded in nature and therefore able to go deeper with people, and hear pain more easily. Or experience it as less overwhelming as I do in the hospice, where there is no relief.

Listening, silences, 'cueing' talking, questioning is like a dance. Daring to go further, deeper, knowing when to step back, knowing when to change direction.

There is a challenge to hold them, so having taken them there, that you don't leave them there, that you can hold them in that place for as long as they need to be, and bring them back out again. It easier here, in nature.

Its not just profound, its more than that. Its more like going into a sacred place – and at that level you find yourself saying things and you don't know where its coming from.

The closeness to people who are dying inevitably brings the facilitators closer to shadow feelings of fear, death, loss.

And I thought I might get hardened and build up resistance to it and that hasn't happened, and its scary, an awareness that someone is an individual and precious and I want to listen attentively, and yet I get so tired.

At times I get overwhelmed by the amount of illness and death.

If I get cancer what will I feel – not what would I feel.

Sometimes it feels safe and secure, sometimes its scary.

We witness and share deep parts of ourselves, and that changes the relationship, travelling with people to their death, or near death. Sometimes I feel tired: the constant cycle of dying and new people coming, and loss.

We purposefully develop a profound relationship with people who are going to die.

It teaches me constantly about facing death and dying and at times I want to get away from it – yet there is a place within me that knows how great a teacher death is and how the world seems so big and rich.

And sometimes I can feel so intensely connected to someone's story and feeling that I'm being taken into Hades, and then I remember to breathe and look at the sky, or the swaying trees and I'm pulled back to life, or perhaps can hover at the edge, seeing both ways.

Boundaries

Researchers experienced a sense of equality in the woods. Whereas the hospice sets boundaries, roles, expectation, the woods provide none.

> Something about equality, so being in nature brings me to a more equal place. It isn't owned by anyone, it's all of ours. It belongs to us all, we belong to it, so it sets us off in a different place.

They experienced a change in professional boundaries:

> Just walking towards the labyrinth we were walking together and that felt so different, a freedom.

> Just two souls meeting.

> I'm aware of holding a boundary, but its more subtle, knowing my responsibilities and holding, yet being at ease and a fellow traveller.

> You need a higher level of self-awareness and of your own boundaries.

And the subject of the group belongs to us all. We're all going to die.

If you work with someone who has appendicitis or schizophrenia, the chances are you won't experience these things, but we will all die, so there is no difference other than the question of when death may come.

Their Journey, Not Ours

It was important for the researchers to recognize that as facilitators, each could travel alongside a group member and share their mortality, and yet they were also separate. Being sure of their own boundaries, the facilitators could allow the boundaries to loosen at times. The work involved an awareness and exploration not just of professional boundaries but also the boundary between life and death.

> I suppose, working with people that are dying and then listening to their experiences and feelings, in nature, which is the medium that helps give that freedom … . I feel at ease that I'm going alongside them into dying, but at the same time, I wont take that final step, not yet.

And the management of professional and personal boundaries changes again as the work develops and deepens.

> I see them with different eyes. No boundaries. We drop into life. And I can still contain the day. One foot in the professional world, one in theirs. One foot in life, one in death, or just standing on the threshold looking both ways, like Janus. We peer again at death and the robin sings. Someone says something amazing.

Discussion and Summary

It became clear from the final interview of the research that nothing in the co-researchers' training (nursing and complementary therapy) had prepared them for working in nature, and at this kind of depth. Experiences outside their professional training were more relevant: their childhood love of nature, their self-awareness, their personal journeys and creative exploration plus the accumulated knowledge from the 15 years' experience in these particular projects and in palliative care. For myself, my experiences as a hospice nurse and my personal exploration acted as a foundation to encountering death. My psychotherapy training in the use of arts and imagination, and in group process, helped me ground, contain and develop the work. Access to other streams of knowledge – from ancient Greek myths to the Chinese five elements, to Western folklore and

Celtic wisdom – provided structure, inspiration and vehicles for creative and embodied exploration. Several of the themes which emerged from the research resonate with evidence from the research literature: for example, the relationship between nature and well-being and the boundary shifts in working outside.

The positive effects of nature on body and emotions are widely recognized (e.g. Berger and McLeod, 2006; Linden and Grut, 2002; Mitten, 2009). Although this is normally discussed in terms of benefits to clients, this study showed how healthcare professionals can feel more at ease and at home in a natural environment. Symptoms of stress – 'blurred eyes, tension' – were soothed by contact with nature. The positive effects go beyond this, however, to include nature as a container and resource for therapeutic work. Nature provides a multiplicity of metaphors and analogies, both literal (e.g. in the turning of seasons, the cycle of birth, death and rebirth) and in its associated folklore and myth. For these researchers, accessing this knowledge not only helped their facilitation, as extra 'tools', but also helped them reflect, contain and make meaning of their own experiences around life and death.

Nature, in its containment and holding, offered support for the practitioners, which was not so evident in hospice and clinical environments. Part of this sense of 'feeling contained' was nature's capacity to hold polarities – the light and the dark, death and renewal, health and disease, tragedy and birdsong. Nature can be seen as a metaphor for many positive psychological concepts, such as the secure base, solid ground, the safe container and the good mother. In symbolic and literal form, for these researchers, being in nature was undoubtedly significant in supporting practitioners to be alongside suffering and in dropping into depth. The experience of seeing and hearing more clearly, of communicating without words, assumed, at times, the nature of sacredness, of liminal space. This attunement at a deep level might be seen in terms of Eliade's sacred space, where the threshold divides the profane from the sacred. He notes that woods and trees can take on a religious meaning in their shape and heavenward growth (Eliade, 1987). To the researchers, it seemed that a sense of temenos, of sacred space, was facilitated by the woods, and by the journey to the woods, and by the journey towards death, with each threshold taking the researchers and group participants into more 'sacred ground'.

That therapeutic boundaries change when working outside is expected. The absence of institutional hierarchy, rules and expectations also gave a sense of mutuality and neutrality to our researchers. The sense of travelling alongside was amplified by a perception of mutual suffering (we're all going to die) and by the invitation to be alongside fear and pain rather than to fix these. This aspect is implicit in Kearney's work, where the therapeutic holding becomes, in Jordan and Marshall's terms, more flexible (2010). Jung also echoes this when he writes: 'Learn your theories well, but be prepared to put them aside when you encounter the miracle of the human soul' (1953, p. 4).

It seems to me that if we are to travel alongside people in suffering, to work with 'soul pain', then our approach needs to encompass depth, the way of the soul (Hillman, 1989). The chthonic nature of the earth, the initiation journeys and the earth wisdom of the snake may point our way. Perhaps it is inevitable, in encountering death, loss and suffering, that we 'never afterwards belong to the surface of the earth', but to its depths (Moriarty, 2011, p. 82). The positive sense of nature as grounding, a good mother, a therapeutic container and resource, may prepare the practitioners, and their clients, for those journeys 'into Hades', where, so the myths tell us, we may be transformed.

The Asklepian model invites a holistic approach to healing that prepares an individual to receive 'a visitation from the gods', to encounter healing 'from within'. This approach is not just medical, not just psychotherapeutic, not just physical or spiritual, but an integrated field of creative potential on which the person can draw to facilitate their healing, even into death. Literature, art, body-work, play, dreaming, ancient wisdom, experiencing beauty – these invite an opening to all ways of being, as does our experience of nature. And the ways through nature can lead to extraordinary experiences of life and vitality, unity and eternity, darkness and mystery; it can also teach us that the way down might be the way through.

References

Angelo, M. (2005) 'Splendor Solis: Inviting the Image to Teach', *Harvest*, 51, 13–35.

Angelo, M. (2010) Re-Imagining Research. Unpublished MA dissertation, University of Chichester, West Sussex.

Berger, R., and J. McLeod (2006) 'Incorporating Nature into Therapy: A Framework for Practice', *Journal of Systemic Therapies*, 25, 80–94.

Braud, W., and R. Anderson (1998) *Transpersonal Research Methods for the Social Sciences* (London: Sage).

Braud, W. and R. Anderson (2011) *Transforming Self and Other Through Research* (New York: State University of New York).

Eliade, M. (1987) *The Sacred and Profane: The Nature of Religion* (Florida: Harcourt).

Hillman, J. (1989) 'Cosmology of the Soul: From Universe to Cosmos', *Sphinx: Journal for Archetypal Psychology and the Arts*, 2, 17–33.

Jordan, M., and H. Marshall (2010) 'Taking Counselling and Psychotherapy Outside: Destruction or Enrichment of the Therapeutic Frame? *European Journal of Psycho-therapy & Counselling*, 12, 345–59.

Jung, C. (1953) *Psychological Reflections* (New York: Pantheon).

Kaptchuk, T. J. (1983) *The Web That Has No Weaver: Understanding Chinese Medicine* (New York: Congdon & Weed).

Kearney, M. (1992) Palliative Medicine: Just Another Speciality? *Palliative Medicine*, 6, 39–46.

Kearney, M. (1996) *Mortally Wounded: Stories of Soul Pain, Death and Healing* (Dublin: Marino Books).

Kearney, M. (2000) *A Place of Healing: Working with Suffering in Living and Dying* (Oxford: Oxford University Press).

Kerenyi, C. (1959) *Aslepios. Archetypal Image of the Physician's Existence* (New York: Pantheon).

Linden, S., and J. Grut (2002) *The Healing Fields: Working with Psychotherapy and Nature to Rebuild Shattered Lives* (London: Francis Lincoln).

Mitten, D. (2009, September) The Healing Power of Nature: The Need for Nature for Human Health Development and Wellbeing. Paper presented at The Birth of 'Friluft-sliv': 50-Year Dialogue Conference Jubilee Celebration, North Troendel University College, Levanger, Norway.

Mabey, R. (2010) *A Brush with Nature: 25 Years of Personal Reflections on the Natural World* (London: BBC Books).

May, R. (1985) *My Quest for Beauty* (Dallas: Saybrook).

Moriaty, J. (2011) *Nostos* (Dublin: Lilliput Press).

Moustakas, C. (1990) *Heuristic Research: Design, Methodology and Application* (London: Sage).

O'Donoghue, B. (2013) *A Moriaty Reader: Preparing for Early Spring* (Dublin: Lilliput Press).

Romanyshyn, R. (2007) *The Wounded Researcher: Research with Soul in Mind* (New Orleans: Spring Journal Books).

Tacey, D. (2009) *Edge of the Sacred: Jung, Psyche, Earth* (Einsiedeln: Daimon Verlagh).

7

EXPERIENCING EXISTENTIAL DIMENSIONS IN NATURE-BASED REHABILITATION

Eva Sahlin

In November, I attended the first guided nature walk during my rehabilitation. The guide stopped at a spot in the forest and scratched away the brown autumn leaves which covered the ground and some closely knotted small sprouts that emerged just above the surface were revealed. These are, said the guide, wood anemones awaiting spring and their flowering. Now (in May) on my last nature walk before I left Green Rehab, we visited the same place again and now the wood anemones were in full bloom and when I saw them I realized that it was me – I was the wood anemones.

> (From an interview with a female participant who had just
> completed rehabilitation at *Green Rehab*)

Introduction

This chapter leans on the studies and results that constitute a part of my doctoral thesis, entitled 'To Stress the Importance of Nature – Nature-based Therapy for the Rehabilitation and Prevention of Stress-related Disorders' (Sahlin, 2014). Furthermore, results from analysis of in-depth interviews conducted later with participants in nature-based rehabilitation (NBR) are included. A brief description of the Swedish model of NBR and specifically of the nature-based therapy (NBT) programme Green Rehab is included to give the reader an understanding of the topic of this chapter. For a more detailed description of NBR/NBT, please see Sahlin (2014); Sahlin et al. (2014, 2012); Sahlin, Ahlborg Jr, Tenenbaum and Grahn (2015); and Grahn et al. (2010).

Figure 7.1 Wood anemones in May that have forced through the dry autumn leaves.
Source: Photo © E. Sahlin.

Nature-based Therapy for Stress-related Disorders

The woman quoted in the beginning of this chapter had just completed 28 weeks at Green Rehab, a nature-based rehabilitation programme (NBR) in the Gothenburg Botanical Garden, Sweden. This type of rehabilitation was originally developed at the Swedish University of Agricultural Sciences at Alnarp and directed at individuals on long sick leave because of stress-related mental disorders (SRMD). Many NBRs in Sweden have used the *Alnarp model* (Grahn et al., 2010; see below) as a basis for their NBRs, with adaptation to available local nature and/or staff resources. The lack of established rehabilitation programmes for this patient group has opened up to this rather new method for rehabilitation. NBR in Sweden often embraces two parts: (i) activities, or simply being, in a designed garden or/and a specially chosen nature environment suitable to meet the needs of the targeted patient group, and (ii) traditional medical rehabilitation methods used for SRMD, such as prescribed sick leave, drugs, relaxation, stress management, physiotherapeutic exercises, body awareness, conversational therapy and handicraft, which all are professionally integrated into a nature/garden context.

A nature-based rehabilitation team is comprised of professionals from the medical sector, for example a psychotherapist, a physiotherapist and an occupational therapist; and from the garden/nature sector, for example a gardener, a biologist and/or a nature guide. The content of the programme is planned jointly by all professionals in the rehabilitation team and is based in the evidence-based methods and theories practised within each of the professions.

Grahn et al. (2010) distinguished four rehabilitation phases to describe the participants' inner state observed in the Alnarp therapeutic garden for individuals diagnosed with SRMD; (i) a *contact* phase, when the individual, after a time of disconnection from the self and the surrounding world, finds new ways to establish contact with an inner and outer reality. This phase is characterized by extreme tiredness, where just going to the rehabilitation site is a struggle; participants in this phase have an urge to perform and be 'good'. The second phase is (ii) *breaking the shell*, which includes re-evaluation and re-orientation. In this phase, individuals are opening up more and are more actively participating in activities. They are encouraged to listen to signals from their bodies and to adapt their ambitions accordingly. Thirdly, (iii) the *opening* phase involves feelings and emotions from the past coming to surface, and this can be worked on in the context of participants' recovery at the garden. The fourth phase (iv), *growing*, is characterized by participants gaining acceptance for their situation and reconciliation with their life story and illness.

Green Rehab

The Green Rehab was started by the large public healthcare organization, Region Västra Götaland, to offer additional rehabilitation to its own employees where initial care because of SRMD had not been sufficient, and the rehabilitation process had stalled (Sahlin, 2014; Sahlin et al., 2015). *Green Rehab* also comprises a nature-based stress prevention programme directed at employees at risk of developing more serious and work-inhibiting stress-related mental disorders (Sahlin et al., 2014).

The maximum 28-week rehabilitation programme comprised four half days in small groups of eight participants. The programme included a broad variety of content such as different techniques of guided relaxation, guided therapeutic group and private conversations, and art therapy. The major part (more than 40 per cent of the time, see Figure 7.4) was directly connected to garden and nature, for example garden activities according to the seasons, nature walks and handicrafts with material from nature. The weekly guided nature walks were conducted during a couple of hours in a directly adjacent 225-hectare nature reserve with wild uncultivated nature, for example moorland, ponds and watercourses; mixed coniferous and deciduous forests; and mountainous areas (Figure 7.3). The content of the stress management intervention programme was similar to the content described for the rehabilitation group; however, it was shorter in time and included two sessions per week over 12 weeks' participation.

Figure 7.2 The garden at Green Rehab and, in the background, the nature reserve.

Photo: Green Rehab, Gothenburg.

Figure 7.3 A walk in the nature reserve.

Photo: Green Rehab, Gothenburg.

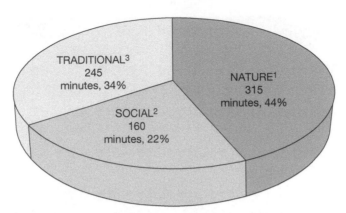

Figure 7.4 Uniting the single items[1,2,3] into the broader groups displaying the proportions of social activities, the more traditional therapeutic activities and the nature/garden activities offered during a week in Green Rehab (Sahlin, 2014).

The Participants

This chapter is based on 35 in-depth interviews which were carried out at the end of the participants' rehabilitation at Green Rehab. The participants had been on sick leave for more than three months (mean, approximately 20 months) because of SRMD and diagnoses such as burnout, exhaustion disorder, depression and/or anxiety. Consequently all participants had lived through a crisis that had shaken their lives and had affected not only their cognitive capacity and executive functioning but also their self-esteem, self-confidence and how they looked upon their future. Some expressed a fear that they had an incipient dementia, and some had a sense of aloneness concerning their condition. They had experienced depersonalization and exhaustion, without a capacity to take charge of their lives. They lacked the energy to maintain and take hold of any kind of responsibility for work and home life and to manage these basic tasks. All of them had withdrawn from others, even from their family, and suffered from social isolation. They had lost a sense of who they were in the world and felt very depressed, as expressed by one female participant: 'I had nothing left. I had no hope; I had no wishes for the future, no plans. Why should I get up in the morning? (Sahlin el al., 2012) The participants in the stress management course had, before starting on the course, increasing stress-related symptoms and/or repeated short-term sickness absence.

Experiencing Existential Dimensions during NBR

Two factors influenced the participants' experiences of existential dimensions during their NBR: nature and significant others (the rehabilitation team as well as other participants in the programme. See Figure 7.5).

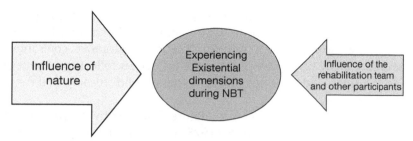

Figure 7.5 Existential dimensions were influenced by nature experiences (which had the strongest influence, as illustrated by a larger arrow) and by the rehabilitation team and the other participants.

The Influence of Nature

In nature the participants found peace and quiet which, according to the participants' narratives, was a condition for the existential reflections to occur. Experiencing nature's richness gave an expanded perspective. Below I outline some of the themes encountered here.

Education About Nature

During the nature walk the guide, a biologist, pointed out and described details and phenomenon in nature and exploring it in a way that was described by the participants as absolutely fascinating, which awoke curiosity and awe and made them forget about their own situation. The nature walks and the education were described lyrically, often almost euphorically:

> The biologist told us in a fascinating way about different processes in nature; about plants, squirrels, yes a lot around this. It was very entertaining and very inspiring at the same time, because: when you find yourself in this situation [Being sick and recovering] you become so amazed about how fantastic this life is. And when you get the opportunity to learn more about nature this knowledge strengthens these experiences [i.e. about how fantastic life is].

Feelings of Connectedness and Spiritual Reflections

Nature was explained by the NBR participants as a strong resource to find and develop spiritual growth. Heinzman (2009; 2000) sees spirituality as important and central for the individual's well-being. Kaplan's (1995) theory on restorative environments also proposes how restorative environments in nature provoke feelings of 'being away' from situations or settings connected to causes of stress and pressure. In this way, being away in nature allows people to distance themselves from a stressful situation. Restorative environments, according to Kaplan, also give opportunities for deeper reflections about one's priorities and goals and offer possibilities to get rid of disturbing and ruminating mental garbage.

The experiences of the impact from nature described by the participants in the NBR are in line with Wuthnow's (1978) report from a large study on the frequency of peak experiences (often described as feelings of great happiness, ecstatic moments of awe, e.g. a beautiful nature experience). A majority of the thousand participants in the study experienced being deeply moved by nature's beauty. Half of them reported feelings of being in harmony with the universe, and half of this group reported that these experiences had had lasting effects on their lives. Spiritual experiences in a wilderness project have been described by Talbot and Kaplan (1986) as a major contribution to enhancing well-being and self-image. Participants in their study reported a better understanding of their own thoughts as a result from their stay in the wilderness. It is possible, then, that nature allows people to become more reflexive. In nature the NBR participants experienced feelings of connectedness to a larger whole, a sense of coming home and a kinship with nature (also described by Wilson, 1984). In nature they felt a greater sense of self-acceptance which promoted a feeling of restoration. Cosgriff et al. (2010) have described a deep connection to nature for women during nature-based leisure activities. The importance of attachment, not only to significant others but also to the natural environment, during childhood as well as during adulthood, has been elaborated by Jordan (2009) who describes how a feeling of security in contact with nature can be seen as representing a secure base for a healthy development. This was explicit in the narratives from the NBR participants. Ottosson's and Grahn's (2008) study on the role of natural settings in crisis rehabilitation showed that experiencing nature was of specific value for individuals highly affected by crises, as was the case for the participants when starting the NBR programme.

A female participant in a nature-based stress management course expressed her reflections on her experiences connected to the nature walks:

> Now, let me say that I'm a deeply devoted atheist so I do not believe in any Creator, but nonetheless I can almost have one of those religious experiences from being in nature, think it's fantastic. And they've (the team) indeed conveyed that very well … That you're part of a context – making you new.
>
> (Sahlin et al., 2014)

This can be compared to Uddenberg's (1995) study on the relation between spiritual well-being and nature experiences, where the author made interesting remarks about the study participants' use of religious words and language when describing emotions and experiences in nature. It was as if the use of every-day language did not cover what the participants wanted to express.

Finding Models and Metaphors for the Own Life

Nature opened up, enabling existential reflections to emerge which affected the participants' self-image and also how they looked upon their life and their situation. Experiences during the guided nature walks opened the participants' eyes and mind to the beauty of nature and to nature's faceted and ingenious interplay. The participants saw themselves mirrored in nature's processes and found models, symbols and metaphors relating to their own life world. This gave comfort and hopes for the future and also helped them to see their situation in new and constructive ways.

> The one minute nature is sparkling with beautiful colours and the next it is rotten and dead. This makes me reflect a lot about that it may be okay to have a period in your life when you are in dissonance with yourself and not feeling so good, not having the same strength as before. Because nature is formed in that way – one maybe need[s] to hibernate for a while in order to bloom again.
>
> (Sahlin et al., 2012)

A description of a garden activity during NBR involving replanting small seedlings could be interpreted as a symbol of self and the participants' vulnerable state in the rehabilitation process, as expressed by one participant: 'And you must be careful of the little plant that is to be replanted so that it has the strength to keep on growing' (Sahlin et al., 2012). This female participant had just started to return to work after a long period of sick leave. Her narrative could be interpreted as a conscious or unconscious wish to be met with the same care as she herself had given to the seedlings when she now was stepping out from the safe and undemanding period of rehabilitation back into the 'real' world with its harder pace and its demand for efficiency. The quote revealed a desire to be met with understanding and tolerance in the workplace, to be able to adapt to working life again; to be replanted, nourished by understanding from her environment, thus making it possible to continue to regain health and strength.

New Perspective

Nature experiences contributed to a new perspective on life, and this was reflected in how the participants described a sense of gratitude for just 'being' and for the ability to experience the beauty in nature. The narratives reflected shifts in what was perceived as important in life; feelings that could be transferred into their everyday lives and the ability to discover new ways of relating to others, as voiced by one participant:

I feel grateful for being able to experience this beauty. If I can have peace and harmony [in the experience of nature] and if I can carry with me the fascination about
the small things around me, I can discover and appreciate small things in other people and therefore I can tolerate them in a more positive manner.

(Sahlin et al., 2012)

Finding and Refinding Meaning in Life

According to Frankl (1962), meaning in life is essential for all individuals. Nature
allowed the NBR participants to find peace and quiet not only in managing
stress but also in reflecting on their lives. Nature experiences had a deep impact
in finding or refinding values and meaning in life. Some participants found that
their life had been given new meaning through sickness. This is in line with
Jacobsen's (2008) description of cancer patients who felt that because of their
disease, they had found new values in life. One NBR participant's account exem-
plifies this: 'While it [the illness] is the worst that I've been through it has also
been the best.' It continues by describing how the 'old' performance-based
view on one's value as a human being had evolved towards a new perspective
where 'this devilish force to perform' had been replaced by appreciation of
emotions and empathy, and tranquillity and silence (in nature): 'Today I have a
more balanced perspective on life. I appreciate the small things, not the big
things' (Sahlin et al., 2012). New sides have been allowed to come forward
during the NBR, and people have learned to understand themselves as well as
to look upon themselves from a new point of view, leading to better quality of
life. This was attributed to the enriching experiences in nature because of 'opening of their eyes' during the guided nature walks which enabled them to more
fully perceive nature. Some of the participants also explained that new insights
gained through therapeutic painting had revealed new and positive sides to
themselves, leading to personal growth and new priorities. Descriptions of
nature as a therapeutic environment have been presented by Snell and Simmonds (2012), who also demonstrated long-lasting impact on individuals'
psychological well-being and self-perceptions through nature experiences.

Body and Soul

The close discoveries of details in nature gave rise to individuals experiencing
humble, harmonious and hopeful reflections about their life, the past and the
future, and were explained as an overwhelming positive and secure feeling of
being a part of 'something bigger' where one could rest and revitalize. This was
explicit throughout, as exemplified by the following quotes:

- *Thoughts on experiencing positive bodily sensations in nature and the garden were recorded:*
  The green parts (the parts in the programme connected to nature and garden) have helped me and maybe the most important thing has been to be in a rather harmonious state of mind – that the body has been allowed to remember how it is to be harmonious. Because this is easily forgotten. And even though it is for just a few hours, those hours are extremely important and this has helped me – to be reminded about [how it was to be] feeling good and experiencing beauty.

- *Comments on thankfulness, harmony and peace and sensorial experiences connected to nature commonly occurred:*
  I get a feeling of contentment. It could be harmony, peace ... I feel happy when I touch the magnolia buds and look at the leaves. I feel good on the inside, some kind of thankfulness ... thankfulness for all the beauty and being able to experience this beauty (Sahlin et al., 2012).

- *Religious reflections emerged:*
  I find it restful just to be in nature, I see God very much in nature, it is calming also to be near God.

- *Spiritual reflections connected to nature experiences were frequent in the narratives:*
  Sitting here out in the sunshine, hearing and seeing nature, it is like a shower in the inside. To give the brain a shower. It is like lotion after a shower. In some way it is purifying, actually I'm almost touched. One gets this feeling of an almost spiritual peacefulness (Sahlin et al., 2012).

The Influence of the Team and Other Participants

The supportive rehabilitation team and the other participants in the group (Figure 7.5) also influenced experiencing existential dimensions during the NBR. To see the more experienced participants' progress opened up hope that progress was possible for the other participants. It was also described as very satisfying to know that, as experienced participants, they played a role for and had a positive influence on new participants in the group, which boosted self-confidence and sense of self-worth.

Self-acceptance and Restoration of Self

The participants gained self-acceptance in the programme, which was attributed to feelings of trust and safety conveyed by the rehabilitation team and the other participants; feelings of being allowed to be just the way they are; and being encouraged to practise inward listening and to follow their own needs and to limit engagement accordingly. To be recognized and confirmed by a qualified rehabilitation team was vital for the restoration of self.

> The importance that I have felt during the whole period [is] the meeting with other persons and to be taken care of. When I started here I was in great need of being confirmed, not taken care of but that there was somebody who saw me, always; confirmed me and [I was also in need of] belonging to a context. And *those* things are of utmost importance in the process of coming back. And I feel that when I came here it was precisely in that way, it gave me strength, and it has given me courage to look beyond today ... it may sound unbelievable but it made me feel that I existed, it may sound unbelievable but it was a confirmation that I existed.
>
> (Sahlin et al., 2012)

The acquired self-acceptance was also attributed to the nature content in the programme. 'To be in nature or in the garden is not so much about performance but to find yourself a bit' (Sahlin et al., 2012). The value of mirroring in others with similar experiences was stressed. There were rich descriptions of the importance of having been met with empathy and respect in a tolerant and permissive environment where self-confidence and self-image were encouraged and had been restored.

> The important thing from the beginning was actually to come here, you didn't have to come and perform. That was enormously important for me ... a spirit of permissiveness and from the team a strong support. I feel that there is someone who understands or several that understand. I have not met with that before.
>
> (Sahlin et al., 2012)

Existential Health: Meaning in Life and Well-being

The education during the guided nature walks opened the participants' eyes to the beauty of nature and nature's interplay, which was of help in finding meaning and coherence in life and existence, which, according to Antonovsky (2003) are important for staying healthy and to regain health. Finding meaning in life is of vital significance for health and well-being and is a basic human need which has been described by, for instance, Jacobsen (2008) and Melder (2011) and expressed by Frankl (1962): 'Man's search for meaning is the primary force in his/her life ... this meaning is unique and specific in that it must be searched by the individual himself and realized by him' (1962, p. 98).

Eight Foundations for Existential Health

Existential health includes the individual's philosophy of life, finding meaning in life, priorities, hopes, values, and acceptance of our vulnerability and human limitations. Fleck and Skevington (2007) and Melder (2011) have described the importance of human health related to the eight existential dimensions in the WHOQOL–SRPB (WHO, 2002). The presence of the following dimensions are crucial for the individual's overall health: *feelings of connection to something greater* (spiritual connection); *meaning and purpose in life*; *a feeling of wonder at life* (feeling inspired and grateful in the presence of our environment, nature, art and music); *unity* (a conviction that thoughts, feelings, actions, psyche and the spirit are united); *spiritual strength* (finding ways to get over difficulties and feel calm); *harmony and inner peace*; *hopefulness and optimism*; and a *personal faith* (but not necessarily religious). All eight dimensions were found within the NBR participants' narratives and have been highlighted in this chapter.

Summary

Deep interviews with participants in nature-based therapy in Sweden showed that nature experiences had significant impact on the rehabilitation process from stress-related mental disorders. In nature existential reflections emerged and developed. Through guided nature walks and garden activities, the participants found or refound values and meaning in life. Reflections on one's place and role in life, what decisions to make about one's life, a sense of coherence, self-image, new views on life, and spiritual and religious reflections about being a part of 'something bigger' were frequently expressed. The support from significant others (the rehabilitation team and the other participants in the group) was of importance for the rehabilitation; the need to be confirmed and recognized by others was met by the professional multidisciplinary team and other group members.

Acknowledgement

I want to express my gratitude to Professor Patrik Grahn at the Swedish University of Agricultural Sciences at Alnarp, Sweden for his valuable comments.

References

Antonovsky, A. (2003) *Hälsans mysterium* [Unravelling the mystery of health] (Stockholm: Natur och kultur).

Cosgriff, M., D. E. Little and E. Wilson (2010) 'The Nature of Nature: How New Zealand Women in the Middle to Later Life Experience Nature-Based Leisure', *Leisure Sciences*, 32, 15–32.

Fleck, M. P., and S. Skevington (2007) 'Explaining the Meaning of the WHOQOL-SRPB', *Revista de psiquiatria clínica*, 34(1), 67–9, http://www.scielo.br/scielo.php?script=sci_pdf&pid=S0101-60832007000700018&lng=en&nrm=iso&tlng=en.

Frankl, V. E. (1962) *Livet måste ha en mening* [Life must have a meaning] (Stockholm; Verbum).

Grahn, P., C. Tenngart Ivarsson, U. K. Stigsdotter and I.-L. Bengtsson (2010) 'Using Affordances as a Health-Promoting Tool in a Therapeutic Garden', in C. Ward Thomson, P. Aspinall and S. Bell (eds) *Innovative Approaches to Researching Landscape and Health* (Abingdon: Routledge) pp. 120–59.

Heintzman, P. (2000) 'Leisure and Spiritual Well-Being Relationships: A Qualitative Study', *Loisir et Société/Society and Leisure*, 23(1), 41–69.

Heintzman, P. (2009) 'Nature-Based Recreation and Spirituality: A Complex Relationship', *Leisure Sciences: An Interdisciplinary Journal*, 32(1), 72–89. doi:10.1080/01490400903430897.

Jacobsen, B. (2008) *Existensens Psykologi – en introduktion* [Invitation to existential psychology – A psychology for the unique human being and its applications in therapy] (Stockholm, Sweden: Natur och Kultur).

Jordan, M. (2009) 'Nature and Self – An Ambivalent Attachment?', *Ecopsychology*, 1(1), 26–31.

Kaplan, S. (1995) 'The Restorative Benefits of Nature: Toward an Integrative Framework', *Journal of Environmental Psychology*, 15, 169–82.

Melder, C. (2011) 'Vilsenhetens epidemiologi – En religionspsykologisk studie i existentiellfolkhälsa' [The epidemiology of lost meaning: A study in psychology of religion and existential public health in a Swedish context], PhD dissertation, Acta Universitatis Upsaliensis, Psychologia et Sociologia Religionum, Uppsala. (English summary pp. 248–65).

Ottosson, J., and P. Grahn (2008) 'The Role of Natural Settings in Crisis Rehabilitation: How Does the Level of Crisis Influence the Response to Experiences of Nature with Regard to Measures of Rehabilitation? *Landscape Research*, 33(1), 51–70.

Sahlin, E., J. Vega Matuszczyk, G. Ahlborg Jr. and P. Grahn (2012) 'How Do Participants in Nature-Based Therapy Experience and Evaluate Their Rehabilitation?', *Journal of Therapeutic Horticulture*, 22, 8–22.

Sahlin, E., G. Ahlborg Jr., J. Vega Matuszczyk and P. Grahn (2014) 'Nature-Based Stress Management Course for Individuals at Risk of Adverse Health Effects from Work-Related stress – Effects on Stress-Related Symptoms, Workability and Sick Leave', *International Journal of Environmental Research and Public Health*, 11, 6586–611.

Sahlin, E. (2014) 'To Stress the Importance of Nature – Nature-Based Therapy for the rehabilitation and Prevention of Stress-Related Disorders', PhD dissertation No. 2014:98, Swedish University of Agricultural Sciences Alnarp, Sweden, Acta Universitatis agriculturae Sueciae, http://pub.epsilon.slu.se/11651/1/sahlin_e_20141113.pdf.

Sahlin, E., G. Ahlborg Jr., A. Tenenbaum and P. Grahn (2015) 'Using Nature-Based Rehabilitation to Re-start a Stalled Process of Rehabilitation in Individuals with Stress-Related Mental Illness', *International Journal of Environmental Research and Public Health*, 12, 1928–51.

Snell, L., and J. G. Simmonds (2012) '"Being in That Environment Can Be Very Therapeutic": Spiritual Experiences in Nature', *Ecopychology*, 4, 326–35.

Talbot, J. F., and S. Kaplan (1986) 'Perspectives on Wilderness: Re-examining the Value of Extended Wilderness Experiences', *Journal of Environmental Psychology*, 6, 177–88.

Uddenberg, N. (1995) *Det stora sammanhanget* [The larger context] (Nora, Sweden: Nya Doxa).

Wilson, E. (1984) *Biophilia – The Human Bond with Other Species* (Cambridge, MA, and London: Harvard University Press).

World Health Organization (2002) *WHOQOL Spirituality, Religiousness and Personal Beliefs (SRPB) Field-Test Instrument.* Department of Mental Health & Substance Dependence, World Health Organization, Geneva, Switzerland, http://www.who.int/mental_health/media/en/622.pdf.

Wuthnow, R. (1978) 'Peak Experiences: Some Empirical Tests', *Journal of Humanistic Psychology*, 18(3), 59–75.

Notes

1 Guided nature walks, walks, garden activities and handicraft were merged into the group 'Nature'.

2 Morning gatherings, coffee/tea, chats and short mindfulness relaxation and extended break with coffee/tea and sandwiches were merged into the group 'Social'.

3 Guided relaxation (different techniques), guided (therapeutic) group conversations, art therapy and reflections on the past week were merged into the group 'Traditional Rehabilitation Activities'.

8

A SALUTOGENIC APPROACH IN NATURE-BASED REHABILITATION (NBR) FOR INDIVIDUALS WITH STRESS-RELATED MENTAL DISORDERS

Anna María Pálsdóttir

Introduction

This chapter is based on the doctoral thesis 'The Role of Nature in Nature-Based Rehabilitation for Individuals with Stress-related Mental Disorders. Alnarp Rehabilitation Garden as Supportive Environment' (Pálsdóttir, 2014). The aim of the thesis was to increase the understanding of supportive outdoor environments, especially the role of the natural space (nature) and the essential qualities that can support the rehabilitation process. The study is based on 59 interviews with former clients after 12 weeks of NBR and was performed between 2007 and 2012 (Pálsdóttir, 2014). Alnarp Rehabilitation Garden was established in 2002 (Stigsdotter and Grahn, 2003) as a Living Lab on nature-based rehabilitation (NBR) for individuals suffering from stress-related mental disorders, mainly exhaustion disorders (ICD 43.2) (Glise, 2014).

The concept of nature can be problematic (Jordan, 2014), but in this context nature-based rehabilitation is defined as the phenomena where the natural space is the bearing element of the rehabilitation and where it takes place. Hence, the term *nature* is used as an overall term for the natural space in the healing garden.

The Healing Garden in Alnarp

The 2-hectare garden was designed according to theories on nature restorative and salutogenic effects (Grahn et al., 2010; Stigsdotter and Grahn, 2002). The garden contains places for work as well as rest and contemplation (doing and being). It is divided into two major areas: the *nature-garden* area (top area on Figure 8.1) and the *cultivation and gardening* area (bottom area on Figure 8.1).

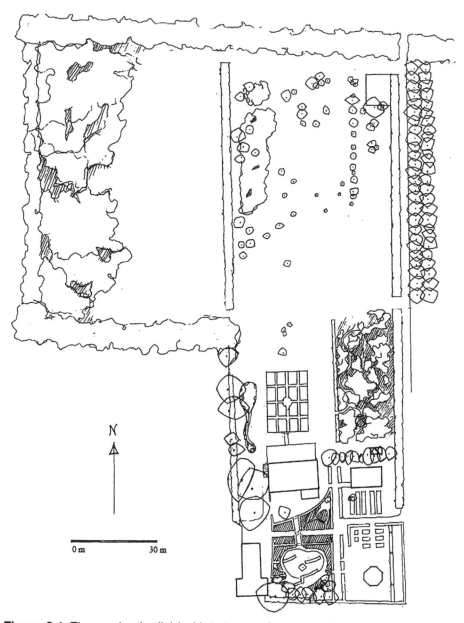

Figure 8.1 The garden is divided into two major areas: the nature garden (less formal structure) and the cultivation and gardening area (formal structure).

Illustration: Petra Thorpert and Anders Busse Nielsen, 2014.

These areas are further sub-divided into different garden rooms, with different qualities intended to support the client's rehabilitation process. The garden is planted with evergreen and deciduous trees and shrubs as well as a vast variety of perennials and annuals, with an emphasis on seasonal variation. To stimulate and awaken the different senses, the size, height, form, texture and fragrance of plants differ. However, the colour scheme is dominated by soft hues, with strong hues limited to certain places in the garden (Pálsdóttir, 2014). There are three glass buildings in the garden that were used, interchangeably, for horticultural proposes, personal relaxation and/or individual/group therapeutic sessions (Pálsdóttir et al., 2014). The garden is fenced and was closed to visitors during the NBR (Tenngart Ivarsson, 2011).

Nature-based Rehabilitation Programme

The NBR was designed as group therapy and was supported by the multimodal rehabilitation team, integrating four major therapy forms: occupational therapy, physiotherapy in the form of Rosen therapy, psychotherapy and horticultural therapy (Lavesson, 2013; Grahn et al., 2010). The aim of the NBR was to enhance a salutogenic processes to improve individuals' health and well-being with firm support from natural space (Tenngart Ivarsson, 2011; Grahn et al., 2010).

Table 8.1 The Weekly Schedule for the Nature-based Program in Alnarp Rehabilitation Garden*

	Monday	Tuesday	Wednesday	Thursday
Session 1	Morning tea and gathering	Morning tea and gathering	Morning tea and gathering	Morning tea and gathering
Session 2	Relaxing exercise	Relaxing exercise	Relaxing exercise	Relaxing exercise
Session 3 – the main focus for the day	Creative occupations (indoors or outdoors depending on weather).	Individual meeting with the psychiatrist (30 minutes). Before and after: garden and horticultural occupations (in a group or by oneself).	Individual meeting with the physiotherapist (30 minutes). Before and after: garden and horticultural occupations (in a group or by oneself).	Garden and horticultural occupations (in a group or by oneself).
Session 4	'Closure' with light refreshments	'Closure' with light refreshments	'Closure' with light refreshments	'Closure' with light refreshments

* Sessions 1, 2 and 4 are the same for each day, but session 3 varies from day to day (light grey colour).

Over one year, the NBR was divided into four rehabilitation periods (I–IV) of 12 weeks each: I, winter to spring; II, spring to summer; III, summer to fall; and IV, fall to winter. The weekly programme was managed by an occupational therapist assisted by a horticulturist. All occupations were performed outside except when the weather was unfavourable; in such cases, they took place inside, preferably in one of the glass buildings. The programme was scheduled for four days a week, each day lasting three and a half hours. In the first week, the participants attended the therapy for one day, and over the following weeks increased their attendance to four days a week. Each day had the same basic structure, with four themed sessions led by an occupational therapist assisted by a horticulturist. Sessions 1, 2 and 4 were the same on all four days, whereas the third session varied each day.

The first themed session was the morning get-together, with a cup of tea, allowing the participants to 'catch their breath' and settle down before entering the second themed session, a relaxation exercise performed either indoors or in the garden. The third themed session varied each day. On Mondays, it consisted of creative occupations performed either indoors or in the garden; on Tuesdays, the participants were invited to meet individually with the physiotherapist for a 30-minute session on bodily awareness; on Wednesdays, they were invited to meet privately with the psychotherapist for a 30-minute counselling session. Before and after these sessions on Tuesdays and Wednesdays, the participants could participate in horticultural occupations led by the occupational therapist assisted by the horticulturist, or stay in the garden, resting or enjoying the surroundings. On Thursday the themed session included garden and horticulture occupations. The fourth and final themed session was 'closure' for the day, in which all participants gathered for light refreshments (often something harvested from the garden, fresh or preserved) before going home. Also, at this time the participants could discuss the morning's events, reflecting on their own experiences from the themed sessions (Pálsdóttir et al., 2014).

Health-promoting Design

The term *salutogenic* derives from the Latin word *salus* ('health') and the Greek word *genesis* ('origins') and refers to the origin of health (Antonovsky, 1979). Aaron Antonovsky introduced the *salutogenic model*, handling aspects as stress, coping and health. The model focuses on the direction towards health instead of ill health and diseases, that is, the *salutogenic* approach (Lindström and Eriksson, 2009). It consists of two concepts: (i) generalized resistant resources (external and internal resources) and (ii) sense of coherence (SOC), which in turn consists of three components: meaning (subjective and a motion-driven component), comprehensibility (a cognitive component) and manageability (the ability to act and meet challenges). SOC is determined by our ability to cope and maintain good health (Lindström and Eriksson, 2009; Antonovsky, 2007).

The *salutogenic* approach in health design focuses on elements that can promote improved mental and physical health (Souter-Brown, 2015; Westlund, 2010). Grahn et al. (2010) argue that a supportive environment is an important part of salutogenesis and is needed in order to maintain good health. The theory of supportive environment (SET) explains that people need supportive environments to develop physically (senses, muscles, locomotion) and mentally (the ability to feel and think) (Grahn et al., 2010). SET discusses that the need for supportive environments will be different depending on a person's physical and mental capacity, situation and state of mind; that is, *a scope of meaning*. This term indicates that there exists a scope in which nature, culture and people can change meaning (comprehensibility, manageability, significance) for an individual, depending on his or her mental and physical resources at the moment (Pálsdóttir, 2014; Grahn, 1991). When people become ill or experience a life crisis, they need strong support from the environment in order to regain their health and wellness. However, they often experience a change in how they perceive the environment; their scope of meaning has changed. Phenomena they previously experienced as comprehensible, manageable and meaningful (and that even provided valued support in their daily lives) can suddenly be perceived as chaotic or even threatening (Ottosson, 2007). They often have great difficulty understanding and managing people, whereas physical environments – especially natural ones – are easier to understand and manage (Ottosson and Grahn, 2008; Ottosson, 2007). The more a person feels pressured, insecure and/or lost, the greater the need is to find salutogenic environments (enriched social, physical environments) that support healing processes. This is illustrated as a pyramid of supportive environments (Pálsdóttir et al., 2014; Grahn, 1991). The pyramid is divided into four levels of executive functions, the lower part symbolizing low capacity of executive functions and characterized by inward involvement and a high need for a supportive environment. Conversely, the higher levels symbolize higher capacity of executive functions and are characterized by active or outgoing involvement and less need of a supportive environment. Based on their situation, SET argues, people try to self regulate find environments they perceive as supportive and secure. Sensory impulses in a supportive environment can give rise to salutogenic effects regarding, for example, senses, hormones, emotions and cognition, which affect function, feelings and behaviour (Grahn et al., 2010).

Three Themes on the Role of Nature in Relation to the Rehabilitation Process

Based on the findings, an explanatory model of nature-based rehabilitation is presented for explaining and illuminating the role of the natural environments in relation to three main themes; *Prelude*, *Recuperating* and *Empowerment* (Table 8.2). The themes are presented in the chronological order in which the participants described them occurring.

Table 8.2 The Three Main Themes on the Role of Nature in Relation to the Rehabilitation Process of Individuals Undergoing Nature-based Rehabilitation at Alnarp Rehabilitation Garden*

Superordinate themes	Subthemes	Dimensions
Prelude	Alliance	Establishing contact
	Permissiveness	Taking armour off
Recovery	Restoration	Being in the present in nature
		Being one with nature
		Feeling peace and tranquillity in nature
	Awakening & processing	Entrusting nature
		Being inspired by nature
Empowerment	Moving on	Challenging oneself

* The themes are presented in the chronological order in which the participants described they occurred.

The theme *Prelude* describes the importance of settling safely into the new context before starting to take notice of everything around oneself. The following theme, *Recuperating*, describes the intimate and embracing interaction between the participants and nature during the rehabilitation period that supports different therapeutic processes. The third theme, *Empowerment*, describes how the garden supports the participants taking control over their own health and life.

These findings partially confirm earlier findings of Grahn and colleagues (Grahn et al., 2010). However, there are some crucial differences, which apply mainly to the finding of the *Prelude* not earlier described and the theme *Recuperating* that resembles the phases earlier described by Grahn et al. (2010), that is, the phases of Contact (with the external world and themselves), Breaking the shell (starting to re-evaluate their situation) and Opening (processing). Also, a new component of restorative environment was identified, that is, *Social quietness*, as an important component facilitating personal and intimate engagement with the natural environments in the *Recuperating* and *Empowerment* phases (Pálsdóttir et al., 2014).

Social Quietness – Pre-requisite for Intimate Engagement with Nature

The participants specifically expressed a strong need to be alone with nature, in a self-chosen supportive location in the rehabilitation garden, undisturbed by the presence of others when resting or handling all the emotions evoked in the rehabilitation. This essential quality of a supportive environment is hereby defined as *Social quietness* and seemingly one of the important qualities of supportive environment in nature-based rehabilitation. It was expressed as an important quality for engaging in intimate communication with the natural environment. The profound non-verbal communications with nature, in the garden, seem not only to be a source of restoration but also to reconciliation's complex mental processes evoked by the professional rehabilitation team. Solitary engagement with nature was negatively affected when others entered the scene because of both the noise from other people and the actual presence of another person in the surroundings. The participants expressed that the possibility to instantly act on the emotions evoked was crucial in order to move on with the recovery processes, and not to be left with these emotions. This, the participants often repeated, was not possible in the usual healthcare facilities, and participants said that nature could meet them where they were emotionally, and this without words or judgement. 'To cry in despair and let go of all the tension that was inside of me; I felt bad and it felt like there was no point living with this. I didn't want to let go of these feelings in front of other people, but the garden and nature could take it.'

Nature Supports and Embraces the Rehabilitation

Several areas in the garden were experienced as having strong attributes of nature and being rich in species, and were repeatedly sought out during the theme of *Recuperating*. The participants found garden rooms and supportive locations where they felt safe and were in tune with their state of mind. Participants sought the prospect of *refuge*, that is, where one could 'see but not be seen' (Appleton, 1975), where one could hide from others. The common physical features of the supportive locations are as follows: a firm and solid support from the sides and the back as well as a (canopy) roof; alternative paths ('escape exits'); varied ground cover (e.g. soft bark, gravel); sufficient distance from the user to passers-by, with the area in between planted with lush vegetation in a soft colour scheme (e.g. white, purple, blue, variations of green and grey); plants of varied textures and shapes, giving the eye a resting point; comfortable sitting facilities; and a mixture of stone, water and plants. Other important qualities were comfortable temperatures, nice fragrances and considerable quiet (though the sounds of nature were acceptable). Soft shapes and curves were perceived as less demanding structures than strict lines and a hard surface structure. A balanced and coherent colour scheme, with soft colours such as lilac, pink, white and blue, was perceived as calming and as not 'bothering' tired minds. Pleasant plant fragrances and the sounds of nature, such as birds twittering and the wind sweeping softly through the leaves, were perceived as soothing and calming. Locations with a clear and firm structure and the attributes of prospect and refuge as well as escape routes were highly regarded as supportive environments.

The seasonal changes reminded the participants of eternity and their being part of a bigger whole. It also demonstrated that nature cannot be rushed; it has its own rhythm that the participants expressed as a peaceful and calming experience. Stones, water, plants, small animals, birds and insects – all these wonders of nature represent the origin of humans. It gave participants a strong feeling of being in tune with nature. This allowed them to get closer to their inner feelings and to stay with them without demand from the surroundings. This was in contrast to their experience of everyday life that was more or less dominated by expectations and demands from others and hence even themselves.

The participants explicitly expressed that a natural environment in the garden gave the impression of taking care of itself and that they did not have to take responsibility for anything else than themselves. That in turn, gave them the feeling of *just being* in the present and resting without effort. The *nature-like* and *rich of spices* attributes gave the feeling of lush greenery where the participants could be alone with nature without the disturbance of others. The *nature* dimension represents the force and power of nature – not human-made, but on nature's own terms (Grahn et al., 2010) – and seems to neither dominate the participants' thoughts nor demand their *direct attention*. Instead, mental recovery is facilitated through *soft fascination* (Kaplan, 2001).

The participants frequently mentioned the importance of permissiveness from the surroundings and that access to the garden was a vital resource of mental restoration and processing emotions. This was always preferred in solitude, without the disturbance of others. Social interaction demanded attention and depleted their fragile source of energy, but the interaction with nature did not.

Nature in Everyday Life

After nature-based rehabilitation, the participants in this study included more nature-related activities in their everyday life as both restorative and pleasurable experiences. These changes seem to have been initiated in the NBR. The participants re-engaged in or introduced new occupations into their everyday life. These occupations were characterized by enjoyment, pleasantness and creativity, all of which have been described as meaningful (Pálsdóttir et al., 2014). Nature's role as a supportive environment was extended into everyday life in order to maintain and improve health and well-being. This emphasizes the need for close connection to nature in everyday life and that access to everyday greenery can be a key to better mental health.

References

Antonovsky, A. (1979) *Health, Stress, and Coping* (San Francisco: Jossey-Bass).

Antonovsky, A. (2007) *Hälsans mysterium* [*The mystery of health*] (Stockholm: Natur och Kultur). (In Swedish).

Appleton, J. (1975) *The Experience of Landscape* (London: Wiley).

Glise, K. (2014) 'Exhaustion Disorder – Identification, Characterization and Course of Illness', PhD thesis, Institute of Medicine at the Sahlgrenska Academy, University of Gothenburg, Gothenburg.

Grahn, P. (1991) 'Om Parkens Betydelse' ['On the meaning of parks'], Stad and Land nr 93, PhD thesis No. 93, Alnarp: Swedish University of Agricultural Sciences. (In Swedish).

Grahn, P., C. Tenngart Ivarsson, U. K. Stigsdotter, and I-L. Bengtsson (2010) 'Using Affordances as a Health-Promoting Tool in a Therapeutic Garden', in C. Ward Thompson, P. Aspinall and S. Bell (eds) *Innovative Approaches to Researching Landscape and Health. Open Space: People Space 2* (New York: Routledge) pp. 116–54.

Jordan, M. (2014) *Nature and Therapy: Understanding Counselling and Psychotherapy in Outdoor Spaces* (London: Routledge) pp. 18–20.

Kaplan, S. (2001) 'Meditation, Restoration, and the Management of Mental Fatigue', *Environment and Behaviour*, 33, 480–506.

Lavesson, L. (2013) 'A Pilot Study of Rosen Practitioners' Experiences Receiving a Modified Form of Rosen Method Bodywork in a Garden Setting', *Rosen Method International Journal*, 6(1), 5–16.

Lindström, B., and M. Eriksson (2009) 'The Salutogenic Approach to the Making of HiAP/ Healthy Public Policy: Illustrated by a Case Study', *Global Health Promotion*, 16(1), 17–28.

Ottosson, J. (2007) 'The Importance of Nature in Coping: Creating Increased Understanding of the Importance of Pure Experiences of Nature to Human Health', PhD thesis No.115, Swedish University of Agricultural Sciences, Alnarp, Acta Universittis agriculturae Sueciae.

Ottosson, J., and P. Grahn (2005) 'Measures of Restoration in Geriatric Care Residence: The Influence of Nature on Elderly People's Power of Concentration, Blood Pressure and Pulse Rate', *Journal of Housing of the Elderly*, 19 (3/4), 229–58.

Pálsdóttir, A. M. (2014) 'The Role of Nature in Rehabilitation for Individuals with Stress-Related Mental Disorders. The Alnarp Rehabilitation Garden as Supportive Environment', PhD thesis No. 45, Swedish University of Agricultural Sciences, Alnarp, Acta Universitatis agriculturae Sueciae, http://pub.epsilon.slu.se/11218/.

Pálsdóttir, A. M., D. Persson, B. Persson, and P. Grahn (2014) 'The Journey of Recovery and Empowerment Embraced by Nature – The Clients' Perspective on Nature-Based Rehabilitation in Relation to the Role of the Natural Environments', *International Journal of Environmental Research and Public Health*, 11, 7094–8015.

Souter-Brown, G. (2015) *Landscape and Urban Design for Health and Well-Being. Using Healing, Sensory and Therapeutic Gardens* (Oxon: Routledge) pp. 201–44.

Stigsdotter, U. A., and P. Grahn (2002) 'What Makes a Garden a Healing Garden?', *Journal of Therapeutic Horticulture*, 13, 60–9.

Stigsdotter, U. A., and P. Grahn (2003) 'Experiencing a Garden: A Healing Garden for People Suffering from Burnout Diseases', *Journal of Therapeutic Horticulture*,13, 38–48.

Tenngart Ivarsson, C. (2011) 'On the Use and Experience of a Health Garden. Exploring the Design of the Alnarp Rehabilitation Garden,' PhD thesis No. 89, Swedish University of Agricultural Sciences, Alnarp, Acta Universitatis agriculturae Sueciae, http://pub.epsilon.slu.se/8388/1/tenngartivarsson_c_111018.pdf.

Westlund, P. (2010) *Salutogen design är framtidens äldreboende* [*Salutogenic design is the future nursing home for elderly*] (Solna: Fortbildning AB). (In Swedish).

Wilson, N. W., R. Jones, S. Fleming, K. Lafferty, L. Knifton, K. Catherine, and H. McNish (2011) 'Branching out: The Impact of a Mental Health Ecotherapy Programme, *Ecopsychology*, 3(1), 51–7.

9

GROWING TOGETHER: NATURE CONNECTEDNESS, BELONGING AND SOCIAL IDENTITY IN A MENTAL HEALTH ECOTHERAPY PROGRAMME

Matthew Adams and Martin Jordan

Introduction

This chapter recounts the findings of a unique collaboration between the University of Brighton's School of Applied Social Science and the charitable organization *Grow*. *Grow* is dedicated to providing outdoor mental health support. Their provision is designed to provide people with diverse lived experiences of mental distress the chance to experience the well-being benefits derived from being in nature in a safe and supportive group. The collaboration involved teaming up a research psychologist and psychotherapist from the University with coordinators, volunteers, former and current participants in a *Grow* season. The main purpose of the collaboration was to explore the positive improvements in mental health and well-being reported by participants in the scheme to date, as recorded anecdotally and in the organization's own feedback mechanisms. We worked towards this aim by collating and thematizing the preliminary evidence already generated by those involved in *Grow*, devising a set of research questions with the project's co-coordinators, subsequently carrying out some targeted qualitative research; and by contextualizing the findings in existing literature. Finally, we considered the implications of our results for mental health practitioners, policy makers and other decision-makers. In what follows we outline literature addressing the relationship between mental health and natural settings before providing an overview of our approach, findings and discussion.

Mental Health and Ecotherapy

Mental health problems and associated distress are a vitally important issue in today's society. From a personal, community and social point of view mental illness exacts enormous costs. Up-to-date figures suggest that mental health problems affect an increasing number of people in the United Kingdom, somewhere between as many as one in four and one in six are likely to experience mental health problems in any given year (Mental Health Network, 2014). Layard goes as far as to claim that 'in Britain mental illness has now taken over from unemployment as our greatest social problem' (Layard, 2006, p. 1030). An increase in the prevalence of mental health problems at a national and global level is associated 'with significant impacts on health and major social, human rights and economic consequences in all countries across the world' (World Health Organization, 2014); permeating human endeavours as diverse as employment, housing, relationships and physical health. In the United Kingdom this increase is occurring against a backdrop of far-reaching reform and cost reductions imposed on health service and welfare provision, ongoing controversy regarding both the efficacy of medication to treat psychological problems, and the quality and accessibility of psychological therapies (e.g. Petrioni, Griffiths and Steen, 2013).

One area in particular has garnered increased attention as a potential adjunct or even alternative to existing treatment programmes – ecopsychology and ecotherapy (Chalquist, 2009). Ecopsychology, at its simplest, is the study of the relationship between humans and nature – an often-neglected aspect of psychology (Metzner, 1991; Schroll, 2007). Ecopsychology is also often considered as a foundation for an advocacy of the positive benefits of this relationship, and explores the various aspects of how contact with the natural world is central to psychological well-being (e.g. Barrows, 1995; Messer Diehl, 2009; Santostefano, 2008; Strife and Downey, 2009). Doherty, for example, states that ecopsychology's 'mission' is 'to validate that an emotional connection to nature is normal and healthy' (Doherty, 2009, p. 2); and a range of empirical studies in ecopsychology explore this connection in relation to various health measures further (e.g. Howell et al., 2011; Maller et al., 2006; Mayer and Frantz, 2004; Nisbet et al., 2011; Wolsko and Lindberg, 2013).

Grow, Ecominds and Mind

Via its 'Ecominds' programme, the UK national mental health charity Mind, with National Lottery support, has funded environmental projects in England that 'provide a range of outdoors green activities for people with mental health problems' (Mind, 2013). Projects are geared towards improving confidence, self-esteem, and physical and mental health, and reflect Mind's commitment to ecotherapeutic practices (Bragg, Wood and Barton, 2013; Mind, 2007). *Grow* was originally funded as one of these projects, though it now operates independently as a charitable organization, with its own funding secured via the Big Lottery fund.

Grow is designed to support people with diverse lived experiences of mental distress to experience the significant well-being benefits of being in nature in a safe and supportive group. Each day with *Grow* is structured around a 'check in' session when people arrive and a 'check out' session at the end of the day. Participants are offered the choice of a range of activities to suit varying levels of mental and physical health in rural Sussex. Options include guided walks, conservation activities, green woodworking, environmental art, mindfulness, healthy lunches, fireside tea and conversation. Participants meet fortnightly for three-month 'seasons', and are welcome to attend however they feel and whether or not they wish to be involved in any activities. Transport to and from the site is provided, travelling together by minibus.

Each *Grow* season has included participants experiencing a range of difficulties – including bi-polar, borderline personality disorder, schizo-affective disorder, schizophrenia, delusions, psychotic episodes, hearing voices, depression, anxiety, PTSD, eating disorders, OCD and self-harm. The two project staff and additional volunteers offer a high level of support alongside the peer support that develops within the group. Service-user involvement has been central to the subsequent development of *Grow*. Previous participants have been recruited as volunteers, and a user-led development group has been integral to the project design and delivery for forthcoming seasons of *Grow*, including the structure of sessions, which activities are chosen, how participants are supported, volunteer roles, and the design and development of methods of monitoring and evaluation. After being part of a closed group Season people can continue on to *Grow*'s 'drop-in' days, which also offer a wide variety of nature-based activities as well as close links to other nature-based community projects.

That the programme has had positive effects for those involved was widely acknowledged by past and present participants, volunteers and coordinators, and was reflected in the project's own measures of well-being. While there would be value in further quantifying aspects of well-being, the outcome of the project's own feedback mechanisms identified the need for more qualitative data; a requirement recognized more broadly in this area of research (Wilson et al., 2010). As a result the project founders and the research team were in agreement that the priority for a small-scale project of limited duration was to explore peoples' own perceptions of the positive effects of participating in *Grow* in more depth. To this end an initial decision was made to adopt an explorative and qualitative approach to evaluation.

Our Research

The research focuses on the most recent *Grow* programme at the time of writing ('season 5'), consisting of eight weekly day-long sessions involving a range of outdoor activities, for a closed group of ten participants identifying as suffering from moderate to severe forms of psychological distress. Data collection comprised of three elements: semi-structured interviews, open-ended questionnaires and a focus group. All season five participants had the option to participate in evaluation and choose the form of responding they felt most comfortable with. All ten participants responded across the three evaluation options. The group was made up of four men and six women, aged between 26 and 65. Nine participants identified as White British, one as White Irish/gypsy.

To maintain some parity across the evaluation formats, there was a parallel schedule for the focus group, interviews and questionnaires (see Table 9.1). A sequence of eight explorative questions was posed. Following Wilson et al.'s guidance (2010, pp. 7–8), the questions were 'designed to be open, neutral, non-directive and free of jargon'. They were geared towards exploring participants' own perceptions of the benefits of involvement in *Grow*, and were broadly consistent with a phenomenological approach (Wilson et al., 2010, 2011). The focus groups and interviews were recorded and transcribed verbatim.

In approaching analysis, we adopted a version of Gordon, Holland and Lahelma's (2000) three-stage process of interpretative thematic analysis (see also Adams and Raisborough, 2010). The first stage (thematic) denotes immersion in the data for the purpose of identifying emerging themes. The second stage (interpretative) requires a return to the data to now interpret content through the themes identified in the first stage. The third stage involves the extraction of illustrations and examples of those themes. Building on the authors' previous experience, we modified these stages by cross-referencing between emerging themes to try and capture, the ways in which aspects of participant's talk spoke to multiple themes simultaneously. Findings were subsequently organized around five themes: positivity, nature connectedness, autonomy, belonging and social identity. Though we recount them briefly here, we

Table 9.1 Questionnaire, Interview and Focus Group Schedule

Number	Question
1	Can you put into words what it is about being in nature that is helpful to your emotional and mental health?
2	What kinds of personal changes do you think being in nature with *Grow* has encouraged?
3	Can you talk about the difference it makes that the *Grow* project is outdoors?
4	Can you say how it was for you to have a choice of things to do each day?
5	Were there specific activities you enjoyed and why?
6	Could you say how being in a group at *Grow* was for you?
7	How would you describe the benefits of being in nature, with a project like *Grow*, to someone who has never experienced it?
8	Finally is there anything else you'd like to say about *Grow*?

have elaborated on the first three themes in some detail elsewhere (Adams et al., 2014). In this chapter we pay particular attention to the final two themes.

Positivity and Nature Connectedness

A primary finding was a reiteration of what *Grow*'s existing feedback had strongly indicated: participant's experiences of *Grow* were overwhelmingly couched in positive terms. In fact most of the subsequent themes are effectively elaborations on perceived causes and detail of the positive experiences. Nonetheless something can be said about the particular qualities of this experience in general terms. Positivity cohered around related terms of gentleness, stillness, peace and calm.

> The peaceful environment helps your mind become peaceful in contrast to the hectic city environment which seems to make your mind more hectic.
>
> Life is at a gentler pace than in the town.
>
> It helps my mind become more peaceful and calm.

The positive emotions and experiences described here are often accompanied by an acknowledgment of their contrast – urban life in the above quotes, or more specifically, 'normal' mental health provision settings:

> Indoors is really claustrophobic and clinical.
>
> [At *Grow*] there are no tables which always seem like such a barrier.
>
> It's much more formal indoors.

This theme relates to an observation regarding an interesting element of the methodology of the influential Mind report (2007) that was not explored by the authors, discussed in more detail later in this chapter. The report is based in part on a study that measures the mood of two groups of mental health service clients before and after a walk. The first group walked in a country park, the second in a shopping centre. The reduced stress and increased well-being of the first group was interpreted to be an indicator of the positive benefits of the natural setting. Findings here seem to tentatively support the notion that what is also important about natural settings is how they *contrast* with everyday contexts such as shopping centres.

Other comments incorporated peace, stillness and quiet in tandem with the opportunity to focus mind or senses on nature, which leads us to our second theme, nature connectedness. Expressions of a felt sense of connection to nature were often accompanied by hesitation and uncertainty – that this was a difficult experience was put into words. Not surprisingly participants often cited feeling connected to nature as an important part of *Grow*:

> Nature walks – learning about the different plants etcetera – it helps you get connected to nature.

> I really liked foraging and finding things like the wild garlic.

> The peacefulness and the quietness and the spaciousness and the birds and the sky. The quality of the air was so gorgeous.

> I just love being around the animals, hearing the birds singing and breathing in the fresh air.

The emphasis in the final quote on a relational sense of well-being rather than a dyadic 'individual–nature' connection is elaborated in the theme of belonging. These first two themes support existing research highlighting the capacity of natural settings to reduce stress (e.g. Kaplan, 1993). Clearly it is possible that people may find natural settings uncomfortable or anxiety inducing, at least initially, especially if they have had little prior experience of such settings (Bixler and Flood, 1997).

Autonomy

As noted above, an important element of *Grow* is the inclusion of service-users in the decision-making processes around how the project is run. Previous and current participants have been involved in planning and organizing *Grow* seasons. Participants also have the freedom to engage, or not, with the activities on offer on any given day without judgement; to be separate (while support is on hand) or together; and to discuss preferences for future activities. However the provision of choice was not expressed as an unequivocal 'good':

> Sometimes I like someone to tell me what to do but I did appreciate the choices given – it helped me be able to make more choices.

> Sometimes the choices made me a bit anxious. I was also anxious about missing out on activities if I made 'the wrong choice'.

Nonetheless autonomy appeared to be highly valued in most participants' accounts of *Grow*, particularly if it was understood as genuine choice.

> The choice whether to do an activity or not meant that negative feelings don't escalate. For example there was one exercise which we did one morning... I didn't feel like doing... at all because I didn't feel great and having the choice not to do it made

me feel not quite so bad and so feelings that could have escalated and got worse quickly just went away.

There are several really deep messages which *Grow* has reminded me of and made clear to me again and again, in different states and levels of illness and wellness. One of the key messages was – 'come as you are', 'please come as you are however you are', 'please come', 'we would love to have you however you are'.

It's a group out in nature doing some really nice activities but with unconditional acceptance. I was a bit confused by the choice, freedom and complete acceptance of the group to start with because it was so unusual.

All three quotes here indicate that the positive value attributed to autonomy occurs alongside experiences of unconditional acceptance. This lack of judgement seems vital, as it embraces and encourages choice without normative expectations or interpersonal penalties. It also elides with what we consider to be a progressive recovery model advocated by the Mental Health Foundation among others (Mental Health Foundation, 2013; Wilson et al., 2010). The recovery model moves away from a focus on symptom reduction/removal towards a way of being in the world and the hope for optimal functioning given the vicissitudes of an enduring mental health problem.

Belonging

As stated at the outset, the intention in this chapter is to focus in more detail on the related but less well-understood dynamics of therapeutic green care programmes reflected in the last of our two themes, belonging and social identity. The group therapeutic element of ecotherapy is much less well documented, despite the fact that group green care programmes are often advocated in this area (NICE, 2004), and are predominant in practice. Social contact *is* now emerging as an important dimension of people's own understandings of the benefits of ecotherapy projects they are involved in (Bragg, Wood and Barton, 2013), but less so as a central component of green care and ecotherapy provision (though see Sempik et al. [2010] for discussion of the holistic benefits of green care). Social contact is a significant element of *Grow*. Participants frequently voiced what felt good about *Grow* in terms of attachments – a sense of belonging, acceptance, safety, that applied to the group.

Support from my peers has been really beneficial.

Grow has helped me enjoy meeting new people and made me realise that I'm not so alone – that there are others who have been through similar things.

I enjoyed being able to wander off alone and take pictures but know that I had people to come back to and have the safety of the group.

Safety and security are clearly key leitmotifs, and many participants suggested that this sense of feeling 'held' was in turn a secure basis for some affirming self-reflections, for example:

> I used to be a sociable person but when I had my breakdown 2 or 3 years ago people stopped getting in contact with me. I was getting more and more isolated and coming to *Grow* has made me realise that I can form relationships with people again.

On the other hand, it must be noted that the social contact integral to *Grow* was sometimes experienced as difficult:

> I find it hard in a group sometimes but it's good to challenge yourself.

> Check-in and check-out is challenging sometimes.

It is potentially significant that despite the attendant challenges, for our participants the positive value of belonging and the natural setting were often articulated as interdependent:

> The natural environment is safer (than) consultation rooms, hospitals are a problem rich area dealing with crisis, that environment is a tricky one to visit because there are so many problems all in one place. Being in an natural environment those problems are all out so its safer there isn't the concentration (of) issues which are spread out a lot wider than it would be in a room and I think that's a big factor being outdoors.

The ways in which positive group dynamics interweaves with experiences of natural settings take us beyond the consideration of 'social contact' as separate benefit or variable of group-oriented green care (Bragg, Wood and Barton, 2013). The appreciation of belonging recounted was often entwined with expressions of feelings of acceptance and openness here aligned with the themes of nature connectedness and autonomy. It is a fascinating area for future research, and one that we address further in our concluding discussion.

Social Identity

Broadly speaking, social identity refers to a person's sense of who they are based on their membership of a group (Tajfel and Turner, 1979). In placing emphasis on the role of the group, it is claimed that social interactions between two or more people can be viewed as expressions of both interpersonal and intergroup dynamics (Tajfel, 1981). The social cognitive origins of social identity theory have given way to many variations on the concept of social identity. Contemporary understandings of social identity tend to incorporate some of the core tenets of social constructionism, allowing for a more fluid, dynamic and situational conceptions of social identity. The challenge here is 'to replace the traditional assumption of individual selves with a vision of self as an expression of relationship' (Gergen, 2009, p. 124). Thus, following Gergen, the term 'relational self' perhaps better captures the aspects of social identity we consider salient in the context of this study.

When asked about previous experiences of mental health service provision, participants commonly elaborated on the previous themes by talking about the kind of experience of self *Grow* as an environment encouraged, often in contrast to the normal environments, habitually indoors, that were supposedly therapeutic.

> I don't feel like I'm here because I've got mental health issues and so it changes the way I see myself.

> With indoor mental health services you are constantly reminded of mental health issues, diagnoses, labels – this isn't the case outdoors. This was a bit strange for me at first – I wanted to talk about my 'label' but now I don't.

> It's more about focusing on nature rather than mental health – you only start thinking about mental health issues and your problems when you get near to home again.

> You are also not surrounded by posters displaying a whole range of things… All these problems that people can have are there in front of you. Being in an environment where you are not bombarded with problems, there is no clock ticking, that takes way a lot of the pressure and stress.

Participants here express the value of *Grow* in terms of it offering an escape from the social and cultural markers of mental ill health, often, ironically, compacted in normal (and indoor) therapeutic settings. Here we potentially broaden our understanding of the benefits of providing nature connectedness, beyond individual psychological functioning, and the supportive dynamics of the immediate group, to the 'softening' of social and cultural reference points that might normally position a person's health as problematic more 'sharply'. This finding again adds to emerging findings in ecotherapy that social contact, and more specifically, *supporting and feeling supported by others*, both contributes to and is an outcome of the process of reconnecting with nature (e.g. Burls, 2007).

Culture, Nature, Identity

The natural setting of *Grow*, intertwined with the themes discussed above, appeared to combine to provide an alternative social environment, or set of relations, out of which to forge a sense of self. This is neither to underestimate the obdurate nature of relationship, norms and expectations outside of the setting, nor to make unfounded or exaggerated claims about the endurance of alternative configurations beyond the setting. Nonetheless, participants' own words seem to us to speak to the possibilities of an alternative identity closely tied to the relational dynamics. The informality, 'softness' and openness of the natural settings are expressed as integral to the possibility of alternative under-standings of self. At the very least it seems to signify a temporary escape from the relationships, symbolism, and discourses of everyday life – a social identity – that routinely 'trap' participants in a particular identity.

Simultaneously, the positive benefits of the natural setting were intertwined with the experience of a supportive group and the exercise of a degree of autonomy not routinely experienced elsewhere. This discovery combines emerging findings that social contact is vital to the process of reconnecting with nature touched upon earlier in this chapter (Bragg, Wood and Barton, 2013). It also connects to developments in social theory, human geography and else-where that emphasize the importance of social and cultural dynamics in shap-ing experiences of nature (e.g. Castree, 2005; Heim, Waterton and Szerszynski, 2003; Kidner, 2007).

There is of course a great deal of variation in what 'social' and 'cultural' is taken to signify, and how these phenomena intersect with each other. There is also a great deal of debate about the extent to which nature is socially mediated or constructed (e.g. Crist, 2004). There is not the space here to even begin to address these concerns. Our intention instead is to flag up the possibility that the value of natural settings is derived, in part, by experiencing them as anti-thetical to everyday social and cultural contexts. This point can perhaps be bet-ter illustrated via a brief example from an earlier study of the benefits of ecotherapy (Mind, 2007). In this study, researchers were keen to measure the health outcomes of being in nature. To this end, in one study, two groups of mental health service users went on a walk. One group walked in a shopping centre, the other a more natural park setting. Mood and well-being was meas-ured before and afterwards for both groups. From similar baselines, the group walking in nature reported significant improvement on a range of outcomes related to well-being compared to the group in the built-environment. The lat-ter actually reported deterioration on a number of indicators. The project's authors saw this as evidence of the benefits of a natural setting.

While we would not dispute this finding, the contrast in settings for each group is a useful illustration of suggesting why more complex dynamics might be at play. Sociologists of consumer culture such as Zygmunt Bauman argue that consumption, or more accurately consum*erism*, is a primary social and cultural constellation via which we are encouraged to navigate our identities in contempo-rary neo-liberal economies (Bauman, 2007). Consumerism is 'a culturally manu-factured, socially constructed and economically mandated desire for and preoccupation with endless acquisition of consumer goods and experiences' Humphery (2011) (Lewis and Potter, 2009, p. 42). According to many sociolo-gists, it has become the template which we use to make sense of our selves, the 'default philosophy for all modern life' (Campbell, 2004, pp. 41–2; Lawson, 2009).

The extent and nature of our consumption is claimed to reflect a powerful fusion of individual investment and social and cultural validation. Accordingly, consumption practices are granted a pivotal role in creating and maintaining an individual's identity.

In this context, a shopping centre is not a neutral or non-specific exemplar of a 'built' environment in contrast to a 'natural' one. In fact it carries a great deal of symbolic and semantic load, a place embedded in a range of sociocultural expectations and embodied in myriad of practices. This space, in turn, invokes various forms of identification, recognizing certain aspects of self *or their lack*. A sociological perspective here is not tangential; it helps explain the dis-identification that may be experienced as discomfort in places such as shopping centres, compounding a heightened sensitivity to crowds and noise, and perhaps to the performance of the aforementioned 'preoccupation'. A shopping centre, in other words, is a place laden with normative social and cultural expectations about how to be; and that afford autonomy and choice but only if one has the requisite psychological, economic, social and cultural capital to 'belong'. At stake here is the potentially spoiled identity of a 'flawed consumer' (Bauman, 2007, see also discussions in ecopsychology literature on consumer identities, e.g. Kanner and Gomes, 1995).

On the other hand, natural settings are less saturated with such expectations. This is not to say that how we come into natural settings is free of normative expectations, or what we experience *as* nature escapes such mediations. It permits, again potentially, a form of intersubjectivity less dependent on sociocultural prescriptions we may feel we have already been judged by and failed to match up to. Combine this possibility with a supportive group structure and a sense of being held, a form of intersubjective recognition, is mutually reinforcing.

Returning to our participant's talk, we can make a more specific point along similar lines. *Grow* participants often commented on how the usual trappings of service provision often reinforced their sense of being unwell. The rich opacity of the natural setting, alongside the supportive group dynamics, seemed to offer a basis for engagement on a spectrum other than illness-well-being. There is potential for further work here, on the value of non-statutory settings for mental healthcare (Walker, Hanna and Hart, forthcoming). This has a bearing on the implications of our findings – not just about benefits of nature; about value of radical and marginal alternative spaces.

Conclusion

We have no hesitation in adding to the increasing calls for ecotherapy to be recognized as a clinically valid treatment for people with diverse lived experiences of mental distress. Access to natural settings and green space is a marker of health inequality (Mitchell and Popham, 2008), so it is equally important that access to these spaces is extended to more people, more of the time. This study is another voice, however small, that contributes to the chorus proclaiming the psychological benefits of nature connectedness under the right conditions. What we hope to have suggested in this chapter is that those conditions involve social processes of belonging and identity.

The themes of belonging and social identity suggest that more than nature connectedness is involved in successful ecotherapy programmes. The talk of our participants articulates the importance of the relationship between natural settings, psychology and the social and cultural contexts that shape identity. More specifically, our participants describe the way users of indoor NHS services are situated within certain frameworks and narratives of understanding, and how, by regularly attending supportive groups and activities outdoors, alternative frames and narratives can be initiated and explored.

In conclusion, a number of interrelated practices seem to make *Grow* a success. If an environment can be fostered where access to the setting is made relatively easy and routinized; where a sense of safety, love and belonging through effective interpersonal structures and practice is established; then it is likely that an effective holding environment is created. This, in turn, is the basis for exploration of the wider environment – natural, personal, social and the countless points at which they merge. This exploration is, in effect, a form of self-expansion, a basis for experiencing differently who we are in relation to our own understandings, other people and the natural setting. The potential for exploration and expansion is important in the context of mental health if we accept that entrenched, negative and narrow self-understandings are central to the experience of mental ill-health, reinforced in the norms, narratives and practices of everyday life in relation to others, and social and cultural life more generally.

References

Adams, M., M. Jordan, J. Wren and J. Wright (2014) *The Grow Project. A Report on the Well-Being Benefits of Nature Connection for People with Experience of Mental Distress* (Brighton: University of Brighton), http://www.growingwellbeing.org.uk/grow%20report%20final%20version.pdf.

Adams, M., and J. Raisborough (2010) 'Making a Difference: Ethical Consumption and the Everyday', *British Journal of Sociology*, 61(2), 256–74.

Barrows, A. (1995) 'The Ecopsychology of Child Development', in A. D. Kanner, T. Roszak and M. E. Gomes (eds) *Ecopsychology: Restoring the Earth/Healing the Mind* (San Francisco: Sierra Club Books) pp. 101–10.

Bauman, Z. (2007) 'Collateral Casualties of Consumerism', *Journal of Consumer Culture*, 7(1), 25–56.

Bixler, R. D., and M. F. Flood (1997) 'Nature is Scary, Disgusting and Uncomfortable', *Environment and Behavior*, 29(4), 443–67.

Bragg, R., C. Wood and J. Barton (2013) *Ecominds Effects on Mental wellbeing: A report for Mind* (London: Mind) http://www.mind.org.uk/media/354166/Ecominds-effects-on-mental-wellbeing-evaluation-report.pdf.

Burls, A. (2007) 'People and Green Spaces: Promoting Public Health and Mental Well-Being through Ecotherapy', *Journal of Public Mental Health*, 6(3), 24–39.

Campbell, C. (2004) 'I Shop Therefore I Know That I Am', in Karin M. Ekström and Helen Brembeck (eds) *Elusive Consumption* (Oxford: Berg) pp. 27–44.

Castree, N. (2005) *Nature* (London: Sage).

Chalquist, C. (2009) 'A Look at the Ecotherapy Research Evidence', *Ecopsychology*, 1(2), 1–10.

Crist, E. (2004) 'Against the Social Construction of Nature and Wilderness', *Environmental Ethics*, 26, 5–24.

Doherty, T. J. (2009) 'Editorial: A Peer Reviewed Journal for Ecopsychology', *Ecopsychology*, 1(1), 1–7.

Gergen, K. J. (2009) *Relational Being: Beyond Self and Community* (Oxford: OUP).

Gordon, T., J. Holland and E. Lahelma (2000) 'Friends or Foes? Interpreting Relations Between Girls in Schools', in G. Walford and C. Hudson (eds) *Genders and Sexualities: Studies in Ethnography in Education* (London: JAI) pp. 689–706.

Heim, W., C. Waterton and B. Szerszynski (eds) (2003) *Nature Performed: Environment, Culture and Performance* (Oxford: Blackwell).

Howell, A. J., R. L. Dopko, H. Passmore and K. Buro (2011) 'Nature Connectedness: Associations with Well-Being and Mindfulness', *Personality and Individual Differences*, 51(2), 166–71.

Lewis, T., and E. Potter (2011) 'Introduction', in T. Lewis and E. Potter (eds) *Ethical Consumption: A Critical Introduction* (London: Routledge) pp. 2–23.

Kanner, A., and M. Gomes (1995) The All-Consuming Self', in T. Roszak, M. Gomes and A. Kanner (eds) *Ecopsychology: Restoring the Earth, Healing the Mind* (London: Sierra Club Books) pp. 77–91.

Kaplan, S. (1993) 'The Restorative Benefits of Nature: Toward an Integrative Framework', *Journal of Environmental Psychology*, 15(3), 169–82.

Kidner, D. (2007) 'Depression and the Natural World: Towards a Critical Ecology of Psychological Distress', *International Journal of Critical Psychology*, 19, 123–46.

Lawson, N. (2009) *All Consuming* (Harmondsworth: Penguin).

Layard, R. (2006) 'The Case for Psychological Treatment Centres', *British Medical Journal*, 332, 1030–32.

Maller, C., M. Townsend, A. Pryor, P. Brown and L. St Leger (2006) 'Healthy Nature, Healthy People: "Contact with Nature" as an Upstream Health Promotion Intervention for Populations', *Health Promotion International*, 21(1), 45–54.

Mayer, F. S., and C. M. Frantz (2004) 'The Connectedness to Nature Scale: A Measure of Individuals' Feeling in Community with Nature', *Journal of Environmental Psychology*, 24, 503–15.

The Mental Health Foundation (2013) *Recovery*, http://www.mentalhealth.org.uk/help-information/mental-health-a-z/R/recovery/.

Mental Health Network (2014) *Key Facts and Trends in Mental Health – 2014 Update*, http://www.nhsconfed.org/resources/2014/01/key-facts-and-trends-in-mental-health – -2014-update.

Messer Diehl, M. R. (2009) 'Gardens That Heal', in L. Buzzell and C. Chalquist (eds) *Ecotherapy: Healing with Nature in Mind* (San Francisco: Sierra Club Books) pp. 166–73.

Metzner, R. (1991) 'Psychologizing Deep Ecology: A Review Essay', *ReVision*, 13(3), 147–52.

Mind (2007) *Ecotherapy: The Green Agenda for Mental Health*, http://www.ecotherapy.org.uk/files/ecotherapy/home/ecotherapy.pdf.

Mind (2013) *Ecominds*, http://www.mind.org.uk/ecominds.

Mitchell R and Popham F. (2008) Effect of exposure to natural environment on health inequalities: an observational population study. *The Lancet* 372,1655-1660.

National Institute for Clinical Excellence (NICE) (2004) *Depression: Management of Depression in Primary and Secondary Care* (London: NICE).

Nisbet, E. K., J. M. Zelenski and S. A. Murphy (2011) 'Happiness Is in Our Nature: Exploring Nature relatedness as a Contributor to Subjective Well-Being', *Journal of Happiness Studies*, 12, 303–22.

Petrioni, P., S. Griffiths and S. Steen (2013) Improving Access to Psychological Therapies (IAPT) Programme – Setting Key Performance Indicators in a More Robust Context: A New Perspective, The Centre for Psychological Therapies in Primary Care, University of Chester, http://www.chester.ac.uk/sites/files/chester/IAPTpape1sg18.06.13.pdf.

Santostefano, S. (2008) 'The Sense of Self Inside and Environments Outside: How the Two Grow Together and Become One in Healthy Psychological Development', *Psychoanalytic Dialogues*, 18, 513–35.

Schroll, M. A. (2007) 'Wrestling with Arne Naess and Ecopsychology's Origins', *The Trumpeter: Journal of Ecosophy*, 23(1), 9–38.

Sempik, J., R. Hine and D. Wilcox (eds) (2010) *Green Care: A Conceptual Framework, A Report of the Working Group on The Health Benefits of Green Care*. COST Action 866, Green Care in Agriculture (Loughborough: Centre for Child and Family Research, Loughborough University).

Strife, S., and L. Downey (2009) 'Childhood Development and Access to Nature: A New Direction for Environmental Inequality Research', *Organization and Environment*, 22, 99–122.

Tajfel, H. (1981) *Human Groups and Social Categories* (Cambridge: Cambridge University Press).

Tajfel, H., and J. C. Turner (1979) 'An Integrative Theory of Intergroup Conflict', *The Social Psychology of Intergroup Relations*, 33, 47.

Walker, C., P. Hanna and A. Hart (forthcoming) *Democratising Distress: Reforming Approaches to Suffering Through Community Mental Health* (London: Palgrave MacMillan).

Wilson, N. W., S. Flemming, R. Jones, K. Lafferty, K. Cathrine, P. Seaman and L. Knifton (2010) 'Green Shoots of Recovery: The Impact of a Mental Health Ecotherapy Programme', *Mental Health Review Journal*, 15(2), 4–14.

Wilson, N. W., R. Jones, S. Fleming, K. Lafferty, L. Knifton, K. Catherine, and H. McNish, 'Branching Out: The Impact of a Mental Health Ecotherapy Program', *Ecopsychology*, 2011, 3(1), 51–57.

Wolsko, C., and K. Lindberg (2013) 'Experiencing Connection with Nature: The Matrix of Psychological Well-Being, Mindfulness, and Outdoor Recreation', *Ecopsychology*, 5(2), 80–91.

World Health Organization (2014) *Mental Disorders*, http://www.who.int/mediacentre/factsheets/fs396/en/.

PART III   PRACTICE

10

PRESCRIBING NATURE: TECHNIQUES, CHALLENGES AND ETHICAL CONSIDERATIONS

Patricia Hasbach

Introduction

A growing body of evidence demonstrates that direct exposure to nature is good for our psychological, emotional and physical health. Yet, most traditional therapy occurs in indoor office spaces and focuses on issues that stop at the urban boundary. Grounded in ecopsychological theory, ecotherapy is an emerging therapeutic modality that enlarges the traditional scope of treatment to include the human–nature relationship. This chapter discusses several techniques that invite the natural world into the therapeutic process, including expanding the intake interview to account for the human–nature relationship; making use of nature metaphor and nature imagery in a therapeutic context; assigning nature-based homework to clients; incorporating a 'nature language' (an articulation of human–nature interaction patterns) to deepen and strengthen therapeutic interventions; and moving therapy outdoors, where nature becomes a partner in the therapeutic process. The chapter concludes with a discussion of ethical considerations involved in the practice of ecotherapy.

Expanding the Scope of Therapy

Grounded in ecopsychological theory, ecotherapy enlarges the traditional scope of treatment to include the human–nature relationship (Hasbach, 2012). When we consider the various aspects of therapy, we often think about the intrapsychic processes at work, including unconscious motivations; we consider interpersonal relationships that the client is involved in; we often examine the family systems that the client grew up in and the one he or she is currently living in; and we recognize the social and cultural influences in the client's life. We can view all of these parts of the client's life like the lens of a camera, each expanding the scope of treatment focus. Ecotherapy expands that focus one step further to recognize the ecological system that the client evolved out of and now lives in and is touched by.

At the heart of ecotherapy is the recognition that for hundreds of thousands of years, our species came of age interacting with nature that shaped the human psyche. With our increasingly urban lifestyle and technological focus, the distance between then and now is large. With that distance come psychic costs, often unrecognized (Hasbach, 2012). By expanding the scope of treatment to include the human–nature relationship, ecotherapy makes these issues relevant topics for the therapeutic process. It also allows for clients to express their grief and feelings of despair related to the degradation of the environment, to the loss of special places and the extinction of species, and the helplessness many people feel to affect a change on these issues.

The Intake Interview

During the intake interview, therapists learn about the issues that have brought clients to therapy and gather information about clients' physical and mental health, their education and work history, their current living situation, and their family of origin. To understand the broader context of nature in my clients' lives, I weave into the intake interview several nature-oriented questions. These questions (i) explore recollections of being outdoors in nature as a child; (ii) inquire about how family members viewed the natural world; and (iii) ask about what the client likes to do outdoors now, as well as how often he or she gets to do it. Answers to these questions provide me with initial information about the client's historical and current relationship with nature and the ways that he or she orients to it, values it and engages it. Over the years, clients have shared stories about their relationship with a favourite pet, recollections of hunting with their grandfather, memories of gardening with their mother, stories of family camping trips and powerful accounts of hiding in the woods outside their childhood home during times of family strife. In sharing these and other accounts, clients talk about childhood memories of pleasure, awe, fear and compassion; and in the telling, often seem more relaxed during that initial counselling session. Our discussion also opens nature as an appropriate topic for therapy and lays the groundwork for future discussions and nature-based assignments (Hasbach, 2012, 2013).

Making Use of Nature Imagery and Nature Metaphor

Clinicians have long employed the use of metaphor as a tool to access a client's conceptual world view and to deepen the therapeutic process. Metaphors frame our understanding of one thing (that is known or recognized) in terms of another (that is new or perhaps challenging to articulate).

Clinicians who practice ecotherapy listen for metaphors that clients use that come from nature, and employ nature metaphors to deepen the therapeutic discussion and enrich the nature-based experiences we assign to clients between sessions. A couple of examples from my own practice that I have previously written about follow (Hasbach, 2012).

A successful, middle-aged man in a stable marriage presented with mild depression and feelings of 'being bored with life'. He began one session talking about his tendency to make safe decisions and take the middle of the road. Knowing he was an avid hiker (from the intake interview and earlier sessions), I asked him about mountain trails he had taken, his experiences of walking trails that are sometimes narrow and his feelings about what it meant to him to get to edges when hiking. He talked of how he had to be more aware and felt 'more alive' and present when he was walking an edge than when he walked the middle of a wider path. We returned to a discussion of 'edges and centres' many times as he explored the safer decisions he was prone to make and often regret.

I keep a box of found nature objects in my office. It includes shells, rocks, seeds, sticks, bones, mosses, leaves and feathers. Sometimes, when clients seem to be stuck or at a loss for words, I'll invite them to select an item they are drawn to from the box. One young woman, who was seeing me for depression and issues related to a recent break-up with her boyfriend, was having difficulty articulating her feelings. When given the opportunity to select an item from the nature box, she chose a vine that had formed a hollow ball. She said it represented the emptiness she felt inside and the tangles she felt in her life. The vine ball provided a useful prop for her to describe her feelings.

Other metaphors that have come up in the course of therapeutic discussions include sinking in quicksand, being caught in the undercurrent, swimming upstream, feeling bright and sunny, feeling dark, and being left high and dry. These outer mappings of inner experiences provide rich descriptors to deepen therapeutic discussion (Conn, 1998; Hasbach, 2012).

Nature imagery can also be employed to enhance the therapeutic office. There is ample evidence that viewing real nature and exposure to nature imagery benefits people physically and psychologically (Heerwagen, 1990; Ulrich, 1984). Based on research findings, healthcare settings such as hospitals, physician offices, dental offices, and nursing homes and assisted living communities are increasingly incorporating nature and images of nature in the design of their facilities. As a clinician, I am mindful of what my clients look at while seated in my office. From my second-floor office space, clients view an abundance of trees at the canopy level from four large office windows. Because the office is on the second floor, providing natural privacy, and is north facing, window blinds can remain fully open. Art in the office includes images of a sunrise and a sunset as well as those of a calm water scene. A small stone fountain provides water sounds, and natural textures and colours are used throughout.

Assigning Nature-based Homework to Clients

Many therapists assign homework to their clients between sessions to extend the therapeutic work, practise a new behaviour or create time to reflect on an identified issue. Ecotherapy extends this practice to include nature-based assignments that often encourage the client to move outdoors or to interact with some element of nature in a specific way (Burns, 1998; Clinebell, 1996; Hasbach, 2012). By moving out of their daily routine and unplugging from technology, clients have the opportunity to connect with a deeper internal knowing.

In my practice, I regularly assign tasks that take clients outdoors between our scheduled sessions. One assignment I often suggest to both clients and my graduate students is a guided experience called the Special Place assignment. Clients select a special place that they agree to visit several times a week for a period of a month. They are asked to form a relationship with this place and to spend time in it during varied weather conditions and at different times of the day. To focus their time initially, I ask them to reflect on these questions:

1   How do you feel when you settle into this place?

2   What is the nature of your relationship with this place?

3   What relationships do you recognize in this place?

4   What senses are activated when you are here?

5   What do you feel compelled to write about or reflect on when you are in this place?

6   What are you curious about regarding this place?

Over the course of a month, this exercise fosters a gradual deepening of experience, a heightened sensitivity and sensory perception, an expanded knowledge of the place and a sense of belonging. It invites a conscious communion with the natural world (Hasbach, 2012).

Other nature-based activities I have assigned to my clients include asking them to take a 'contemplative nature walk' that has a specific ritualized beginning and ending; to bring back a found object that drew their attention or held special significance to them when spending time outdoors; to spend time alone in a natural setting, such as sitting by a lake or stream or walking along the water's edge at the beach; to become involved in a restoration project in their community; to journal on an issue of concern during a transition time of nature such as an evening sunset; or to plant a garden or tend to a potted plant or window box. Experiences like these encourage a heightened sensory awareness and an opportunity for thoughts, feelings and ideas to become more embodied. They provide rich images and metaphors and new experiences to work with during subsequent therapy sessions (Burns, 1998; Hasbach, 2012).

Incorporating a nature language into the Therapeutic Process

Elsewhere, I have introduced the concept of a 'nature language' (Hasbach, 2012; Kahn, Ruckert and Hasbach, 2012) and discussed how it might be utilized in our work with clients (Hasbach, 2012). A nature language can be defined as a way to speak about the rich and diverse ways we experience and affiliate with the natural world, and is composed of *interaction patterns* which represent fundamental ways we interact with features of nature that engender meaningful human experience.

Many of these interaction patterns developed during our species' evolutionary history as we coevolved, embedded, in the natural world. Examples of interaction patterns include *sitting by fire, sleeping under the night sky, walking the edges of nature, being immersed in water, recognizing and being recognized by non-human other* and *caring for another being.* Interaction patterns such as these can be experienced on a continuum of wild manifestations to more domestic ones. For example, a wilder manifestation of the interaction pattern *sleeping under the night sky* might entail sleeping outdoors without a tent during a back-country trip. A more domestic manifestation of that same interaction pattern might entail sleeping in a tent in the back yard. A nature language provides a systematic way of thinking about what elements of nature or what experiences in nature might be most potent for a therapeutic exercise.

Therapists can incorporate a nature language into the therapeutic process by listening deeply for interaction patterns in our clients' stories and creating opportunities for encounters between the client and nature that deeply, subtly *touch on* or *attend to* an issue they are working on. One way this is accomplished is by moving the therapy session outdoors or by assigning meaningful, directed nature-based homework. For example, if the therapist would like to encourage a shift in perspective, she might suggest an activity to the client that involves the interaction pattern *being at the edges of nature.* This could be accomplished by asking the client to take the issue he or she is focused on outdoors where the water meets the land or where the forest meets the meadow.

Another example follows that incorporates the interaction pattern *interacting with the periodicity of nature.* The therapist might suggest a contemplative walk or a journaling exercise to be done at a transitional time of the day, such as at sunrise or sunset, to a client who is working through a life transition issue.

By incorporating a nature language into therapy and consciously working with interaction patterns and their wide range of instantiations, we can begin to speak more systematically about behaviours that we engage in with nature and address the meaning, the emotions and the psychological experiences that ensue. In doing so, we create opportunities for clients to reawaken deeper feelings of connection, belonging and awareness (Hasbach, 2012).

Moving Therapy Outdoors – Unique Features and Ethical Challenges

Some ecotherapists accompany clients outdoors during the therapy session. Though interest in this practice is still relatively small among private practice clinicians, there are a growing number of therapists interested in moving sessions outdoors. Several logistic challenges must be considered, such as scheduling concerns, the location of the office and its proximity to a natural space that works for therapy, and unpredictable weather conditions. There are also several ethical concerns that must be considered.

In my own practice, I recently opened a new office in a building that is located in a quiet, wooded area and is situated along a walking/biking path that runs along the Willamette River. This location offers the opportunity to walk right out of the office and onto a safe, pleasant walking path to the river, where I can sit with a client or perhaps 'walk and talk' for a part of our session. But there are few office settings that are amenable to this practice. Most ecotherapists schedule time in a local park or at a specific meeting place each week, and meet their clients at that designated spot. Others see clients at their home office and have a garden area in which to hold their sessions (Buzzell, 2009).

Though perhaps logistically challenging at times, the unique features of outdoor therapy can be well worth the effort. Some of the special features of nature-based therapy include the following: (i) There is an emphasis on direct contact with nature, resulting in heightened sensory awareness and perceptions that connect our inner world with the outer landscape; (ii) the pace slows; (iii) we have the opportunity to frame the client's issues within a wider and deeper context, thus gaining a different perspective; (iv) spontaneous interactions with elements of nature often emerge that influence the therapeutic process and the client's perspective; (v) the place becomes a witness to the client's story, and nature becomes a partner in the therapeutic relationship; (vi) because we are meeting in a place that is neither the client's nor the therapist's, the shared situation provides the opportunity for a co-created therapeutic experience (Burns, 1998; Hasbach, 2012, 2013; Jordan, 2015; Rust, 2009).

This last feature presents new challenges for the therapist regarding the boundaries of a shared experience and maintaining the asymmetry of the therapeutic relationship (Hasbach, 2012; Jordan and Marshall, 2010). Although some practitioners call for a new code of ethics to address the unique concerns of ecotherapy (Berger, 2008), others are concerned that applying a specific code of ethics would further 'professionalize' the practice of ecotherapy (L. Buzzell, personal communication, 10 January 2012).

From my years of practice and from discussions with colleagues who incorporate nature-based practices in their work, I have concluded that there are three overarching areas of ethical concerns that involve confidentiality, avoiding harm and competency. These areas are discussed in the existing codes of ethics held by the American Psychological Association (APA, 2010), the American Counseling Association (ACA, 2014) and the National Association of Social Workers (NASW, 2008). I make the assumption that the European counterparts to these professional groups hold similar standards. My familiarity is with the US associations; therefore, I will reference them as I highlight how these three ethical areas apply to the practice of ecotherapy.

Confidentiality

The APA Code of Ethics (2010) addresses the issue of confidentiality (4.01 Maintaining Confidentiality) and directs psychologists to discuss the limitations to confidentiality with their clients/patients (4.02 Discussing the Limits of Confidentiality). The ACA Code of Ethics (2014) is particularly relevant for ecotherapists as they address the issue of confidentiality when leaving the confines of the clinical office, indicating that practitioners should consider situations where confidentiality might be breached (B.1.d. Explanation of Limitations).

Before moving the therapy session outdoors, the clinician should raise the issue of confidentiality with clients and understand how they want to handle certain situations that might occur. For instance, I ask clients how they would like to handle the situation of encountering a familiar person while outdoors together. I also raise the question of how we will manage sensitive material if someone approaches or passes us on the trail or walking path. It is the therapist's responsibility to raise these potential situations and to support the client in making informed decisions about these important issues (Hasbach, 2013).

Avoiding Harm

Most of the ethical codes require that clinicians avoid harm to their clients. Clinicians work hard to provide a safe psychological space for the people we work with, and we generally intend to provide a safe physical space as well. We generally assume that our office spaces and school, health clinic or agency settings provide a reasonably safe environment for our clients and ourselves. But when we move our therapeutic work outdoors, we must do so mindfully and ask what might pose some danger to clients and raise those concerns with them before leaving the office. For example, the therapist should ask clients if they have any physical conditions that could affect their safety while outdoors, such as allergies, asthma, cardiac conditions, muscular-skeletal problems or other health concerns. The therapist should also go prepared. When I move outdoors with clients, I carry a light backpack containing bottled water, a basic first-aid kit and a lightweight emergency blanket. I take my cell phone in case of an emergency (Hasbach, 2013).

Safety concerns may be a fairly minor issue in a nearby park or walking path or garden. But when therapy moves into a wilder environment, therapists must be prepared and raise these safety concerns with their clients.

Competence

The APA Code of Ethics (2010) states, 'Psychologists provide services ... only within the boundaries of their competence, based on their education, training, supervised experience, consultation, study or professional experience' (2.01.a. Boundaries of Competence, p. 5); and 'In those emerging areas in which generally recognized standards for preparatory training do not yet exist, psychologists nevertheless take reasonable steps to ensure the competence of their work and to protect clients/patients ... from harm' (2.01.e. Boundaries of Competence, p. 5). The ACA (2014) and NASW (2008) advocate similar guidelines for therapist competence.

As the field of ecopsychology grows and interest in the practice of ecotherapy expands, there are more opportunities for clinicians to acquire relevant training through professional development workshops, conferences and graduate pro-grammes. There is also a growing body of literature that addresses the evolving theory of the human–nature relationship and the practice of ecotherapy.

Clinicians need to recognize their limits of competence related to the thera-peutic issues of this emerging field, and they also need to be clear about their level of competence related to the outdoor environment in which they are conducting their work. It is incumbent upon the therapist to assess the level of risk and the client's level of competence and confidence to handle that environ-ment. Once again, if the outdoor experience involves nearby nature, such as a walk on the bike path beyond the office building, there is relatively little risk involved. But if therapy moves to wilder environs, the clinician must be clear about his or her own competence and thoughtfully assess the client's level of ability and comfort (Hasbach, 2013).

Documentation

It is important that clinicians document the preparatory discussions that they have with their clients before leaving the office setting. Documentation require-ments are often determined by the agency or organization where the clinician is practicing. Private practitioners must decide how best to document the issues discussed and the decisions reached. Some practitioners outline the issues dis-cussed in a formal document and ask the client to sign it. Others document the discussion and decisions reached by including the details in the session notes of the client's chart.

Our Ethical Responsibility to the Natural World

As I have written elsewhere (Hasbach, 2013), a final area of ethical concern is not articulated in any of the codes of ethics by which we practice. Because nature becomes a partner in the therapeutic process, it is important to recognize not only the utilitarian value of nature in therapy but also its intrinsic value. This connection to and valuing of the natural world encourages human flourishing in a way that acknowledges our deep kinship with the more-than-human world. I have called this kinship our 'totemic self' (Kahn and Hasbach, 2012). This relationship involves reciprocity and challenges us to consider our ethical responsibility to the natural world in which we work and of which we are a part.

Conclusion

In this chapter, I have shared several techniques that clinicians might consider as they expand the traditional scope of treatment to include the human–nature relationship. These techniques include broadening the intake interview to account for the client's past and current relationship with nature; making use of nature metaphor and nature imagery in a therapeutic context; suggesting nature-based homework assignments to clients; and moving therapy outdoors where nature becomes a partner in the therapeutic process. I introduced the idea of a nature language as a systematic way to speak with clients about their interactions with the natural world and as a tool for clinicians to deepen and strengthen therapeutic interventions. Finally, I discussed several ethical considerations related to the practice of ecotherapy.

Even as the field is evolving and best practices are being defined, the emerging practices of ecotherapy have much to offer. This treatment modality touches the deep roots of human evolution within the natural world, and because of that, fosters human flourishing.

References

American Counseling Association (2014) *Code of Ethics* (Alexandria, VA: ACA).

American Psychological Association (2010) *Ethical Principals of Psychologists and Code of Conduct* (Washington, DC: APA).

Berger, R. (2008) 'Developing an Ethical Code for the Growing Nature Therapy Profession', *Australian Journal of Outdoor Education*, 12, 47–52.

Burns, G. (1998) *Nature-Guided Therapy: Brief Integrative Strategies for Health and Well-Being* (London: Taylor & Francis).

Buzzell, L. (2009) 'Asking Different Questions: Therapy for the Human Animal', in L. Buzzell and C. Chalquist (eds) *Ecotherapy: Healing with Nature in Mind* (San Francisco: Sierra Club Books) pp. 46–54.

Clinebell, H. (1996) *Ecotherapy: Healing Ourselves, Healing the Earth* (Minneapolis, MN: Fortress Press).

Conn, S. (1998) 'Living in the Earth: Ecopsychology, Health, and Psychotherapy', *The Humanistic Psychologist*, 26, 179–98.

Hasbach, P. H. (2012) 'Ecotherapy', in P. H. Kahn Jr. and P. H. Hasbach (eds) *Ecopsychology: Science, Totems, and the Technological Species* (Cambridge, MA: MIT Press) pp. 115–39.

Hasbach, P. H. (2013) 'Moving Therapy Outdoors: Techniques, Challenges, and Ethical Considerations', *Voices: The Art and Science of Psychotherapy*, 49, 37–42.

Heerwagen, J. (1990) 'The Psychological Aspects of Windows and Window Design', in K. H. Anthony, J. Choi and B. Orland (eds) *Proceedings of the 21st Annual Conference of the Environmental Design Research Association* (Oklahoma City: EDRA) pp. 269–80.

Jordan, M. (2015) *Nature and Therapy: Understanding Counselling and Psychotherapy in Outdoor Spaces* (London: Routledge).

Jordan, M., and H. Marshall (2010) 'Taking Counselling and Psychotherapy Outside: Destruction or Enrichment of the Therapeutic Frame?', *European Journal of Psychotherapy & Counselling*, 12, 345–59.

Kahn, P. H., Jr., and P. H. Hasbach (2012) 'Introduction to Ecopsychology: Science, Totems, and the Technological Species', in P. H. Kahn Jr. and P. H. Hasbach (eds) *Ecopsychology: Science, Totems, and the Technological species* (Cambridge, MA: MIT Press) pp. 1–21.

Kahn, P. H., J. H. Ruckert and P. H. Hasbach (2012) 'A Nature Language', in P.H. Kahn Jr. and P. H. Hasbach (eds) *Ecopsychology: Science, Totems, and the Technological Species* (Cambridge, MA: MIT Press) pp. 54–77.

National Association of Social Workers (2008) *Code of Ethics* (Washington, DC: NASW Press).

Rust, M. (2009) 'Why and How Do Therapists Become Ecotherapists?', in L. Buzzell and C. Chalquist (eds) *Ecotherapy: Healing with Nature in Mind* (San Francisco: Sierra Club Books) pp. 37–45.

Ulrich, R. S. (1984) 'View Through a Window May Influence Recovery from Surgery', *Science*, 224, 420–21.

11

A VITAL PROTOCOL – EMBODIED-RELATIONAL DEPTH IN NATURE-BASED PSYCHOTHERAPY

Hayley Marshall

Introduction

I knew I would become an outdoor psychotherapist when, with the sea on one side, and the mountains on the other, the wilderness immersion group I was a member of began to reflect on the powerful happenings from the previous two hours. We had just experienced a turbulent journey by canoe around a headland where the sea had become a bit rougher than anticipated; and although there was a lot of anxiety and anger being expressed in the group about the practicalities concerning this, people were also directly in touch with some very profound personal issues. At the time, I was in contact with a sense of my own physical inadequacy and vulnerability in the world in a way I'd never quite managed to access in the many years of personal therapy I'd undertaken by this point. I was both disturbed and amazed at the immediacy of this process.

As I write this now, I realize just how much I have assimilated the learning from this experience within my body. Essentially, I think this was because of the group's live focus on physical engagement with the landscape and the resultant group process. This seemed to offer a direct route into what I would view as the fundamental aspects of my sense of self. I am also conscious of how much I associate this life-changing experience with the landscape it took place in; this is very much part of the embodied learning that happened for me at the time.

My decision to go on the immersion trip was prompted by a desire to breathe new life into my work. After many years as a Transactional Analysis psychotherapist, I was struggling with the sedentary nature of the work – I knew I wanted to get moving. There were also aspects to the therapeutic process that felt frustrating to me, specifically in terms of helping clients access and transform what I would term the deeper aspects of their personal process – their intrinsic 'ways of being' in the world. I knew I needed to work in a more relationally active way.

The experience I had on that trip firmly laid the foundations for my current outdoor clinical focus, which essentially contains two strands. Firstly, an interest in the way we organize our personal experience in the somatic (of the body) non-conscious domain; and how these aspects may be evoked and worked with in outdoor psychotherapy through an emphasis on movement and vitality. And secondly, the dynamics that come alive in the relational matrix when working with nature – what I would term a *living third*. Both of these aspects relate to the notion of embodiment in therapy, that is, giving a shape or form to personal experience that didn't have this before.

In this chapter, I follow the first of these two interweaving paths and attempt to shine a light on the process of outdoor therapy as viewed through an embodied-relational lens. Referring to some of the subtleties and intimacies from an actual outdoor therapy case, I explore how taking therapy out into nature offers potential to evoke early relational experiences and traumas through the sensory impact on the body–mind and the increased physical movement within the therapeutic relationship. In addition, I link findings from environmental psychology concerning our innate responses to nature to how the natural setting can both aid the process of affect regulation (soothing) in therapy and facilitate an expansion of internal space for reflection on and assimilation of emerging experience.

My Outdoor Therapeutic Space – Setting the Scene

Figure 11.1 My outdoor therapeutic space.

Over the past eight years following the formative experience described above, I have gradually developed an outdoor clinical practice. I work with individuals for psychotherapy and supervision in my local landscape. I have worked with groups of both adults and young people out on wilderness trails in wilder terrain; and I also now provide training for therapists who want to develop their outdoor practice.

With individuals, my work is nested within my local environment in a large area (approximately 150 acres) of open access land on the edge of the town in northern England where I live. For me this landscape forms an important part of the holding I experience when I'm working outdoors (Marshall, 2014). The setting consists of large tracts of mixed woodland incorporating some very old beech trees; some flatter ground with tracks and paths; lots of streams and waterfalls; a nature reserve with ponds of still water; and some steeper climbs up to wilder open moorland and rocky edges, affording wide-ranging views across the wider landscape. There are often some people walking their dogs and running here, but there are also plenty of secluded areas in which to gain more privacy.

Most of the work in this place is conducted on the move; there is some sitting and standing, but usually we are walking and talking, interacting with the landscape and the happenings around us, where that seems important. The environment described in bald terms above certainly flows in and out of the conversation in an explicit sense. However, I also understand it to be part of the implicit (non-conscious and wordless) dialogue that is going on in the therapy all the time. Therefore, although the natural setting forms a significant relational element in some aspects of my work, its vibrancy infuses the therapy throughout. This influences both the people I work with and myself, on major physiological and psychological levels.

This has had important implications as it has inevitably brought my fuller attention to the somatic element within the therapeutic process. A significant theme centres on how some clients connect physically with key, profound, emotional experiences in relation to the environment and to me, the therapist. These appear to be intensified by interaction with the dynamic processes of the natural world and are often experienced with a sense of immediacy.

A therapy where considerable therapeutic potency was gained through attending to these somatic, more non-conscious processes was with my client Fiona.

Fiona struggled in her adult life with generally feeling worthless and physically 'useless'. She had strong feelings about her body, feeling that 'it is ugly and lets me down'. She described feeling emotionally and physically vulnerable around others. She reported that although she often felt 'closed down', she had a strong spiritual connection to nature, it being the one place she felt 'vaguely okay' about herself.

Fiona – Sensory awakenings

It's mid-spring and in a session early on in the work, we are walking up the track. Fiona is commenting on how happy she is that there are so many trees in this place and how loudly the birds are singing. She is feeling really excited by the noisy cascading water that is in evidence, owing to recent heavy rainfall. She says she feels that she 'is opened up and alive' when she's out here. She feels more alive in this therapy than she has before, comparing it to some previous indoor therapy. I am noticing how excited I feel about being out here with her today, even though I've just had a session with another client, in this same place, where I'd felt rather flat. I note that I too am feeling very tuned in to the vigour present in the environment. She also notices this, smiling as she says to me at one point, 'You really seem to like it out here!' As well as listening to her, I am also aware of her style of movement. She seems eager to keep up with me, yet at the same time not quite certain of where to place herself. She keeps trying to turn sideways and adjust her pace to match mine. I begin to experience a sense of unease and awkwardness in my own body and feel unsure about whether to keep my own pace or try to match hers. As a result, our walk up the path, although enthusiastic, is also somewhat stilted!

Vitality

In the traditional therapy room, there is a limited range of movement, textures, colours, sounds and smells to focus on. This offers a particular type of relational attention necessary for some clients in order to help them to connect with their internal experience. By contrast, in outdoor work the physical 'container' for the therapy is a range of dynamic and living processes, brimming with motion and vitality. This setting calls for a sharpening of the senses – an organismic 'switching on' – involving a more active level of engagement for both therapist and client. Like Fiona, many clients report a sense of 'coming alive', particularly in the early stages of the work, as they relate with the world around them through increased sensory interaction and awareness. The example illustrates that this also happens for the therapist too. My experience has been that working outdoors supports my vitality within the therapeutic process. This, then, is therapy in a vitalizing space, where I think that the participants are effectively being 'tuned up' to hone in on movement and process.

In his writing about forms of vitality, Stern (2010) elegantly portrays how we relate to and make meaning of the world surrounding us through the cross-modal (multisensory) languages of movement. In foregrounding the primacy of movement in our basic sense of who we are, Stern argues that vitality forms provide the fundamentals of our felt experience. They are the 'how' or 'style' (not content specific) of what happens as we think, feel, speak, move and relate. This is part of our non-conscious sensing of others and the world around us, the manner in which we know the movement essence of others and reveal ours to them. He describes our experience of vitality as 'a fundamental dynamic pentad.' This consists of *movement*; bringing with it a perception of *force(s)*; then a sense of *space* in which the movement happens; also a sense of *time* profile; and finally, a *direction or intentionality* (going somewhere).

The vignette above illustrates the early stages of a vital bond with the place in which the therapy takes place. Although Stern does not discuss our connection with the natural world through vitality forms, he does ponder briefly on the fact that they do probably 'correspond with realities in nature that may not exist independent of the mind', positing that we do tend to see all dynamic events in these terms. As the natural environment is already on the move, the therapeutic dyad is certainly surrounded by many different forms of vitality. There is therefore much to attune to, as the other-than-human forms of life layer their way into our minds and bodies. This vital resonance is a significant part of building what I term the *vibrant alliance* between client, therapist and the setting in outdoor work. With Fiona I also think it was important that I experienced the space as full of excitement and vigour as she did, as it proved to be a way of forming the human-to-human aspect of the outdoor therapeutic alliance.

The important consideration in the forging of the vibrant alliance, though, is that it seems to root both therapist and client more firmly in their bodies, offering instant access to the immediacy of bodily experience. Returning to Stern's ideas concerning vitality forms, this potentially places the therapist in a position of being able to really feel and understand the live 'movement signature' of the client they are working with, and all that can offer. As concerns Fiona, with feeling the vitality of the setting I also felt a heightened sense of her physical style as we walked. As a result, I began to catch her movement process through observing her awkwardness and feeling a resonance with this in my own body. My hunch was that this seemed to reflect part of an issue she came to therapy with, namely her relational vulnerability. I view all this as an enlivening of my somatic countertransference through the sensory contact with the setting and as opening a powerful channel for really 'knowing' my client.

The vitality in the outdoor space invites a dynamic resonance that has the power to evoke all kinds of important experiences, offering, I think, therapeutic access to the more implicit, non-conscious layers of experience of both client and therapist.

Non-conscious, Implicit 'Knowings'

The implicit memory system is the realm in which our earliest experiences of the world are processed and organized. It contains sensorimotor, sub-symbolic (Bucci, 1997) and emotional processes, essentially forms of 'knowing', such as implicit relational knowing (Lyons-Ruth, 1998). Allen (2009) describes these early organizing mental processes as 'prerepresentational protonarratives, relational knowings involving self-with-others [which] may later be expressed in sensations, feelings, and interpersonal behaviours, but the person involved has no sense that he or she is remembering' (Allen, 2009, p. 187).

These non-conscious, somatic, non-verbal ways of organizing experience continue on throughout life and are experienced with immediacy in the here and now. They coexist with the later developed explicit memory systems. The latter forms the basis for our conscious factual, autobiographical and verbalizable perspectives on our world, which bring with them an internal sense of something being recalled.

The implicit aspect of our functioning, although out of awareness, is systemic and organized, and provides important channels of learning, sensing and being that continue to develop throughout life, forming a significant aspect of everyday functioning. However, non-conscious experience also contains kernels of past experiences that are more fixed, unprocessed and dissociated. These are the elements that are often the most influential in terms of problems we bring to therapy and typically out of awareness, the most difficult to access and transform. Known in Transactional Analysis theory as the protocol, they correlate to the repressed dynamic unconscious.

Fiona – 'hostile' stirrings

On a chilly autumn day, Fiona and I are sitting on a rock by the side of one of the streams. We are both engrossed in her story about something that has happened for her recently at home. However, I suddenly become aware of how cold I feel, and then, with a jolt, I realize that she doesn't have a coat on! I feel a bit appalled that I hadn't noticed this until now and start wondering about the significance of this 'ignoring' of the situation. I notice how she's pulling her cardigan gradually tighter and tighter around her, and ask her how she's doing with the temperature out here. She smiles, saying that she's absolutely fine and that she doesn't feel the cold. She flatly refuses the tentative offer of my scarf! As we continue to sit, my discomfort grows as she seems to be 'holding herself together' against the increasingly inclement weather.

Soon it begins to drizzle, and I suggest we go back and sit in one of the cars as I am concerned that she will get too cold.

Back in her car, Fiona describes how after trying to ignore things, she had eventually begun to connect with just how cold she was feeling and reported experiencing a strong sense of the 'hostility' of the environment. She cries as she realizes it felt like being 'under attack'. She also reported that she felt she couldn't admit to me that she needed to get warm. It was like it wouldn't be okay to do this as I might also 'turn on her', even though I'd seemed concerned about how she was doing. She says that what is powerful for her right now is the fact that she was in touch with all of this through her body.

In this session in relation to the weather, Fiona really began to connect on a felt level with a sense of being attacked by others. This, it transpired, was something that she'd not really ever fully accounted for before, and there was a clear link with her early history, that is, being in a family where bullying was the relational norm.

The Protocol Concept

Eric Berne (1972), writing about the unconscious organization of early childhood experiences, described 'primal protocols' evocatively as 'echoes of the original situation'. I understand protocol as an unconscious aspect of non-conscious experience reflecting traces and shadows of problematic past encounters with self, others (human and non-human) and the physical environment. I relate this to Cornell's (2010) thinking that protocol represents an 'incorporation of the environment that the child grows up in'. Providing the essence for the later-formed life script (Erskine, 2009), these experiences are deeply held within our sub-symbolic (nonverbal) body–mindscapes. They profoundly influence our everyday functioning, as well as offering invaluable information about the relational atmosphere of our earliest times.

Fiona's experience on this level was the beginning of an understanding within her body of early relational trauma – a 'somatic knowing' (Allen, 2003) – a felt sense of the nature of *how things are in the world*. I view this process as the unearthing of a deeply embedded way of being on a protocol level. In our session, she had a lived experience of 'needing' (and the associated 'ignoring' of this by both her and me) in the midst of a hostile environment (the weather). In essence, she was gaining a physical glimpse of the relational environment of her childhood.

In my work outdoors, I have noticed that access to protocol experiences generally appears to occur more readily and spontaneously as a result of the impact of a dynamic natural environment on the human body–mind. Through encountering the natural world with an increased sense of immediacy, the therapeutic dyad has a potential new pathway into the world of the client's protocol. There is a more direct access to the sensory shapes of protocol experiences as they begin to reveal themselves from a stimulated non-conscious layer in an intensified form. In Fiona's case this manifested as her sense of being 'under attack'.

Due to it being part of the implicit memory system, our experience of protocol is present centred; so as happened with Fiona, this is a living process rather than something just talked about, although this may well happen too. Bringing protocol alive involves activation, and an opportunity to work with what Bucci (2008) calls 'the affective core' of the internal relational world, through sensory and bodily experience.

Interaction

There are also implications for outdoor work at the protocol level once the therapist is involved in an even more active physical process with the client. In my experience and that of other practitioners (Holland, 2010; Jordan and Marshall, 2010; Ray, 2010), there is further potential for an increase in immediacy once this occurs, as the therapy is now an active process – therapist and client out together in the world.

It seems that moving together in a terrain where the body is already highly stimulated by the context puts us in a prime position to access more of our somatic experience. A huge amount of 'information' is now available both to the client and the therapist in the form of a vast range of somato-sensory phenomena – our breathing, muscle tone, pulse, skin colour, mucous membranes, facial expressions, smells, pulse and style of movement, bodily tension, and so on. Although clearly also evident in the therapy room, once moving within a vital living environment, both client and therapist's 'somatic infrastructure' (Cornell, 2003) are revealed in an intensified active form, and so here again I think that there is ample potential space for exploration of protocol experience.

Returning to Stern, I find the vitality forms concept useful in understanding the 'language' of protocol, particularly when working on the move outdoors. With reference to the work of the Boston Change Process Study Group (2010), Stern elaborates on the role of vitality dynamics in how we internalize and identify with the 'other' involved in an experience, clarifying that what we actually take in are dynamic forms of vitality (the movement styles, shapes and essences) from an interactive experience. So this includes how others were when around us, reflected through behaviour, feelings and attitudes; and as can be seen in the next case example, how they have made us feel in response. This is the *felt shape* of relating.

Stern views dynamic forms of vitality as pathways to access non-conscious experience and therefore as an important way of opening up the past. Following the trail of a facial expression, breathing style, bodily gait and emphasis through speech or hand gesture can open up a whole landscape of past experience. Traces of these past vitality forms are held in our implicit memory system, so 'the sharing of another's vitality forms is probably the earliest, easiest, and most direct path into another's subjective experience' (Stern, 2010, p. 43).

I think that in outdoor therapy, therapists have golden opportunities to explore a somatic immersion in the dynamic experience of their clients, consequently finding out more about the lived physical reality of their past and present worlds.

Fiona – 'the runt of the litter'

Throughout our work to this point, we had explored Fiona's relationship with her own body, which she felt to be letting her down much of the time.

In a winter session several months into our work, Fiona and I are walking a narrow path up the hill; she is talking about events in her week. However, what is standing out for me is a sense of her straining her body to keep up, even though we are moving slowly. I begin to feel tightness in my stomach, as she seems to be trying to shove her body forward alongside mine. I am suddenly aware that I feel very physically capable and powerful. I muse on the significance of all this happening in my body as she continues to talk, and I notice that I am also beginning to feel some level of irritation with her and, interestingly, an urge to push her!

I reflect aloud about some of my experience with her. There is a moment of silence in which she appears to flush, and I wonder if this has been too much, too soon. However, she seems to take my lead and also begins to recount her experience of her body, especially in relation to mine. She says that she experiences mine as a strong, competent body capable of walking with ease up the hill, and hers as a useless body that lets her down at every juncture. She says, 'I'm letting you down, because I can't even walk up this hill properly.'

We stop, as she begins to feel 'shaky and nervous' about sharing these feelings with me. We stand together as I invite her to stay with what's happening, and then she cries, expressing frustration and hatred of her body that 'won't do what it's meant to' and how she feels 'useless'. In this moment, she connects to being what she eventually describes as 'the runt of the litter' in her large family and to her physical sensations of being violently rejected: 'It's like I'm no good ... and the others are always after me,' she says.

For Fiona, this is a fuller expression of her protocol level. Through her manner of moving her body (the straining and shoving) as a way of keeping up with me, I seemed to sense something powerful from her. Pursuing this path led to her connecting with her early way of being in the world in relation to other more domineering members of her family.

As described in the previous examples, Fiona's protocol was present in embryonic form in the early sessions (as we first walked up the track) and gradually became more and more embodied throughout the therapy. At this point in the work, her sense of worthlessness, physical weakness and vulnerability in relation to others is captured with greater physical intensity in the course of our walk up the hill.

In terms of my somatic countertransference, I think both my feeling a level of aggression towards Fiona within my body and my external reflection upon this were significant in her accessing her protocol experience. I think that this demonstrates the potential increased capacity of the therapist to 'know' the client through moving around in this type of therapeutic setting. As we walked up the hill, I really got a strong sense of how Fiona functioned with others in the world, influenced by her protocol. So the therapist can use his or her own moving and enlivened body to help make sense of what's happening for the client on a protocol level. This involves working in what is effectively an intensification of the somatic transferences between therapist and client.

If Fiona and I had been working in a room, we may well have come to this same point, but I believe we arrived there more quickly via a direct physical route outdoors, and in a way that was hugely powerful for this client's therapy, as significantly, her story was about living in a physically threatening world.

Nature – A Space for Regulation and Reflection

One of the important implications of working outdoors with protocol in the manner explored in this chapter involves thinking about how to support clients to regulate and assimilate their previously dissociated experiences. Although the relationship with the psychotherapist is, of course, important in this, natural settings, as well as offering their green potency in evoking these depth processes, can also provide some assistance in managing what Bucci (2008) calls the *referential process*.

Research evidence, much of it from the field of environmental psychology (Herzog, Black, Fountaine and Knotts, 1997; Kaplan, 1995; Heerwagen and Orians, 1993; Wilson, 1993; Kaplan and Kaplan, 1989; Ulrich, 1983), demonstrates that part of the sensory engagement we experience in relation to nature seems to happen for us as innate restorative responses to the variety of natural stimulus presented. We are naturally equipped to function and to 'survive' in these settings, so we are predisposed to focus on natural living processes (Wilson, 1993). This in turn restores our brain functioning and physiology (Kaplan and Kaplan, 1989; Ulrich, 1983), readying us for effective responses to the immediate demands of our environment. From this ever-growing body of research, there are two key concepts that I think are useful in relation to outdoor psychotherapy, as they provide some clue as to how the natural environment may help us to self-regulate in relation to our traumatic experiences and bring a new 'way of being with' our protocol.

Firstly, Ulrich's (1983) psychophysiological stress recovery theory highlights the genetic ability we have to affect a swift recovery from the fight-or-flight response to threat. Involving the limbic system of the brain, natural settings, or even pictures or sounds from nature have been shown to lower heart rate, reduce blood pressure, lower anxiety and increase feelings of well-being. I think that this process is probably relevant in helping us to regulate affect (Jordan, 2009; Allen, 2003; Fonagy, Gergely, Jurist and Target, 2002) while in a state of arousal, which can occur when protocol processes are surfacing. Although this regulatory process is ongoing throughout an outdoor therapy on the implicit level, there are times when a more specific focus on the client's connection with the setting can also be beneficial.

Fiona – supportive other

It's a warm summer day, and Fiona and I are standing on the side of a hill. She is express-ing some sadness about the losses connected with living in such a hostile family environ-ment, but seems to me to be holding her body rather tensely. Thinking that she may need more support, I offer her the opportunity to sit down in the bracken surrounding us. We both sit down, and as Fiona decides to really lie back in the bracken, she moves more deeply into what she's feeling.

Later she reports that she felt she could really let go and feel what she needed to, knowing both that I was there and that the environment was supporting her.

The second significant concept is 'soft fascination', developed by Kaplan and Kaplan (1989), whereby the natural environment is found to offer the optimum conditions for attentional recovery within the brain (occurring in the frontal cortex) and also for clearing the mind, thus providing increased internal space for absorption of and reflection upon emerging experience. I think that this is important, as our natural response to being out in this environment can then facilitate the potential to bring a more conscious and new symbolic processing to protocol experience (Bucci, 2008).

Fiona – an overview

In summer, towards the end of our sessions, Fiona and I decide to walk halfway up the hill. As we look out together over the landscape, she reflects on where she's been, both physi-cally and emotionally. She points out the places we've done particular bits of work when some things 'had felt almost unbearable' and comments on what happened and what's changed for her as result. She reflects on how she can still revisit 'these places' (pointing out certain ones) but that she can also 'get up high and gain perspective' and so respond differently to others and to herself.

Bringing all this together, I find the work of Allen (2009) useful here in his thinking about different therapeutic emphases relating to three different neu-ral networks in the brain. He considers that the greatest psychological growth occurs through 'simultaneous activation' and integration of limbic (subserving attachment, emotion and safety), neocortical (for cognition), and medial pre-frontal (concerned with response-ability, intuition, mentalizing, mindfulness, introspection and autobiographical processes) networks. I consider the natural environment to have a significant positive impact on this integrating process as we facilitate the opening of the protected landscapes of protocol to a new kind of 'knowing'. It appears that the qualities and processes contained within the external spaces of natural environments can help promote an expansion of an *internal space* that incorporates both self-reflective processes and an internal ability to regulate internal states. This allows for a new kind of relating, specifically to self, as the natural setting may help facilitate clients to find a more fluid response to the trauma of dissociated protocol experience.

Transformation at Protocol Level

Moving around out in the world seems to bring the protocol aspect of our psyche alive. As the elements of our protocol tumble their way out of our internal landscape, they are played out within the external landscape – reflected though our bodies and in our style of relating with environment and the therapist. As demonstrated in the work with Fiona, my experience has been that working outdoors can help facilitate clients to inhabit the shape – the dynamic vitality – of their protocol, felt within their body. I see the nature of outdoor psychotherapy at this level as an exploration of clients' process, that is, of how things 'happen' for them, as well as a provision of a space for them to develop a new kind of 'knowing' of themselves, others and the world around them. Cornell and Landaiche (2006) state that protocol can 'be brought into awareness, understood and lived within', and as a result, opened 'to new experience and action'. In this sense, then, change at protocol level is a form of reorganization on a sub-symbolic implicit level.

Fiona – Changes

In a final session, as we move around the place saying our goodbyes, Fiona reflects on how she's developed a stronger connection with her own body. This means both a realization of how she's been treating it and also how she's begun to take care of herself better. For her this has simply 'started to happen', as she's gradually felt better about herself. She's also feeling 'slightly stronger' in her relationships with others, more able to ask for what she needs and feel okay about doing that. For her, all of these changes are not so much conscious behavioural ones, but seem to arise from a more 'solid place' inside of her. She comments on how important the relationship with me has been in this process, but that also she feels very physically connected to the place we've worked in and that this is something she will also be holding inside her as she leaves therapy.

An important element in this final vignette is the significance of the natural setting in the reorganization process for Fiona, and how it seems that this vibrant 'other' has now become part of an new embodied sense of herself.

Conclusion

Introducing nature into the therapeutic encounter can provide for some powerful possibilities, especially at the depth level of personal transformation. An unseating of protocol evoked by walking out of the therapy room and into the surrounding natural environment potentially enables the therapeutic dyad to engage with robust direct experience.

Our innate responses to being outdoors can elicit somatic knowing not always easily accessible in the more static environment of the therapy room. This, coupled with a more physically active therapeutic experience, can offer up an increased sense of immediacy and vitality within the process. In an outdoor therapy clients are prompted to open themselves to new experience – to begin to breathe the flow of life into their halting self-limiting processes. Out in the world 'anything can happen'; and so, both the creative ways in which they hold the world at bay and also new prospects can be clearly felt and explored. The perpetual relationality in the living context effectively moves us into a process-oriented mode, enabling a richly embodied intelligence to be brought to the work.

References

Allen, J. R. (2003) 'Concepts, Competencies, and Interpretative Communities', *Transactional Analysis Journal*, 33, 126–47.

Allen, J. R. (2009) 'Constructivist and Neuroconstructivist Transactional Analysis', *Transactional Analysis Journal*, 39, 181–92.

Berne, E. (1972) *What Do You Say After You Say Hello?* (London: Corgi Books).

The Boston Process Change Study Group (2010) *Change in Psychotherapy: A Unifying Paradigm* (New York: Norton & Company).

Bucci, W. (1997) *Psychoanalysis and Cognitive Science: A Multiple Code Theory* (New York: Guildford Press).

Bucci, W. (2008) 'The Role of Bodily Experience in Emotional Organisation: New Perspectives on the Multiple Code Theory', in F. Sommer Anderson (ed.) *Bodies in Treatment: The Unspoken Dimension* (New York: Analytic Press) pp. 51–76.

Cornell, W. F. (2003) 'Babies, Brains and Bodies: Somatic foundations of the Child Ego State', in C. Sills and H. Hargaden (eds) *Ego States (Key Concepts in Transactional Analysis Contemporary Views)* (London: Worth) pp. 28–54.

Cornell, W. F., and M. Landaiche III (2006) 'Impasse and Intimacy: Applying Berne's Concept of Script Protocol', *Transactional Analysis Journal*, 36(3), 196–213.

Cornell, W. F. (22 June 2010) *Protocol*. Workshop presentation in Mobberley, Cheshire, UK.

Erskine, R. (2009) 'Life Scripts and Attachment Patterns: Theoretical Integration and Therapeutic Involvement', *Transactional Analysis Journal*, 39(3), 207–18.

Fonagy, P., G. Gergely, E. L. Jurist and M. Target (2002) *Affect Regulation, Mentalization, and the Development of the Self* (New York: Other Press).

Heerwagen, J. H., and G. H. Orians (1993) 'Humans, Habitats and Aesthetics', in S. R. Kellert and E. O. Wilson (eds) *The Biophilia Hypothesis* (Washington: Island Press) pp. 138–72.

Herzog, T. R, A. M. Black, K. A. Fountaine and D. J. Knotts (1997) 'Reflection and Attentional Recovery as Distinctive Benefits of Restorative Environments', *Journal of Environmental Psychology*, 17, 165–70.

Holland, H., personal communication, 22 February 2010.

Jordan, M. (2009) 'Nature and Self – An Ambivalent Attachment?', *Ecopsychology* 1(1), 1–6.

Jordan, M., and H. Marshall (2010) 'Taking Counselling and Psychotherapy Outside: Destruction or Enrichment of the Therapeutic Frame?', *European Journal of Psychotherapy & Counselling*, 12(4), 345–59.

Kaplan, R., and S. Kaplan (1989) *The Experience of Nature: A Psychological Perspective* (Cambridge: Cambridge University Press).

Kaplan, S. (1995) 'The Restorative Benefits of Nature: Toward an Integrative Framework', *Journal of Environmental Psychology*, 15(3), 169–82.

Lyons-Ruth, K. (1998) 'Implicit Relational Knowing: Its Role in Development and Psychoanalytic Treatment', *Infant Mental Health Journal*, 19(3), 282–9.

Marshall, H. (2014) 'The View from Here – A Sustaining Transaction', *The Transactional Analyst*, 4(3), 40.

Ray, N., personal communication, 10 May 2010.

Stern, D. (2010) *Forms of Vitality: Exploring Dynamic Experience in Psychology, the Arts, Psychotherapy, and Development* (Oxford: Oxford University Press).

Ulrich, R. (1983) 'Aesthetic and Affective Responses to the Natural Environment', in I. Altman and J. F. Wohlwill (eds) *Behaviour and the Natural Environment* (New York: Plenum) pp. 85–125.

Wilson, E. O. (1993) 'Biophilia and the Conservation Ethic', in S. R. Kellert and E. O. Wilson (eds) *The Biophilia Hypothesis* (Washington: Island Press) pp. 31–41.

12

FEET ON THE GROUND AND BRANCHING OUT: BEING WITH NATURE AS A TOOL FOR RECOVERY IN CRISIS WITHIN NHS MENTAL HEALTH SERVICES

Vanessa Jones, Brian Thompson and Julie Watson

Introduction

Outdoor therapies, ecotherapy and ecopsychology share a common understanding: that working therapeutically in and with nature offers a vital opportunity to heal spiritual, psychological and ecological wounds. A common premise within ecotherapy is that, as a species, human beings have evolved in relation to their natural environment and the movement away from the natural world, brought about through the processes of industrialization, consumerism and Westernization, and that this is a cause of personal stress and collective human distress (Buzzell and Chalquist, 2009). Linda Buzzell's work reminds us that we are basically primates who are not biologically evolved for the pace of modern, industrialized and technological life.

Reviewing ecotherapy literature, Martin Jordan reveals that there is neither a unifying model of ecotherapy practice nor an 'overarching definition of outdoor therapy', instead, a 'field of practice' has grown, where practice is shaped as much by the individual therapist's background, psychotherapeutic training and modality as it is by theoretical underpinning (Jordan, 2014).

This essay describes our contribution to the field – a group developed to meet the needs of a particular clinical group in a particular location in London. It is primarily a mindfulness-based approach integrating the knowledge frameworks of its facilitators – an art psychotherapist and an occupational therapist, who are both mindfulness practitioners and trained instructors of mindfulness. The group has evolved from a process of co-therapist review and service user feedback over a two-year period. This essay is co-written by its facilitators and a previous group member in answer to the question: How does a shared experience of being in nature support recovery from acute mental health crisis?

Figure 12.1 Ash tree on Woolwich Common.
Photograph © Vanessa Jones.

In writing it, we weave together experiences, thoughts and reflections of participants and facilitators in identifying what appear to be the key benefits of taking an ecological stance. Interviews with participants several months after discharge add supporting evidence that their experience in the group stimulated an ongoing and sustainable positive change beyond the life of the group. We find that helping people build (or re-experience) a personal connection with nature can help reduce distressing symptoms associated with acute mental health problems. Equally, by working in green space locally, we see members' increased appreciation of the local area enabling their confidence to return on their own, post-therapy.

Most ecotherapy literature (Plotkin, 2013; Vaughan-Lee, 2013; Siddons Heginworth, 2008; Metzner, 1999; Abram, 1997) describes approaches that are particularly suited to private woodland, mountain or wilderness settings, allowing people to actively engage with wilderness or secluded nature and to explore deep personal issues, sometimes using ritual and sensate experiencing to access a deeper sense of listening and relating to nature's wisdom (internally and externally). Such an approach works on a spiritual or soulful level and often invites people to explore wider eco-grief and eco-rage as part of the process in order to make real change in the way they live in relation to nature (Rust and Totton, 2012; Buzzell and Chalquist, 2009; Roszak, Gomes and Kanner, 1995).

Our work does not fit these models in an obvious way, taking place within a mainstream, inner-city mental health service with people who are recovering from acute mental distress, often in crisis states. You might say these more known models for ecotherapy seem incongruous to this setting. Yet we believe its validity lies in a wider premise which extends therapeutically beyond the isolated individual ego towards a theory of connectedness and relationality where sharing a direct experience of nature is the common denominator.

Sitting within Day Treatment services, the ecotherapy group represents a potential addition for patients receiving a personalized programme of thera-peutic groups for 12 consecutive weeks. Through a combination of psychologi-cal therapy groups, skills training, activity-focused groups and individual support, interventions aim to build greater awareness of relapse prevention, manage crisis and symptoms of illness, and promote contingency plans for a sustained recovery.

The group takes place on Woolwich Common, South London. Although fairly small, its paved footpaths around the parameter and wild, overgrown areas of shrub land within the interior provide opportunity to experience a remarkable variety of landscapes including small wooded areas, tall grasses, brambles, edible fruit bushes and some fruit trees. There are many species of birds, insects and small mammals. At the same time, Woolwich Common is a seemingly uninspiring piece of common land in Woolwich, London, where local people walk dogs, jog and pass through rather than 'come to'. It is sited directly opposite the hospital, where the NHS adult acute in-patient wards and other crisis teams are based, and is flanked on its other side by a major arterial road.

Outline of Sessions and Structure

Each session lasts one and a half hours. We offer a regular weekly structure, with a defined start, middle and end, but therapists work responsively in relation to the needs of participants, weather and ever-changing flora and fauna. The group flow moves like this:

- Opening circle – introduction – slowing down stage

- Arriving at the oak

- Guided mindful meditation practice

- Verbal inquiry into experience of practice

- Quiet aware walking within interior of common

- Focused sensory exercise

- Focused creative exercise

- Reflecting on and looking at creative artworks/found objects/sensory experience

- Closing circle and thoughts about session

Opening Circle

In the poem 'The Peace of Wild Things', Wendell Berry writes: 'For a time I rest in the grace of the world, and am free.' Poetry like this creates an expansive starting point from which we invite members to turn off their mobile phones, step out of the usual 'doing' frame of mind and simply experience being in this natural environment. Clarifying boundaries for the session, as we would for any traditional therapy group, we encourage participants to experience directly how it is to be out on the Common today, in this moment, free from expectations.

Mindful Meditation

Walking on into the Common, we stop at a very young oak tree in a clearing, the place where we practise guided mindfulness meditation together. We note how the tree is each week as we settle into our bodies, consciously arriving on the Common.

The guiding therapist for the week invites participants to meet internal experience gently, through the safety of the instructions and rhythm of the human voice, which acts as a bridge of connection to the mindfulness practice. Acknowledging the effort it has taken for each one of them to get here today, participants are then guided to the physical experience of standing, breathing the air, feeling into the body with feet on the ground and the soft grass below. Noticing the tilt of the land, maybe feeling deeper into the soil and clay of the earth. Grounding in the physical reality of being here in this moment, in this landscape, all the while noting, without judgement, thoughts as they arise, returning to the direct experience of the moment again and again.

Meditating in a public space may sound challenging for people in crisis. And this is sometimes peoples' initial experience. This is one reason we hold the guided practice to no more than ten minutes. One former group member who suffered from depression described how, in the past, he had frequently come to places like this to drink alcohol. He was extremely anxious about mindfulness practice in public – fearing that passers might call out to insult him or the group. As his confidence grew, rather than fearing the appearance of the odd dog walkers or passers-by, he started to include them in his thoughts during the meditation, actively wishing them well, even noticing a wish for them to join in.

After this short guided practice, we invite people to say a little about their experience of it, sometimes drawing out aspects of what they say, modelling interest in what their genuine experience has been. This inquiry aims to increase self-awareness and curiosity about what this practice of being present is like for them, perhaps noticing its value both in connecting us with nature and in countering the negative effects of ruminations which drive and maintain unhappiness and anxiety. People are often surprised at the level of activity of the mind and the content of their thoughts, beginning to see the grip this has on them.

Mindfulness as a practice offers the opportunity to notice the continuously changing experience of living. Regular practice develops an ongoing habit of being more present within daily life – more embodied, more aware of thought patterns and feelings; building a gentle curiosity towards our inner and outer experiences, and naturally becoming more accepting towards self and others.

There is emerging evidence that acute service users can benefit from mindfulness practice in some forms (Clarke, 2013; Chadwick, 2006), and certainly mindfulness has been integrated into other treatment approaches like dialectic behavioural therapy (DBT), mentalization-based therapy (MBT) and treatments for post-traumatic shock disorder (PTSD) (Rothschild, 2012).

Few of our clients would be able to access more intensive mindfulness courses because of the commitment and emotional stability required; as Kabat-Zinn (2013) writes, ongoing practice 'is not for the faint hearted'. However, in the form we use it in the ecotherapy group, we feel that on the whole it is safe and accessible for most participants, offering a simple introduction to mindfulness which can increase access to a direct experience of nature. Of course, as therapists we must consider each individual's experience, refining our understanding of what helps and what may be harmful to him or her, this being a basic and essential aspect of good clinical practice (Springham, 2008; Roth and Fonagy, 2005).

So in the context of this ecotherapy group, practising mindfulness can create space for the experience of being in nature to reach us. Equally, being in nature can engender mindful awareness. One participant commented that her illness had become unshakeably fixed, and she could not consider that change was possible; yet looking outside herself at the Common from week to week, she could no longer deny change. Seeing it outside, she began to tolerate the idea that it might also be possible inside. Though perhaps only slight at first, this type of shift of perception, whether it is catalysed by the practice of mindfulness or simply by noticing nature's perpetual change, may begin to offer the possibility of a degree of freedom from painful mental and emotional constructs, as well as a sense of possibility for recovery and a meaningful life.

Quiet Aware Walking

We then walk mindfully through the Common; it is generally quite depopulated mid-morning. We usually walk silently, at a slow to moderate pace, led by one of the therapists. In this way participants simply put one foot after the last, bringing mindfulness into an active moving practice, as landscape and scenery shapes and unfolds around them. Service user feedback highlights the importance of the simplicity of this walk, the experience of being able to follow, one step at a time, not needing to think or make choices, simply moving, holding back brambles for each other, gently indicating any hazards in front, or sharing a view. Simple non-clinical acts like these can often hold great therapeutic value as Woods cites in her description of interventions that made a difference during an acute in-patient admission (Woods and Springham, 2011).

Focused Sensory Exercise

At a given point in our silent walk, we pause, come back into a circle before guiding awareness back to the experience of feet on the ground, gently turning our attention to what is here, now, standing on *this* piece of the earth. From a renewed point of stillness, the guiding therapist can lead participants into a focused sensory exercise.

Figure 12.2 The Rough and the Smooth.
Photograph by Vanessa Jones.

Sensory exercises could include exploration of different forms of looking, for example we have practised bringing our awareness to a soft focus gaze (or peripheral vision) to explore the new surroundings we are now in. Participants have also experimented with looking close-up – paying attention to the details of a small area of ground or foliage, or looking across the broad open landscape, homing into a particular object in the distance. The guiding therapist encourages curiosity around any resulting effects this experience brings. We might also guide mindful awareness of touch, smell, taste or sound, giving people opportunities to share with one another verbally during group discussion afterwards.

> The simple experience of being able to look at something, in detail like this helped me experience myself as functioning once more – even if only momentarily – and that made a difference because at the time I wasn't functioning at all.
>
> (Watson, 2015)

Focused Creative Exercises

Next we guide people towards making a creative response to their experience. Image making can deepen personal inquiry, helping to clarify and express further layers of inner experience. Creativity and image making also invite playfulness and spontaneity, often marking a change of pace within the group process, enlivening individual imagination while validating personal experience through mark-making in the landscape.

Often group members are invited to gather natural or found materials to work individually. We also might bring paper, string or clay to work with, making sure not to leave anything behind which may cause harm to the environment. Bringing in new art materials can extend the range and form of expression and generally accentuate the interplay and differences between human experience and the natural world.

Art works made outdoors can be built around, within or on top of living things. They can be placed in considered ways within the surrounding landscape, giving a further dimension for personal and group discovery through the power of grounding our internal experience and sharing this with others. If biodegradable, the creator(s) can choose to leave these structures in situ to be discovered by passers-by or simply to weather on the Common, decomposing back into the earth.

Natural environments are rich in visual imagery, metaphors and symbols to support healing and transformation. As Siddons Heginworth said, 'Wherever we look, whatever we are drawn to, if we allow ourselves to open to the metaphor, we will always meet an aspect of ourselves. As we work

Figure 12.3 *Catching Clouds*.
Artwork printed with permission from artist.

outwardly with that aspect, our inner self is transformed' (Siddons Heginworth, 2008, p. 133).

Externalizing aspects of the internal is very important within the group, and at this stage in treatment the aim is towards noticing, without judgement, what is uncovered through our creative response to this real and living environment. For example, the service user who made the image above described how finding a beer can reminded him of how his own drinking had been a way of retreating from the world. As he spoke about his image in the group, an insect crawled out of the earth within the can. Suddenly, we were all captivated, and in that moment the service user began to laugh, perhaps more able to identify with this tiny (but determined) creature, clambering out of this dark cave, offering a more positive and compassionate image of himself and his efforts. This

Figure 12.4 Untitled artwork printed with permission of artist.

insect revealed something genuinely unexpected and new, which was literally changing before our eyes.

Service users always have the choice to engage in the creative exercise offered. If they do not wish to follow what we have introduced, they can simply look around at what interests them. Some might sit in the sunshine, chase falling leaves, blow dandelion seeds across the field or drink in the aroma of spring blossom. Trusting participants to find what they most need in these therapeutic encounters, and sharing the value of their discoveries, including any difficulty, creates an inclusive and non-shaming approach, enabling people to work at a pace that suits them. Creative writing, in the form of poetry, prose or storytelling, and photography can offer useful additional art forms widening the spirit of inclusivity.

Again and again it is the detail of what people notice in their creative process more than the modality offered. In the photo below, as the group took time to simply notice what was in the vicinity, one participant noticed a discarded can on the grass. Looking closely, he observed that nature was literally growing over and around it, inverting his initial annoyance with people's disregard for the environment into a sign of nature's power and resilience over human carelessness.

Participants seem more confident about making active individual decisions around how they participate in this aspect of the group process. We wonder if

Figure 12.5 *Untitled.*
Photograph by Brian Thompson.

being outdoors, in open space, increases the freedom to choose in ways that indoor clinical rooms cannot. In their classic paper, Jordan and Marshall (2010) argue that taking therapy outdoors democratizes the therapeutic relationship because therapist and client share the natural environment mutually. We have found that being outdoors offers continuous opportunities for democratizing therapeutic process and uncovers fresh insight into what meaningful therapeutic experience might look like for our service users, beyond existing therapist-led construction of value.

We notice that people are often entranced by nature, captivated by the play of shadows across paper or the sway of grass in the breeze. They might be absorbed by the business of bees collecting pollen in the brambles,

Figure 12.6 *Finding the New with the Old.*
Photograph by Vanessa Jones.

or remember a cherished childhood pastime as they place their own freshly gathered objects or handmade art into the nooks of an old ash tree, finding beauty and sometimes joy in the spirit of these actions. As therapists, it is simultaneously humbling and exciting to learn from the personal discoveries our service users share with us in these moments of 'non-compliance', helping us to become better witnesses to what is truly therapeutic.

Verbal or Graphic Sharing of Creative/Sensory Exercise

Sharing experiences in the group allows for a powerful way of 'stepping into other perspectives'. For example, one participant had us stand as a group, at the boundary of the Common, facing South Circular Road, to experience the physical assault of the traffic on our senses. Then, returning to the interior, we looked silently at a single raindrop hanging on a branch, reflecting the sky, discovered by another service user. Sharing such diverse experiences within the group creates the opportunity to put them together as a whole, and inquire together about the breadth of genuine difference.

Figure 12.7 *Where We Meet the Road.*
Photograph by Vanessa Jones.

Closing Circle

We close by verbalizing an appreciation (whether challenging or easeful) of how it was in the group. Regularly, people share that being outside in a group was important, and childhood memories are common, as is the surprise of the unexpected. Service users originating from other countries have said that despite the differences in habitat and landscape, becoming familiar with Woolwich Common helped them feel grounded and 'at home again' in London while also reminding them of the places they had come from. Others say that seeing the beauty of nature makes them appreciate the wonders of nature or the glory of a Creator and gratitude for the divine in line with their spiritual inclinations.

Being in a therapy group on Woolwich Common, although potentially exposing, has often been experienced as liberating, the reality of its challenges becoming a real treasure in some cases. The unexpected reminds us, therapists included, to put aside any preconceptions about what is and isn't useful, and follow what is already unfolding naturally in our shared experience. In a lecture, Iain McGilchrist (2011), author of *The Master and His Emissary*, reminds us that health is not a thing that is 'done to' people, like an injection or insight to cure illness; rather, health systems facilitate helpful relationships.

The multidimensionality of this integrated mindfulness-based approach seems to offer favourable conditions for different layers of connection and relationship to arise. For some, connectivity arises through creativity and playfulness; for others, it may come from simply hearing the sound of crickets together as a group on a hot July morning, or even feeling the cold wind and quietly just being able to snuggle under a warm coat in response. Being outside together mindfully in nature manifests so many relational experiences of interconnectivity that our clinical institutions cannot.

Service User Reflection – Julie

The depression/grief made me feel completely isolated – from family, from friends, from the world, my 'old self' as if on an island with a stretch of water between me and 'normality' or reality. The ecotherapy felt like being ferried back every week to that former life and one of the things that was pleasurable in that life – nature. I remember not even being sure I could get out of bed, where I had been marooned for days and weeks.

When I told someone that I was going to be having ecotherapy on Woolwich Common she exclaimed 'but there's nothing there!' After my Mum died and the depression that her death triggered, I felt barren and empty, as bleak as that person's impression of Woolwich Common. Week by week I was delighted to see that this place was quite the opposite – it was rich and it was constantly changing, with new 'gifts' just there for the taking, laid out by some unseen hand or force for us. One week there were many different grasses to observe, another many butterflies had emerged with their dark chocolate velvet wings … it felt as though my inner empty state, which I was terrified would now never change and heal, was being challenged or woken up and reminded that what seemed dead could be teeming with life, given the right conditions to nourish growth and change.

The fragility of self during and when coming out of depression felt mirrored in the trembling wings of a Speckled Wood butterfly alighting on the path for a few moments or the beads of dew suspended in a spider's web like a 'crystal palace' as one other service user termed it. It was important to break down the isolation of depression by going out into this urban wilderness with others who were similarly fragile and hurting, and to share the worlds that each of them found that day.

Conclusion

Woolwich Common is an edgy place with the quality of a wasteland. Situated in a deprived and troubled part of South London, this bit of land remains largely in its natural, undeveloped state, besides surrounding tower blocks and jangling main roads. Largely untended, the Common offers realism, and over time, a sense of realistic change that is born out of nature's resilience and resurgence.

It could be argued that this ecotherapy group is simply a grouping together of well-known complementary therapeutic mediums and hoping for the best – that is, being in nature, practising mindfulness, using the arts therapies and being part of a group. Hopefully this diversity of practice does offer various 'ways in' to meet the varying needs of participants. However, there is another dimension. Our understanding and to some extent experience of the model is that the whole is greater than the sum of the parts. How this is so is hard to define, but may be intimated by the unpredictability and even outright mystery of nature (like the weather and its relationship with our states of mind; like the insect crawling out of the tin just as we were all watching).

Through co-writing, Julie reflects on her need to begin to allow and notice difficult feelings as part of a whole 'real' emotional life. She wondered if the 'edgy, nearby nature' of the Common seemed better suited to the emotional state of this client group than an idyllic rural setting:

> I have to learn to live *with* my shadows, not attempt to purge them. Resilience rather than 'cure' is perhaps an easier lesson for me to learn in Woolwich Common than in somewhere more pristine. In my crisis everything was so far away, everything felt so unachievable ... When you are really depressed you feel like you are failing at everything. But in this group you weren't failing, I could walk across the road to the common, I could do that. I didn't think I'd find anything there ... but I did and I started to think that if I could find something there, on Woolwich Common, maybe I could find something in myself too.

References

Abram, D. (1997) *The Spell of the Sensuous: Perception and Language in a More-Than-Human World* (New York: Vintage Books).

Buzzell, L., and C. Chalquist (2009) *Ecotherapy: Healing with Nature in Mind* (San Francisco: Sierra Club Books).

Chadwick, P. (2006) *Person-Based Cognitive Therapy for Distressing Psychosis* (Chichester: John Wiley & Sons).

Clarke, I. (2013) 'Spirituality: A New Way into Understanding Psychosis', in E. Morris, L. Johns and J. Oliver (eds) *Acceptance and Commitment Therapy and Mindfulness for Psychosis* (Chichester: John Wiley & Sons) pp. 160–71.

Jordan, M. (2014) *Nature and Therapy: Understanding Counselling and Psychotherapy in Outdoor Spaces* (London: Routledge).

Jordan, M., and H. Marshall (2010) 'Taking Counselling and Psychotherapy Outside: Destruction or Enrichment of the Therapeutic Frame?', *European Journal of Psychotherapy & Counselling*, 12(4), 345–59.

Kabat-Zinn, J. (2013) *Full Catastrophe Living: How to Cope with Stress, Pain and Illness Using Mindfulness Meditation*, 2nd edn (London: Piatus).

McGilchrist, I. (2011, May 23) Things Are Not What They Seem (video file) http:/www.youtube.com:watch per cent3Fv=oXiHStLfjP0h.

Metzner, R. (1999) *Green Psychology: Cultivating a Spiritual Connection with the Natural World* (Rochester, VT: Park Street Press).

Plotkin, B. (2013) *Wild Mind: A Field Guide to the Human Psyche* (Novato, CA: New World Library).

Roszak, T., M. E. Gomes and A. D. Kanner (1995) *Ecopsychology: Restoring the Earth, Healing the Mind* (San Francisco: Sierra Club Books).

Roth, A., and P. Fonagy (2005) *What Works for Whom? A Critical Review of Psychotherapy Research* (New York: Guilford Press).

Rothschild, B. (2012, April 1). Plot Your Course with Mindfulness. Key 1: Mindfulness (Video file) http/:www.youtube.com/watch?v=eR8QZml-Jsc.

Rust, M. J., and N. Totton (2012) *Vital Signs: Psychological Responses to Ecological Crisis* (London: Karnac Books).

Siddons Heginworth, I. (2008) *Environmental Arts Therapy and the Tree of Life* (Exeter: Spirit's Rest Books).

Springham, N. (2008) 'Through the Eyes of the Law: What Is It About Art That Can Harm People?', *International Journal of Art Therapy: Formerly Inscape*, 13(2), 65–73.

Vaughan-Lee, L. (2013) *Spiritual Ecology: The Cry of the Earth* (Inverness, CA: The Golden Sufi Center).

Watson, J. (2015) Unpublished conversation during writing process.

Woods, A., and Springham, N. (2011) 'On Learning from Being the In-patient', *International Journal of Art Therapy: Formerly Inscape*, 16, 60–68.

13

RENEWED BY NATURE: NATURE THERAPY AS A FRAMEWORK TO HELP PEOPLE DEAL WITH CRISES, TRAUMA AND LOSS

Ronen Berger

Introduction

Nature Therapy is a creative and integrative therapeutic method that takes place in nature and functions through direct contact with it. Derived from an ecopsychological perspective, Nature Therapy acknowledges the healing that exists in the relationship between humankind and nature, while also integrating elements from rituals and expressive art therapy. This chapter presents the basic concepts and methods of Nature Therapy, highlighting ways in which it can be used to aid adults and children cope with crises, trauma and loss and to develop from them.

Nature Therapy – A Theoretical and Applied Framework

Nature Therapy, as developed and conceptualized by the author of this chapter, is a creative therapeutic method that takes place in nature while perceiving nature as a partner in constructing a therapeutic setting and process (Berger, 2014, 2009; Berger and McLeod, 2006). It correlates with other nature-based therapeutic approaches, such as nature-guided therapy and ecotherapy (Burns, 1998; Clinebell, 1996), but develops unique concepts and methods. These concepts and methods are based on the author's therapeutic experience doing, teaching and researching Nature Therapy and on concepts and methods from shamanism and drama therapy which were integrated into the creation of Nature Therapy.

Nature Therapy creates a theory, practical models and an ethical code which can help therapists to work in nature, integrating nature in the process. Like other postmodern approaches which have developed social theories in order to explain the expansion of psychological distress such as depression, anxiety and trauma (West, 2000; McLeod, 1997; Gergen, 1991; Cushman, 1990), Nature Therapy developed a theory which views human suffering, illness and healing from a psycho-eco-social perspective. This perspective stems from a perceived connection between mankind's estrangement from nature and the decline of community and spiritual ways of living, leading to the spread of psycho-social distress and manifestations such as loss of meaning, depression, anxiety, loneliness and alienation. In response to these processes, Nature Therapy focuses on methods that attempt to strengthen the body–mind connection, the connection to the inner child and the creative self, as well as interpersonal relationships, self-inclusion and normalization abilities via the strengthening of the connection with nature (Berger, 2014, 2009; Berger and Lahad, 2013).

At the heart of Nature Therapy, and in accordance with ecopsychological ideas such as 'the ecological self' (Totton, 2003; Roszak, 2001; Roszak, Gomes and Kanner, 1995) stands the term *Touching Nature*. This term implies that direct contact with and a connection to nature can deepen a person's sense of his or her basic nature: to feel authenticity and to develop important personal elements and a way of life that might have been difficult to achieve in the intensity of modern life (Berger, 2005). This concept highlights the importance of nature within Nature Therapy.

Related to this term, the second of Nature Therapy's basic concepts was developed: the triangular relationship, that is, therapist–client–nature. This concept seeks to broaden the classical therapeutic relationship between therapist and client by bringing in a third partner – nature. Like the artistic process and the artistic product, which can be addressed as the third element in art therapy (Berger, 2014), the term *triangular relationship* is conceptualized in the unique context of Nature Therapy. It is intended to aid the therapist in relating to nature as an active partner in the process, affecting not only the design of the therapeutic setting but also the therapeutic process itself. In this way it is different from the perception of the artistic product as a third medium in art therapy, since in Nature Therapy nature plays an active role, having an intrinsic value with a life and dynamic of its own. In art therapy, by contrast, the medium is under the complete control of the therapist and/or client (Berger, 2014).

The triangular relationship is intended to support the development of a working approach which gives the therapist greater movement and flexibility in the therapeutic relationship: to take a central role in the relationship and in the interaction with the client and to be assisted by nature as a backdrop or as a supplier of materials. Alternatively, to take a secondary, background role and to serve as a mediator between the client and nature, or as a witness to a process occurring directly with nature. In general, it can be said that when the client or group is involved in investigating processes connected with relationships and 'communication', for example examining questions of trust and control, the therapist can focus on interpersonal interaction and relate to nature as a background or as a supplier of material for a creative exploration. On the other hand, when the client is concerned with comprehensive questions of identity and meaning, the therapist can invite him or her to interact directly with nature, its cyclicality and its perennial sequences, as he or she remains a witness, seeking to intensify the significance that the individual receives from the encounter with nature. Clearly, in many cases, with changes in the dynamics and the issues being examined, the position of the therapist can (and should) change. A change in position and attitude, which may occur several times during the same meeting also enables the client to move along the axis between the interpersonal and the transpersonal, broadening the framework and perspectives regarding the issues being investigated (Berger, 2008, 2009).

In this article, I would like to expand the perception of the triangular relationship to a hexagonal one, made up of two identical triangles in the form of a six-pointed star. At the vortexes of one triangle are the three formerly mentioned terms: therapist, client and nature, and on the three other vortexes are the group (when working in a group), art (and the creative-artistic process) and the spiritual dimension – the relationship with the universe and what is greater than oneself. At the centre of the hexagon, composed of the meeting of all parts, is the process. Maintaining the structure of the two triangles and the movement between them and their vortexes enables the therapist to choose the axis on which to focus at the various stages of the process and how to advance the process.

The Healing Forest – Resilience, Loss and Trauma

The Nature Therapy method has been used for some years, and in that time it has gained extensive experience working with people and communities that have been exposed to trauma, ongoing stress and loss. It has acquired specific methods and protocols that can help people connect with their strengths, develop coping mechanisms and resilience, as well as to deal with, recover and emerge from traumatic experiences and loss. From the research that accompanied this work, it emerges that there are a number of elements in Nature Therapy that support this process in particular (Berger and Lahad, 2010, 2013). The first one relates to the way Nature Therapy refers to nature as a partner in the process and to its independent dynamic and the element of uncertainty and unpredictability in particular. This, occurring alongside the cycles present in nature, can help people develop their flexibility and coping abilities while normalizing, and also give a broader meaning and perspective to difficult stories. A second element present in nature relates to the way nature awakens our senses, inviting us to be present in the moment. This can help people to connect with the 'here and now' and be present in the moment, as opposed to holding on to past experiences and fears. Another contribution of this element relates to the way nature calls for playfulness and creative being: to play children's games, to build castles in the sand and to get involved in physical activities. This connection to the inner-child and to the creative-self has a therapeutic impact (Berger and Lahad, 2013; Berger and Tiry, 2012). It helps people connect to their inner strength, releases difficult feelings and fosters hope. It also allows people to forsake familiar patterns and ways of being and behaving in their everyday environment while exploring and experiencing new modes of behaviour. Spending time in nature and the direct encounter with it, connecting to the feelings and sights afforded by nature, can help the individual to bypass cognitive defence mechanisms and broaden perspectives, both important elements in therapy in general and in the process of recovery from trauma and loss in particular (Berger and Lahad, 2013).

In the context of this chapter, it is important to stress the intimate relationship between Nature Therapy and the resilience and strength of the Basic Ph model (Lahad, Shacham and Ayalon, 2013; Lahad, 2006). According to this model, which was developed in relation to people's coping mechanisms and the ways they deal with and recover from trauma and stress, a person is born with six languages/coping channels: Belief, Affect (feeling), Social, Imagination, Cognition and Physical. Being in contact with these six channels, expressing oneself through them, in addition to the ability to move between them and to integrate them, enables the individual to function better in the world, to deal with and overcome crises. Parallel to technological-scientific development, modern life has emphasized the development of cognitive channels while other channels have been neglected or even ridiculed, and consequently overlooked. Treatment in the spirit of Basic Ph and, similarly, in the spirit of Nature Therapy, does not necessarily focus on developing insight or a psychological conflict solution, but rather centres on the creation of a setting which will encourage remembrance and renewed accessibility to the languages of resilience and the development of a flexibility which will enable movement and integration (Berger and Lahad, 2011; Lahad, 2006).

These elements emphasize the outlook of Nature Therapy, recognizing the independent healing powers of nature and the important contribution of being in direct and creative contact with it. From research that followed Nature Therapy programmes with children, adults and families who were exposed to trauma and stress, it would appear that these are the main elements that supported recovery and healing. It is important to say that these programmes were helpful not only in cases dealing with trauma caused by war, terror or natural catastrophes, but also in cases dealing with sickness or loss.

From Theory to Practice – Examples from Therapy

This unit includes two examples from practice followed by a conceptualization engaging the practice with the theory. The first story demonstrates ways in which Nature Therapy can be used in individual therapy with people dealing with loss. The second shows ways it can be used with groups of young children who have been exposed to large-scale trauma.

With the River's Flow – Example 1

Sharon, a woman in her forties and mother of two children, contacted me after her husband died, asking me to help her process his death. She said that since he had died, six months earlier, she felt depressed and found it hard to function, to work and take care of the children. She told me that she and her husband used to do most things together, and now she had stopped doing many of them. 'Every day we used to go for a walk on the river bank near our home, and every weekend we went there as a family. Going there alone now is too painful as the memories flood me. Every tree and rock reminds me of him, and the longing is too painful. For this reason I have also stopped seeing mutual friends and talking to people about him. I know he is gone. Yet, I am waiting for his return …'

During this telephone conversation Sharon said she wanted to do Nature Therapy as she felt that with the loss of her husband she had also lost her connection to nature and to the landscape she loves so much. She also said that she feels very sad inside but can't find words to describe her sadness, and perhaps the non-verbal and creative ways nature can offer will help her express her feelings. When I asked her where she would like us to hold our first encounter, she said, 'Let's meet on the path to the river, near the graveyard. My husband is buried there …' This statement made by Sharon in our first telephone conversation told me much about the future of our work and process.

The first three sessions took place on a cliff near the path to the river. Overlooking the landscape of the river, the landscape of her life, Sharon told the story of her marriage and family. Telling me about her love of the river she unfolded her love, memories and longing for her husband. Using the landscape as a metaphor and container of stories and memories, a process of intake began. Sharon would point to a specific place and would tell me a personal story related to it. Slowly, we formed a basic contract, defining the aims of the work and establishing a safe place from which to start.

Following this process, Sharon asked me to join her for a visit at her husband's grave. I agreed, and we held the next session in the graveyard. After we watered the flowers she and her children had planted around the grave, we sat near it in silence for a long time. Leaving the graveyard, she thanked me for the quiet way I'd joined her and said, 'It's the first time since he died that I can be here and see the beauty of this place. It's the first time that I can be here in peace and see this beauty without being overcome by sadness and depression.'

The next sessions took place at the same location. After watering the flowers, Sharon collected stones and mud from the flowerbed around the grave and began to create something. At first it was not clear what she was creating; she just enjoyed playful doing and the physical encounter with the natural elements. Later she realized that she was creating a monument. As she placed the last stones on the top of her creation, she said, 'I know that I was physically involved in the planning of his gravestone, but only today, after creating this memorial myself, I feel I have made my first steps of saying goodbye.' Hearing this, I asked Sharon if I could offer her some homework to do until our next encounter. She agreed and I asked her to visit the grave again later in the week, and after water-ing the flowers, to write a letter to her husband and perhaps, reversing the roles, write a letter in his name to her...

At the beginning of the next session, Sharon said, 'Writing the letters, I real-ized it's time to rise up from the grave and step out of the graveyard... I was there for too long. Can we go to the river today?' We made our way to the river quietly. Arriving at a big tree near the water, Sharon stopped. 'This is where he kissed me for the first time,' she said quietly. Then she took off her shoes and went into the water. Crying and washing her face, she stood there for a few long minutes. 'I missed this place; the trees, the water, myself. Can we come here again?' she asked.

In this way each place on the river revealed stories and memories relating to Sharon's life and the life she had with her husband, allowing her to voice these memories and work through the process of mourning. As the stories were being told, it seemed that the memory of Sharon's husband gained a different per-spective, as did Sharon's perspective of her current and future life. A small waterfall and a pond, a place that they used to visit daily, became our meeting place for the next three sessions. Using flowers she had collected, Sharon cre-ated a sculpture symbolizing their family relationship. The sculpture included rocks in the water, connected by four sticks with a flower on top of them. Look-ing at the sculpture made Sharon happy. 'This is us, my family – my husband, the kids and me. This is our home,' she said. Arriving at the same location the week after and seeing the sculpture made Sharon very sad. All the elements of the sculpture were there, but the flowers had dried out and died. 'This is what happened to me. This is the story of my family.' Silently we sat there together, our legs touching the water, throwing stones into it. After a while Sharon stood up and said, 'Look how the water keeps flowing, finding a way around the rocks. This also is my story. It is time to move on...'

The example above illustrates the way in which basic Nature Therapy concepts can be integrated into practice, supporting people on their journey to process and recover from loss. It shows how important the location, that is, the physical places in nature are in the process, and the way that the therapist takes into account the choice of location and its possible impact as part of the planning of the intervention. This was highlighted throughout the story, from the first choice of the meeting place to the way that different places and landscapes were used to evoke different memories and then to process them. It also showed how the connection to nature and the observation of phenomena in nature, for example the flow of the water and the dying of the flowers, gave the client meaning and broadened her perspective. It connected her to a sense of continuity in her life and to the cycle of life and death, which is larger than the self. These issues relate to the concepts of 'touching nature' and 'the three-way relationship' as well as to another concept called 'choosing the right space' (Berger, 2014). Another element that the example illustrates relates to the way that the independent dynamics of nature can be integrated into the process: Sharon confronting the flowers that had died in the sculpture she created. This encounter connected her with a parallel process within her, giving it a wide and holistic meaning which changed Sharon's perspective. The example also touched on the issues of the way Nature Therapy relates to rituals and to the way it supports their spontaneous creation. This relates to the 'art as therapy' orientation of Nature Therapy and to the ways this approach relates to the creative process as healing activity (Berger, 2014). Lastly, Sharon's story shows the soft 'joining and leading' therapeutic approach that Nature Therapy promotes, inviting the therapist to join the client as a witness and supporter on his/her journey to self-recovery and healing in nature.

A Safe Place: Nature Therapy assists children to deal with a traumatic experience – Example 2

In 2006, after the Second Lebanon war in Israel, it was clear that there was an urgent need for a wide and systemic, national therapeutic programme to help the thousands of children who were exposed to the war to deal with and heal from emotional stress. To meet this need The Nature Therapy Center, together with the Israeli Community Stress Prevention Center, designed the programme A Safe Place, which aimed to develop resilience and coping resources in young children. The programme was based on the metaphoric relationship between the damage caused to the forests as a result of the fires during the war and their recovery afterwards. This process paralleled the experiences the children went through in their communities. The programme was built on the outline story of the hero's journey, using healing metaphors from the story to empower the children and support their recovery and development. The story tells of the forest watchmen who cared for the forest, its plants and animals. One day a big fire broke out and burnt down the forest. Although the forest watchmen did all they could to extinguish the fire, many animals ran away, some got injured and a few even died. Slowly the fire was put out, and the animals started to return. Some came back injured, and some did not return at all. The forest watchmen were very happy to meet the animals again and did all they could to help them feel safe. It took time until winter came and it rained again, and until the plants and the forest recovered. The forest watchmen again took care of the forest and its animals and the plants they loved. They played with the animals, and the animals loved them in return.

Relating to the drama therapy basic concept of distancing (Jennings, 1998; Landy, 1996) and via role-play techniques, the programme allowed the children to tell their stories in an indirect and safe manner. Using healing metaphors from the story (the forest watchmen as an authority and protective figure with the power and the ability to help the trees and animals) while playing and acting characters and situations from the story, the programme assisted the children to regain their strength and rebuild a sense of safety. The connection to the universal story about how trees and animals also deal with natural catastrophes helped them to normalize their stories and get in touch with a wider perspective and meaning (Berger and Lahad, 2013, 2011).

The programme begins in a classroom, by reading the story to the children and inviting them to choose one of the characters and to draw it. Then, through ritual, make-up and other accessories, the children enter the characters of the forest watchmen as they leave the classroom and go outside into the surrounding nature. In the next nine to ten encounters, they build the forest protectors' camp, prepare power symbols and conduct activities which enable them to tell their stories and to link up with their strengths. Afterwards, in line with the outline stories – after the fire has been extinguished and when the forest becomes secure again, including the animals which had left – the children plant trees, build and set up feeding stations for birds and, if possible, nesting boxes. In this way, the children do not just connect with their strengths via metaphors and forest protector's role play, but also give of their strength to others, helping nature and the environment. Thus, the ecological, social activity aids them in creating a link to the sense of cyclicality, meaningfulness and value of attachment to the community and to nature.

A Safe Place is a Nature Therapy–recognized programme, which has been in operation since 2006, involving more than 12,000 kindergarten and school children in both normal and special educational frameworks, in Jewish, Arab and Druze schools in the north of Israel. It has been awarded recognition by the Ministry of Education; it has received a recommendation from the Educational

Psychological Services and has won prizes for its contribution to helping trau-
matized children (Berger and Lahad, 2010). Because the programme is based
on the components of drama therapy mentioned above, we can also relate to it
as a drama therapy programme existing in nature, and thus it constitutes an
example of Nature Therapy as a model for drama therapy (Berger, 2014). It is
important to stress that in this protocol programme, independent dynamics in
nature are not emphasized, but rather, the approach relates to nature more as
a backdrop or a stage for a story which has been written in advance. In this
context, there is less flexibility and movement in the 'triangular relationship'
and less reference to spontaneous events which nature makes available. The
side of the 'active partner' of the three-way relationship is hardly related to in
this example. A more flexible approach which integrates the dynamics of nature
in the process and the aspect of nature as an active partner can be seen in the
previous example. It too raises the possibility of approaching Nature Therapy as
a model and an extension of drama therapy and other creative-expressive
therapy, combining various aspects of art in nature-based work (Berger, 2014).

Provisions for the Journey – Discussion and Closer

This chapter presented the basic, theoretical cornerstones and central concepts of Nature Therapy, and delineated a number of possibilities of using it in
therapy with people dealing with loss and trauma. It shows how this concept
could assist the therapist not only to enable creative therapy in nature while
relating to nature as both a setting and as a stage for work, but also to integrate nature as a partner into the therapeutic process and in this way, advance
and broaden it.

The chapter elucidates the outlook of Nature Therapy towards health and
illness, emphasizing the connection to imagination and creativity as a basis for
well-being, happiness and development. It also highlights the focus it puts on
strengthening people's connection with nature and the possibilities for self-
healing and development. It shows the specific contribution that Nature Therapy
can make to these processes and in connection with the cycles of nature, the
normalizing of complex stories. By doing so the chapter showed the uniqueness
of the method in general and in work with people dealing with loss and trauma
in particular.

Considering the self-healing value of nature, and terms such as *ritual, fantastic space* and *distancing*, the chapter presented the relationship between Nature
Therapy and the perceptions of art as therapy. In addition, it presented the
possibility of relating to Nature Therapy as a method in drama therapy and
other methods of art-based therapy, broadening them to the realm of nature.

References

Berger, R. (2005) 'To Be in Nature – Nature Therapy with the Elderly', *Dorot*, 80, 36–41. (In Hebrew).

Berger, R. (2008) 'Building a Home in Nature: An Innovative Framework for Practice', *Journal of Humanistic Psychology*, 48(2), 264–79.

Berger, R. (2009) 'Nature Therapy – Developing a Framework for Practice', PhD thesis, University of Abertay, Dundee, School of Health and Social Sciences.

Berger, R. (2014) 'Nature Therapy – Integrating Nature in Therapy', in R. Berger (ed.) *Arts – The Heart of Therapy* (Kiryat Byalik. Ach Publication) pp. 411–43. (In Hebrew).

Berger, R. and M. Lahad (2013) *The Healing Forest: Nature Therapy and the Expressive Arts in Post-crisis Work with Children* (London: Jessica Kingsley Publishers).

Berger, R., and G. McLeod (2006) 'Nature Therapy – A Theoretical and Practical Framework', *Social Work Journal*, 46, 22–31. (In Hebrew).

Berger, R. and M. Tiry (2012) 'The Enchanting Forest and the Healing Sand—Nature Therapy with People Coping with Psychiatric Difficulties', *The Arts in Psychotherapy*, 39, 412–16.

Burns, G. A. (1998) *Nature-guided Therapy: Brief Intervention Strategies for Health and Well-Being* (London: Taylor & Francis).

Clinebell, H. (1996) *Ecotherapy – Healing Ourselves – Healing the Earth* (New York: Routledge).

Cushman, P. (1990) 'Why the Self Is Empty: Toward a Historically Situated Psychology', *American Psychologist*, 45, 599–611.

Gergen, K. J. (1991) *The Shattered Self: Dilemmas of Identity in Modern Life* (New York: Basic).

Jennings, S. (1998) *Introduction to Drama Therapy* (London: Jessica Kingsley).

Lahad, M. (2002) *Creative Supervision* (London: Jessica Kingsley).

Lahad, M. (2006) *Fantastic Reality: Creative Supervision in Therapy* (Tivon, Israel: Nord).

Lahad, M., M. Shacham and O. Ayalon (2013) *The 'BASIC-Ph' Model of Coping and Resiliency: Theory, Research and Cross-cultural Application* (London: Jessica Kingsley).

McLeod, J. (1997) *Narrative and Psychotherapy* (London: Sage).

Roszak, T. (2001) *The Voice of the Earth* (Grand Rapids, MI: Phanes Press).

Totton, N. (2003) 'The Ecological Self: Introducing Eco-Psychology', *Counselling and Psychotherapy Journal*, 14, 14–17.

West, W. (2004) *Spiritual Issues in Therapy* (New York: Palgrave).

14

EQUINE-ASSISTED THERAPY: DEVELOPING THEORETICAL CONTEXT

Joe Hinds and Louise Ranger

Introduction

This chapter discusses equine-assisted therapy (EAT) as an element of ecotherapy, first by briefly reviewing a selection of allied animal-assisted therapies (AAT) in which it is embedded, before addressing the often overlooked or under-theorized epistemological aspects of these approaches by proposing pre-therapy (Prouty, 2001) as a theoretical frame to further elucidate the widely reported outcomes within the broad AAT literature generally, and EAT specifically. Secondly, due attention will be paid to the specific qualities of EAT that differentiate it from other animal-based therapies, and the concept of *awe* is proposed for consideration. Throughout, conceptual and theoretical ideas are located within a pre-therapy frame using phenomenological, experiential and relational material from a heuristic case study to support their inclusion in a contemporary understanding of EAT.

Despite the large body of writing on AAT and its variants (e.g. pet therapy, animal-assisted interventions, equine-facilitated psychotherapy; see Kruger and Serpell, 2006), which has detailed many of the therapeutic benefits purportedly gained from utilizing the services of animals (Chandler, 2012; Fine, 2006), AAT has been largely absent from ecotherapy, albeit with a few notable exceptions (e.g. DeMayo, 2009). We wish, therefore, to make this connection explicit by summarizing here the body of literature to date, and to further advance current theoretical understanding of the efficaciousness of these interventions.

Many animals provide comfort at a simple psychological and physiological level as 'companions' (Friedmann and Tsai, 2006), whereas other animal-based interventions are targeted to alleviate deeper psychological trauma (Dietz, Davis and Pennings, 2012). Ranging from small and domesticated through to large and wild, this spectrum elicits very different relational qualities and experiences (Siporin, 2012); compare, for instance, being in the company of a whale (DeMares and Krycka, 1998) or goldfish (Cole and Gawlinski, 2000). Typically, pet-animals such as birds (Holcomb, Jendro, Weber and Nahan, 1997), guinea pigs (Kršková, Talarovićová and Olexová, 2010) and, in particular, dogs (Dietz et al., 2012) have been utilized for a range of psychological interventions such as the alleviation of loneliness (Banks and Banks, 2002) and improving general well-being (O'Haire, 2010).

Despite a small number of theoretically informed exceptions (e.g. Karol, 2007), there tends to be only cursory coverage of the theoretical reasons *why* these interventions may work (Kruger and Serpell, 2006). In some cases bio-medical models of stress have been used to explain how dogs reduce anxiety in a clinical setting (Lang, Jansen, Wertenauer, Gallinat and Rapp, 2010). In contrast, others have drawn on traditional therapeutic philosophies. For instance, Dietz et al. (2012) refer, in a person-centred sense, to dogs providing unconditional love and engendering an environment of warmth, acceptance, security, and empathy. In addition, psychodynamic approaches, particularly with children, have conceived animals as unthreatening and can therefore be viewed as transitional objects and as a focus of projection (Karol, 2007; Melson and Fine, 2006), and attachment theories have been used to explain how animals may provide a secure base (Geist, 2011; Zilcha-Mano, Mikulincer and Shaver, 2011).

The evidence for these therapeutic interventions, consisting of a variety of anecdotal and empirical sources, remains disparate (Fine, 2006). Adding further to this growing complexity, some indications suggest that these various approaches may be summative in determining positive outcomes (e.g. develop-ing secure attachment *and* lowering heart rate) and may only be appropriate to certain people at certain times (Berget, Skarsaune, Ekeberg and Braastad, 2007). With this in mind, we wish to draw on our respective strengths and experience here, opting to restrict our discussion specifically to EAT and set in motion a more informed consideration of the theoretical underpinnings of EAT using heuristic case study material in which to ground our epistemological claims. Although others have made implicit references to the importance of non-verbal communication, drawing, for instance, on pre-verbal ideas to explain the utility of horses within a psychotherapeutic environment (Siporin, 2012), we wish to make explicit the links between EAT and pre-therapy (Prouty, 2001). Moreover, we wish to show that the horse is able to elicit awe-like experiences which may explain and underpin some of the theoretical frameworks suggested above.

Heuristic Inquiry

Moustakas's (1990) heuristic process directs researchers to explore their internal experience while being in relationship with the topic of inquiry. This requires an immersion in the subjective experience to deepen understanding by collecting data through self-dialogue and personal journals and to develop a broadening of horizons by engaging in creative exploration. Assuming a relatively unique position, the primary researcher is both a humanistic therapist and an experienced horse handler and therefore is able to be personally involved in the 'search for qualities, conditions, and relationships that underlie a fundamental question, issue or concern' (Moustakas, 1990, p.11). Alongside this personal reflexivity, an open discussion with the co-researcher was utilized to further elucidate those musings, as well as by drawing on client accounts of EAT from the primary researcher's practice. Due to the present parameters, only part of this body of data will be presented here; the process of insight and discovery is still ongoing. All the quotes that appear below are from the primary researcher's own insights and, in some cases, those of her clients.

Pre-therapy: The Non-verbal World

Pre-therapy (Prouty, 2001, 2008) was conceived within a phenomenological and person-centred tradition and was devised for those people that deemed to be outside of normal psychological contact such as for those with dementia and schizophrenia (Dekeyser, Prouty and Elliot, 2008). Contact within pre-therapy may be divided into three types: reality contact is awareness of people, places, things and events; affective contact is awareness of distinct moods, feelings and emotions; and communicative contact is the symbolization of reality contact and affective contact to others (Dekeyser et al., 2008; see also Solomon, 2010). In particular, we are concerned here with the non-verbal contact (e.g. body and face: Prouty, 2001) provided by the 'horse as mirror' (Vidrine, Owen-Smith and Faulkner, 2002), together with the subsequent emotive contacts that develop from this. Being immersed in a real and concrete situation with a horse may elicit immediate experiencing and therefore genuine self-expression and psychological contact (Prouty, 2003). This is not to say that we do not acknowledge the important function of the therapist in the triad and the therapist's role to verbally reflect, communicate and facilitate sense-making (Prouty, 2003); rather, we wish to attend to, and focus on, the specific qualities of the horse that provide these contact reflections.

Increasing evidence indicates that animals in AAT are able to serve as a 'clinical bridge' (Barker and Dawson, 1998) for people who are typically viewed as being beyond 'talking' therapy, such as those who have experienced childhood sexual trauma (Dietz et al., 2012), autistics (Solomon, 2012), schizophrenics (Lang et al., 2010) and people with dementia (Filan and Llewellyn-Jones, 2006). This finding has also been an important consideration for EAT interventions (Ewing, MacDonald, Taylor and Bowers, 2007; Schultz, Remick-Barlow and Robbins, 2007). To date, as far as we are aware, there have been no explicit connections made between pre-therapy as a theoretical frame and animal-assisted therapy. However, the link between the use of robot animals, particularly for people with dementia (e.g. Moyle et al., 2013) and the elicitation of pre-therapy contact reflections has been considered (P. Dodds, personal communication, 15 June 2015).

The horse has, through evolutionary necessity, developed high sensitivity and responsiveness to body language, including humans' (Johansen, Wang, Binder and Malt, 2014). Equally, the human response to a large animal will often be attuned to its physical presence and its movements and may, through the tactile, embodied and physical quality of the animal encounter, enhance important affect expression and build relational aspects of the self that have been thwarted or under-developed (Myers and Russell, 2003; Solomon, 2010; Yorke, 2010). These encounters can provide a 'bodily experience… in an expressive gesturing landscape, in a world that speaks' (Abram, 1996, p. 81; see also Totton, 2011).

Sanders (2003) emphasizes the importance of the richness of human–animal relationships to provide a non-linguistic, cooperative, interpretative process such as through mutual gaze to define 'self' in relationship with 'other'. Some have gone further, suggesting 'animals are critical contributors to the construct of human identity and a "relational self"' and that 'people tend to view animals as they view themselves' (Kalof, 2003, p. 161). There is an importance, implicit here, for personal engagement with the 'more-than-rational' world, to develop a sense of self within a community of inter-subjectivities (Garcia, 2010, p. 86). Social communications are made up of non-linguistic and embodied signals which may be more important to particular people, for instance those with autism, at certain times and within specific contexts (Solomon, 2010). It seems that the strengths of autistics' experiencing (e.g. visual imagery) may make it easier to connect to the non-verbal world of the animal and, in turn, foster the development of empathy and self-expressiveness (Grandin, 1995; cited in Barrett-Lennard, 2013; see also DeMayo, 2009). This process can benefit many; borrowing from Buber, Leontiev (2013) suggests that open, authentic and mutual relationships may be represented by non-verbal dialogue, and this seems to manifest in human–horse encounters:

> I feel much happier being round animals at the moment, there seems to be something so much more real and present and calming for me about the nonhuman world. Human communication is so bloody complicated!

> There is this moment where I stand with my horse and we are together in meaningful silence. He stoops his head down, lip slightly protruding and his whole body sinks down in a relaxed state. I rest my hand on his shoulder and feel utterly content, both of us looking out into the horizon. I know, with absolute certainty, he is enjoying my company and me his. He is standing next to me freely, no head collar or rope restraining him he could walk away at any point. Often these moments only last for several minutes, and occasionally up to half an hour. I feel a sense of relief I don't have to talk,

there are no expectations. He doesn't need or want anything from me at this point in time ... It is strange, when I think about it I do not have this type of interaction with people, and I cannot explain in words why this is so.

[Since childhood] I had spent time in relationships, become close friends with people I didn't particularly like and done countless numbers of favours in martyr like fashion, all to avoid causing [seeing] someone else's disappointment. Somehow, just the simple act of the horses standing and looking at me I was able to access this sudden realisation. It sounds inconceivable this could cause such an insight, but it is true. The horses had inspired within me a perfect moment of non-directive therapy.

Jung speaks of the mystery of this encounter: 'the eyes of the animal ... are full of woe and beauty because they contain the truth of life', an experience that is 'most bewildering', and that is recommended for all people in order to 'find again the connection with the nature within, with one's own nature' (Sabini, 2008, pp. 171–72). The horse acts as an embodied non-talking 'catalyst' and 'metaphor' (Klontz, Bivens, Leinart and Klontz, 2007), which allows a deeper level of relating:

I feel like I'm starting to 'see' Sparkle a bit more, or taking him in more somehow. He is gradually changing from just 'horse' to a personality and a more detailed physical presence. When I think about him now I can picture the texture of his coat and his mane, and the shape of his hooves, and the look in his eye. It feels like a long time since I've seen beyond just horse and felt that sense of actually getting to know and connecting with one.

The horse encourages the client to act and behave in a way consistent with his or her actual thoughts and feelings and this form of congruence may potentially be overlooked or underdeveloped within the environment of a therapist's counselling room (Lentini and Knox, 2009). The horse responds with blatant honesty and without opinion or hidden agenda (Weiss, 2009), reacting to the internal world of the person, regardless of his or her efforts to conceal it, either consciously or unconsciously (Lentini and Knox, 2009; Roberts, 2004); in essence, the horses are 'truth sensers' (Totton, 2011). And indeed, much of the literature on horse–human interaction acknowledges that horses act congruently, responding immediately, clearly and non-verbally (Karol, 2007). This here-and-now immediacy is also transmitted to the person in contact with the horse:

With a horse you can't reflect on challenging behaviour, you need to react to it immediately. And I think this is something that I really need to learn, to have the confidence to act straightaway on my intuition. With people and with horses, because unfortunately if I don't, not only does the difficult behaviour often escalate but my lack of response means that I feel unheard, and I then end up ruminating on what

I actually should have done, and how upset and wronged I feel, for far longer than is good for me!

Direct experiences with a wild animal can produce a deep sense of perceived mutual understanding, an ineffable feeling state (Myers and Russell, 2003). Simply, there is a substitution of verbal cognitive communication for a basic or primal motivational drive that is symbolic and dictates behaviour and communication, something that is evident in autistic children (Solomon, 2012). Direct (in-the-moment) tacit knowledge, brought about through therapeutic animal encounters engenders an embodied and metaphorical experiential 'felt shift or change' equating to the idea of focusing (Bohart, 2011, p. 258). Bringing cognitions together with bodily involvement can elicit important change during therapy outdoors (Corazon, Schilhab and Stigsdotter, 2011) and can prompt authentic moments, thus reiterating Sander's statement that 'actions speak louder than words' (2003), and in our own experience:

> I realized I had been suppressing sadness all day. My horse wandered over to connect with me, rubbed his head on my shoulder, and searched through my pockets for treats. A wash of emotions rose from the depths, and I let the sadness be.

> My horse continues to be a teacher to me, and as long as I listen, as long as I'm clear about my intentions, we get on just fine. If I am not in touch with my emotions, he doesn't want me around, and certainly not on his back. He is not perfect and neither am I. We both have days when either one of us is grumpy or bad tempered, or simply wants to be left alone. That's ok, it makes our relationship authentic.

Awe

Awe is a transpersonal concept that represents deeply meaningful, evocative and ineffable experiences (Bonner and Friedman, 2011) and may effect emotional moments of self-reconfiguration (Schneider, 2011). Furthermore, awe has been defined as 'the thrill and anxiety of living ... the cultivation of the capacity for humility and boldness, reverence and wonder' (Schneider, 2003, p. 135). Wild animal encounters have elicited emotionally profound and intense experiences, including deeply relational and harmonious moments (DeMares and Krycka, 1998; Myers and Russell, 2003; Smith, Ham and Weiler, 2011). What is more, similar therapeutic experiences have been reported with horses (Garcia, 2010). Indeed, being with horses has been described as 'indescribably healing' and 'profound and emotional, almost mystical' which transports people to a place of awe (DeMayo, 2009, pp. 150–52). Moreover, 'Being carried on the back of a 1200-pound vulnerable giant can certainly provide access to core personal issues' (Weiss, 2009, p. 227).

A horse can cause significant damage to a person in an instant, and yet mostly they choose (and even seem to enjoy) being around us peacefully. In the few cases where I have been next to a dangerous horse, it has been absolutely terrifying, and sharply reminded me of my own mortality. Awe in this case is about being in the presence of an animal who chooses not to kill you when it so easily could. There is a real moment when a horse leaves the herd and walks over to say hello (regardless of whether this is simply because they think you might have food), that feels very special. In this case, the awe for me is rooted in the fact that I am significant enough to a different species. At times I do literally feel awestruck by this, much more so than with a small pet like a cat or dog … . So the awe doesn't always come from the size of the animal, but from the choice it has just made to leave its safe base to be with me.

It is possible that such a sense of awe triggers regression to development periods that reflect similar relational experiences during childhood. To revert to a childlike propensity in order to resolve and work through issues does not necessarily require two persons; pre-psychological interaction (contact) may initially involve objects and non-human beings (Dekeyser et al., 2008). This is perhaps why the horse may be deemed the 'ideal' therapist for the transferential relationship (Vidrine et al., 2002); a mixed sense of love and fear (awe), whereby the horse is perceived as a powerful but trusted transitional object. We are in agreement here with others (e.g. Kruger and Serpell, 2006) that once imbued with metaphorical significance and meaning, the horse acts as a transitional object to facilitate movement from one pattern of human relating and behaviour to another, rather than the horse being seen as a substitute attachment figure. This viewpoint has significant parallels with the idea of a transformational object (e.g. a horse) which may be identified, through intense and existential emotional 'remembering', with an earlier powerful parental transformational object (Bollas, 1987). This remembering is not cognitive, but rather engenders a deep, profound and aesthetic familiarity that is reverential, intimate and awe inducing (Bollas, 1987). Similarly, in another act of regression, observing the spontaneity and playfulness of horses, in a carefree, childlike manner, can return the person to past and unresolved parts of themselves:

This morning … they galloped round and round the field together playing racing games. Then they would screech to a halt, stop and eat taking huge mouthfuls of grass, then suddenly start racing again with the grass still half hanging out their mouths. Watching them like this reminded me of being a child, and I wondered at what age I had stopped playing, I had stopped running, and when I had stopped doing things spontaneously just for the hell of it. Their simple love of life lifted my mood … . This brief but joyous moment with the horses had set off a whole host of thoughts in my head, remembering happy times from my childhood I had long forgotten. Having recently lost my Mum, these thoughts were welcome, as I had become bogged down in a myriad of grief and sadness, with repetitive thoughts about her death and the difficult months following ... this was helpful, not to dispel the necessary grief, but as a reminder that I can still have moments of happiness within the grieving process.

I'm still slightly amazed when Sparkle does anything that I'm asking him to, and feel rather like an insignificant weightless bubble that he can nudge around to his heart's content. And that reminds me of another really long-term theme for me that I am invisible somehow, not really seen or heard. Which I guess links in to the theme of authority. I would like to get to a place where I naturally walk more upright and hold myself with a stronger internal energy that horses and people respond to.

The horse–human relationship could be observed and experienced as an indication of attachment issues (Siporin, 2012). Something about working with horses seems to replicate our family scripts. The way the people are around horses, and the way they respond to the horse, seems to mirror the position or role within their family of origin and present relationships. On a basic level people are 'acting out' a script which the horse then reacts to; particularly with people who refer to the horse as 'difficult' or 'naughty' or 'deliberately not doing what I say'. The horse does not have a concept of these terms and is simply responding to an unhealthy psychological communication. Once worked through, these experiences can be applied in other aspects of the clients' lives:

> I had spent the majority of my life being invisible in the world. Sparkle taught me I couldn't be invisible around him, he needed me to be heard. And crucially, I needed to hear him too. I was ignoring his body language, and then getting angry when he didn't do as I asked. The anger often overwhelmed me, and I would find myself shouting at him with pure frustration, then immediately breaking down in floods of tears which I couldn't stem. I had to face up to the big question, who was I actually angry with?

> When I feel like they're going down a familiar route that I know is not for the best. Sometimes I can catch myself and do something different, sometimes I can't. But I'm finding having the visual memories of the work with Sparkle really helps me to behave differently in situations.

Summary

EAT is not necessarily for everyone – *horses for courses* (see Berget et al., 2007). There may be cases where a client simply does not like horses, may be scared of such big animals or cannot see any benefit to working with them. Sometimes the thoughts and emotions horses stir can be so strong and immediate that it can feel extremely uncomfortable and uncontained. Moreover, in counterpoint to much literature regarding animals as representing an unconditional accept-ance, the primary researcher's experience of working with equines has been at times contrary to this proposition – horses are a challenge. Much like person-to-person interactions, the relationship between person and horse can be unique and often complex. If mistreated, over-worked or not listened to, horses can become 'shut down' and unresponsive, engendering countertransference from the client, for example 'No one ever listens to me'. With the aid of an accom-plished and intuitive therapist this important 'difficult' or 'resistance' informa-tion can be better understood.

We do not intend to underestimate either the important role of the natural environment or of the therapist here. Our focus has been on the therapeutic quality of the horse while leaving implicit both the role of the therapist as an important facilitator or 'go-between' in this triadic relationship and the natural environment in which equine-based therapy takes place. We have drawn atten-tion to both pre-therapy and awe as elements for theoretical consideration, and how these relate to animal therapy generally and large animals (horses) specifi-cally, as well as the interplay with other theories. Although the concept of pre-therapy does not relate directly to awe per se, undoubtedly when harnessed with EAT, awe becomes an important part of the non-verbal therapeutic process which may reflect the meeting of a powerful transformational object (Bollas, 1987). Finally, we wish this chapter to be a springboard for greater attention to, and development of, the epistemological foundations of both EAT and AAT, within an ecotherapy frame, so as to validate and promote the practice.

References

Abram, D. (1996) *The Spell of the Sensuous: Perception and Language in a More-Than-Human World* (New York: Vintage).

Banks, M. R., and W. A. Banks (2002) 'The Effects of Animal-Assisted Therapy on Loneli-ness in an Elderly Population in Long-Term Care Facilities', *The Journal of Gerontology*, 57, 428–32.

Barker, S. B., and K. S. Dawson (1998) 'The Effects of Animal-Assisted Therapy on Anxiety Ratings of Hospitalized Psychiatric Patients', *Psychiatric Services*, 49, 797–802.

Barrett-Lennard, G. T. (2013) *The Relationship Paradigm: Human Being Beyond Individu-alism* (Basingstoke, UK: Palgrave Macmillan).

Berget, B., I. Skarsaune, O. Ekeberg and B. O. Braastad (2007) 'Humans with Mental Disorders Working with Farm Animals', *Occupational Therapy in Mental Health*, 23, 101–17.

Bohart, A. C. (2011) 'A Meditation on the Nature of Self-Healing and Personality Change in Psychotherapy Based on Gendlin's Theory of Experiencing', *The Humanistic Psychologist*, 29, 249–79.

Bollas, C. (1987) *The Shadow of the Object: Psychoanalysis of the Unthought Known* (London: Free Association Books).

Bonner, E. T., and H. L. Friedman (2011) 'A Conceptual Clarification of the Experience of Awe: An Interpretative Phenomenological Analysis', *The Humanistic Psychologist*, 39, 222–35.

Chandler, C. K. (2012) *Animal Assisted Therapy in Counselling* (New York: Routledge).

Cole, K. M., and A. Gawlinski (2000) 'Animal-assisted Therapy: The Human–Animal Bond', *Advanced Critical Care*, 11, 139–49.

Corazon, S. S., T. S. S. Schilhab and U. K. Stigsdotter (2011) 'Developing the Therapeutic Potential of Embodied Cognition and Metaphors in Nature-based Therapy: Lessons from Theory to Practice', *Journal of Adventure Education & Outdoor Learning*, 11, 161–71.

Dekeyser, M., G. Prouty and R. Elliot (2008) 'Pre-Therapy Process and Outcome: A Review of Research Instruments and Findings', *Person-Centered and Experiential Psychotherapies*, 7, 37–55.

Dietz, T. J., D. Davis and J. Pennings (2012) 'Evaluating Animal-Assisted Therapy in Group Treatment for Child Sexual Abuse', *Journal of Child Sexual Abuse*, 21, 665–83.

DeMares, R., and K. Krycka (1998) 'Wild-animal-triggered Peak Experiences: Transpersonal Aspects', *The Journal of Transpersonal Psychology*, 30, 161–77.

DeMayo, N. (2009) 'Horses, Humans and Healing', in L. Buzzell and C. Chalquist (eds) *Ecotherapy: Healing with Nature in Mind* (San Francisco: Sierra Club Books) pp. 149–56.

Ewing, C. A., P. M. MacDonald, M. Taylor and M. J. Bowers (2007) 'Equine-Facilitated Learning for Youths with Severe Emotional Disorders: A Quantitative and Qualitative Study', *Child Youth Care Forum*, 36, 59–72.

Filan, S. L., and R. H. Llewellyn-Jones (2006) 'Animal-assisted Therapy for Dementia: A Review of the Literature', *International Psychogeriatrics*, 18, 597–611.

Fine, A. H. (2006) *Handbook on Animal-assisted Therapy: Theoretical Foundations and Guidelines for Practice* (San Diego, California: Elsevier).

Friedmann, E., and C.-C. Tsai (2006) 'The Animal–Human Bond: Health and Wellness', in A. H. Fine (ed.) *Handbook on Animal-assisted Therapy: Theoretical Foundations and Guidelines for Practice* (San Diego, California: Elsevier) pp. 95–117.

Garcia, D. M. (2010) 'Of Equines and Humans: Toward a New Ecology', *Ecopsychology*, 2, 85–9.

Geist, T. S. (2011) 'Conceptual Framework for Animal Assisted Therapy', *Child and Adolescent Social Work Journal*, 28, 243–56.

Holcomb, R., C. Jendro, B. Weber and U. Nahan (1997) 'Use of an Aviary to Relieve Depression In Elderly Males', *Anthrozoos*, 10, 32–6.

Johansen, S. G., C. E. A. Wang, P.-E. Binder and U. F. Malt (2014) 'Equine-Facilitated Body and Emotion-Oriented Psychotherapy Designed for Adolescents and Adults Not Responding to Mainstream Treatment: A Structured Program', *Journal of Psychotherapy Integration*, 24, 323–35.

Kalof, L. (2003) 'The Human Self and the Animal Other: Exploring Borderline Identities', in S. Clayton and S. Opotow (eds) *Identity and the Natural Environment: The Psychological Significance of Nature* (Cambridge, MA: MIT Press) pp. 161–78.

Karol, J. (2007) 'Applying a Traditional Individual Psychotherapy Model to Equine-Facilitated Psychotherapy (EFP): Theory and Method', *Clinical Child Psychology and Psychiatry*, 12, 77–90.

Klontz, B. T., A. Bivens, D. Leinart and T. Klontz (2007) 'The Effectiveness of Equine-assisted Experiential Therapy: Results of an Open Clinical Trial', *Society and Animals*, 15, 257–67.

Kršková, A., L. Talarovićová and A. Olexová (2010) 'Guinea Pigs: The "Small Great" Therapist for Autistic Children, or: Do Guinea Pigs Have Positive Effects on Autistic Child Social Behavior? *Society and Animals*, 18, 139–51.

Kruger, K. A., and J. A. Serpell (2006) 'Animal-assisted Interventions in Mental Health: Definitions and Theoretical Foundations', in A. H. Fine (ed.) *Handbook on Animal-assisted Therapy: Theoretical Foundations and Guidelines for Practice* (San Diego, California: Elsevier) pp. 95–8.

Lang, U. E., J. B. Jansen, F. Wertenauer, J. Gallinat and M. A. Rapp (2010) 'Reduced Anxiety During Dog-assisted Interviews in Acute Schizophrenic Patients, *European Journal of Integrative Medicine*, 2, 123–7.

Lentini, J. A. and M. Knox (2009) 'A Qualitative and Quantitative Review of Equine Facilitated Psychotherapy (EFP) with Children and Adolescents', *The Open Complementary Medicine Journal*, 1, 51–7.

Leontiev, D. (2013) 'The Challenge of Otherness: Relationships, Meaning and Dialogue', in E van Deurzen and S. Iacovou (eds) *Existential Perspectives on Relationship Therapy* (Basingstoke, UK: Palgrave Macmillan) pp. 32–43.

Melson, G. F., and A. H. Fine (2006) 'Animals in the Lives of Children', in A. H. Fine (ed.) *Handbook on Animal-assisted Therapy: Theoretical Foundations and Guidelines for Practice* (San Diego, California: Elsevier) pp. 207–26.

Moustakas, C. (1990) *Heuristic Research: Design, Methodology, and Applications* (London: Sage).

Moyle, W., M. Cooke, E. Beattie, C. Jones, B. Klein, G. Cook and C. Gray (2013) 'Exploring the Effect of Companion Robots on Emotional Expression in Older Adults with Dementia', *Journal of Gerontological Nursing*, 39, 46–53.

Myers, G., and A. Russell (2003) 'Human Identity in Relation to Wild Black Bears: A Natural-Social Ecology of Subjective Creatures', in S. Clayton and S. Opotow (eds) *Identity and the Natural Environment: The Psychological Significance of Nature* (Cambridge, MA: MIT Press) pp. 67–90.

O'Haire, M. (2010) 'Companion Animals and Human Health: Benefits, Challenges, and the Road Ahead', *Journal of Veterinary Behavior*, 5, 226–34.

Prouty, G. F. (2001) 'The Practice of Pre-Therapy', *Journal of Contemporary Psychotherapy*, 31, 31–40.

Prouty, G. (2003) 'Pre-Therapy: A Newer Development in the Psychotherapy of Schizophrenia', *Journal of the American Academy of Psychoanalysis and Dynamic Psychiatry*, 31, 59–73.

Prouty, G. (2008) *Emerging Developments in Pre-Therapy: A Pre-Therapy Reader* (Ross-on-Wye, UK: PCCS Books).

Roberts, F., J. Bradberry and C. Williams (2004) 'Equine Facilitated Psychotherapy Benefits Students and Children', *Holistic Nursing Practice*, 18, 32–5.

Sabini, M. (2008) *C. G. Jung on Nature, Technology, and Modern Life* (Berkeley, CA: North Atlantic Books).

Sanders, C. R. (2003) 'Actions Speak Louder Than Words: Close Relationships Between Humans and Nonhuman Animals', *Symbolic Interactions*, 26, 405–26.

Schneider, K. J. (2003) 'The Fluid Center: An Awe-Based Challenge to Humanity', *Journal of Humanistic Psychology*, 43, 133–45.

Schneider, K. J. (2011) 'Awakening to an Awe-Based Psychology', *The Humanistic Psychologist*, 39, 247–52.

Schultz, P. N., G. A. Remick-Barlow and L. Robbins (2007) 'Equine-assisted Psychotherapy: A Mental Health Promotion/Intervention Modality for Children Who Have Experienced Intra-Family Violence', *Health and Social Care in the Community*, 15, 265–71.

Siporin, S. (2012) 'Talking Horses: Equine Psychotherapy and Intersubjectivity', *Psychodynamic Practice: Individuals, Groups and Organisations*, 18, 457–64.

Smith, L. D. G., S. H. Ham and B. V. Weiler (2011) 'The Impacts of Profound Wildlife Experiences', *AnthroZoös*, 24, 51–64.

Solomon, O. (2010) 'What a Dog Can Do: Children with Autism and Therapy Dogs in Social Interaction', *Ethos*, 38, 143–66.

Solomon, O. (2012) 'Doing, Being and Becoming: The Sociality of Children with Autism in Activities with Therapy Dogs and Other People', *Cambridge Anthropology*, 30, 109–26.

Totton, N. (2011) *Wild Therapy* (Ross-on-Wye, UK: PCCS Books).

Vidrine, M., P. Owen-Smith and P. Faulkner (2002) 'Equine-Facilitated Group Psychotherapy: Applications for Therapeutic Vaulting', *Issues in Mental Health Nursing*, 23, 587–603.

Weiss, D. (2009) 'Equine Assisted Therapy and Theraplay', in E. Munns (ed.) *Applications of Family and Group Theraplay* (Lanham, Maryland: Jason Aronson) pp. 225–36.

Yorke, J. (2010) 'The Significance of Human–Animal Relationships as Modulators of Trauma Effects in Children: A Developmental Neurobiological Perspective', *Early Child Development and Care*, 180, 559–70.

Zilcha-Mano, S., M. Mikulincer and P. R. Shaver (2011) 'Pet in the Therapy Room: An Attachment Perspective on Animal-assisted Therapy', *Attachment and Human Development*, 13, 541–61.

AFTERWORD

Martin Jordan and Joe Hinds

This collection of chapters is not a definitive statement on ecotheapy, but represents an overview of some current approaches within this broad discipline happening in Europe and the United States. The common denominator between the chapters is the central importance placed on the natural world in its myriad forms and its relationship to human well-being and mental health. Although this relationship has traditionally been ignored or underplayed by psychology, recently the importance of it has been gaining greater interest, evidenced by a growing body of theoretical, research and practice initiatives. The book, as well as offering some interesting perspectives on the theory, practice and research within the growing field of ecotherapy, also suggests some future inquiries. For example, we have not stated a definitive evidence base for ecotherapy or stated its efficacy for different client groups or how and why it might work with these clinical populations. With a growing interest among the therapeutic community and beyond, the present collection of chapters will provoke further theoretical, research and practice initiatives which will address explicit questions associated with specific groups and individuals. In keeping with the holistic approach of ecotherapy, we feel the chapters offered here provide an interesting and varied view on ecotherapy which we would like to see encourage further insight and exploration to support the growing research and evidence base for ecotherapy in which we, and the contributors herein, are involved.

Ecotherapy represents a broadening of current theory and practice within the field of counselling and psychotherapy, and in doing so it also offers an important critique of current ways of thinking. By including the physical (natural) environment and the more-than-human world into therapeutic practice, it expands our understanding of relationships and mental health beyond the purely intrapsychic and interpersonal to include a matrix of relationships and their potential for healing. In this sense, it offers a much more holistic and reciprocal understanding of therapeutic practice beyond its traditional conceptions.

The theoretical chapters are an attempt to map out an epistemological basis for ecotherapy, which we believe, given the history of ecotherapy as discipline, is a timely consideration for its development. One issue with the holistic nature of the approach is the problem of arriving at one overarching theoretical underpinning: we recognize that the diversity of ideas and approaches makes the task of outlining one coherent epistemological base impossible. What is apparent in these chapters is that each author presents much more of an onto-logical position. By starting with Thomas Doherty and finishing with Linda Buzzell, we have placed ecopsychology as a central conceptual vehicle through which ecotherapy can be understood and articulated.

The topic of research has been covered in four chapters that offer an eclectic range of distinct yet overlapping qualitative methods within a range of contexts. Deborah Kelly engages in an intimate biographical immersion in order for her to better understand palliative care, using a heuristic methodology, whereas Eva Sahlin and Anna María Pálsdóttir both use in-depth interviews to explore the effects of a structured and time-dependent nature-based rehabilitation pro-gramme using a multi-agency team (see advocates of a similar approach; e.g. Bollas, 2013). Using a similar group-based intervention to cater for a range of mental health issues, Matt Adams and Martin Jordan use a mixed methodology utilizing semi-structured interviews, open-ended questionnaires and a focus group to research a therapeutic outdoor programme. Although these methods cover some ground in terms of approaches and research philosophies, some will undoubtedly wish to make comparisons with other more 'robust' evaluations, such as randomized control trials and the like. Our position here is that there are no perfect 'gold standards' of assessment and that each has its own strengths and weakness; and also that it's through longitudinal follow-up work that the true effect of any intervention may be determined, and we would issue a call for more of this work to be initiated.

The chapters which explore the practice of ecotherapy again give an insight into the diverse nature of approaches and directions taken within ecotherapy. These chapters capture what might be, for some, central concerns in relation to ethical and professional practice. Patricia Hasbach builds upon and further develops ideas concerning the importance of boundaries and ethics for eco-therapy as we seek to develop it as a professional therapeutic practice. Other chapters outline different facets of ecotherapy practice from a range of perspec-tives. An ongoing and evolving issue of whether ecotherapy operates as an add-on to traditional forms of therapeutic practice or presents a unique form of practice is touched upon in Ronen Berger's chapter. There are strong parallels between arts therapies and ecotherapy, and indeed these have been found to be very compatible therapeutic partners (Jordan, 2014). The diversity of prac-tice represented in the book raises further questions about the practice of eco-therapy in relation to well-being and what might be broadly termed 'therapy'. Undoubtedly some forms of 'depth' ecotherapy are akin to psychotherapy, whereas others may represent a new form of psychotherapy practice rather as the arts therapies have done by developing over the last 30 years as unique modalities in and of themselves. Through continued developments and contri-butions in the three areas we have outlined, we wish that ecotherapy may begin to carve its own unique place in the therapeutic world. We hope this book is a contribution to the development of ecotherapy in terms of its theoretical foundations, research endeavours and contemporary therapeutic practices, and we hope it acts as a clarion call for the discipline of ecotherapy, however it is interpreted or enacted, to be further validated as an established and accepted practice.

References

Bollas, C. (2013) *Catch Them Before They Fall* (London: Routledge).
Jordan, M. (2014) 'Taking Therapy Outside: A Narrative Inquiry into Counselling and Psychotherapy in Outdoor Natural Spaces', unpublished PhD thesis, University of Brighton.

INDEX

Note: Page numbers in *italics* indicate figures or tables.